MW00561315

TRANSPERSONAL ASTROLOGY:

EXPLORATIONS AT THE FRONTIER

PRODUCED AND EDITED BY:

ARMAND DIAZ

ERIC MEYERS

ANDREW SMITH

INTEGRAL TRANSFORMATION

Published by Integral Transformation in the United States of America and the United Kingdom

© 2013 Integral Transformation, LLC

Cover Art, Other Worlds, by Isaac Mills, Mugwort Designs
www.MugwortDesigns.com

Cover Produced by Bill Streett

ISBN: 978-0-9894163-0-6

ACKNOWLEDGEMENTS

This work has been a collective effort, the product of vision, persistence and collaboration. True to the scope of the book, it is beyond any individual, but the following individuals graciously gave of themselves to make it a reality: Phoebe Brown for copy-editing, Isaac Mills for the cover art, and Bill Streett for designing the layout of the cover.

Armand thanks Emila Santo for love and encouragement and Nutmeg for her help. Eric thanks Sajit Greene for support, Drew Meyers for the cover picture, and Josh Levin for editing suggestions. Andrew thanks Karen Morgan, Sarah and Maya for their patience and encouragement.

We have gratitude for the communal efforts of the astrological tribe (past and present), continually developing and expanding this sacred knowledge. May we all ride the merry-go-round of cycles within cycles together.

Lastly, of course, are the authors themselves—the writers, astrologers, and thinkers who joined this community. They have so generously contributed to this collection and allowed this dream of ours to ignite.

Benjamin Bernstein, Faye Cossar, Dena DeCastro, Adam Elenbaas, Maurice Fernandez, Adam Gainsburg, Margaret Gray, Mark Jones, Julene Packer-Louis, Jessica Murray, Rafael Nasser, Bill Streett and Sherene Vismaya Schostak. Thank you one and all!

CONTENTS

Introduction

A Transpersonal Perspective

It has become cliché to say the world is changing faster than ever. We frequently hear that we are reaching a crisis point, that some new way of being—or perhaps extinction—lies just around the corner for humanity and our precious planet. In these times of uncertainty, we can learn to see life from a broader and more holistic perspective and, thereby, trust the natural process of evolution. One of the most hopeful currents of our time is what we might call the *transpersonal* perspective.

Transpersonal means "beyond the personal." It includes the ability to comprehend life free of personal attachments—to hold a perspective broader than the self as the center of existence. When our identification shifts from the separate self (personality, ego, body) as the primary reference, we venture into exciting, but less defined, territory. Viewing life through the transpersonal lens opens us to the vast territory of consciousness, which is creative, complex, and unbounded in comparison with the orderliness of the everyday (Saturnian) world. The task is not to disregard the personal, our precious vehicle for growth, but to reposition our frame of reference to that of a spiritual being *within* a physical body. We can maintain and value our uniqueness while also seeing that we are intimately connected to all of life.

The emergence of a transpersonal perspective is reflected across the fields of psychology, spirituality, and the human potential movement. Increasing numbers of scientists, academics and philosophers are encouraging us to incorporate multi-dimensional and multi-leveled perspectives—more nails driven in the coffin of materialist reductionism. There is an increased awareness that life is far more complex than can be appreciated by our immediate senses. More conscious understandings of the universe are also being complemented by direct experience as contemplative practices of many varieties rapidly gain in popularity. There is a palpable eagerness to seek alternative ways to understand the human condition and to expand our experience of life's great mystery. Spiritual growth is on the rise, and the transpersonal is becoming less "fringe" as each year passes.

Yet this revolution in consciousness has made little progress in astrology—which is remarkable, considering that astrology is ultimately transpersonal in scope. We are clearly enveloped within a system not of our design but of an intelligence that transcends and includes us, as if we are each nerve cells in a larger brain. Incorporating the transpersonal perspective is an act of yielding to this broader reality instead of choosing to couch the phenomena of astrology in only familiarly personal ways.

Paralleling the discovery of the three major transpersonal planets (Uranus, Neptune, and Pluto) within the last 250 years, we have experienced a dramatic shift in consciousness and how we perceive the universe and our place therein. Several astrologers have been conscious of this shift and have articulated a less deterministic and more transpersonal perspective, most notably Dane Rudhyar in the first half of the 20th century.

However, prior efforts to incorporate the transpersonal have largely been thwarted by the Saturnian virtues of utility and certainty, to know "what's really real." These values are understandable and necessary in many ways, but they are not the final arbiters of truth. Just as the transpersonal planets orbit beyond Saturn, we can understand the everyday world as existing *within* other dimensions of experience.

The adoption of a transpersonal approach to astrology does not make redundant the many forms of astrology that have existed for millennia. The tension between modern discovery and history reflects the mythology between Uranus and Saturn, which also illustrates the theme of marginalizing the transpersonal. Chronos (Saturn) wielded his scythe and castrated his father Ouranos (Uranus) because of his perceived aloofness and lack of love. Through this act, Saturn asserts his supremacy, but the bargain is steep. In fear of being usurped himself, Saturn is fixated on control, domination, and his own personal interests—in short, literally cut off from the transpersonal.

Now that the outer planets have been discovered and more fully understood, our next task is to integrate them into the Saturnian realm. We may heal this rift and bring "heaven" to "earth." Instead of a wall, Saturn can serve as a gateway or membrane that brings broader perspectives and processes into manifestation. For this to occur, Saturn must yield to a broader reality,

2

while the transpersonal must become relevant and understandable in our everyday lives. The chapters in this book attempt to find that balance.

A major part of this integration is to see astrology as a dynamic, creative, and multifaceted system holding unlimited energetic possibilities instead of concrete and predictable occurrences. Though it might appear that the universe has provided an owner's manual that illuminates the unconscious world, we have the formidable task of interpretation. Ideally, we can bring our sharpest left-brained logic and sense and our most inspired right-brain imagination and creativity to chart analysis. We can exercise our intuition and draw from our well of wisdom and translate through accessible language in everyday and practical ways.

Consistent with the mythic castration, the component of consciousness has been dismissed or seen as cumbersome to address in the context of conventional interpretations. As a result, astrologers tend to focus on questions that serve the ego in the conventional world: a "good" time to launch a project, affirmation that a love interest is worth pursuing, or a way to get an edge in playing the game of life. The usual uses of astrology assume that inflation (or at least maintenance) of the ego is the *primary* goal.

Egoic questions have their relative validity. We can respect the very human and vulnerable tendency that wishes to know more of its plight. The issue is not with ego, as a healthy one is necessary for autonomy and self-definition; we see ego as a radiant reflection of Spirit. The issue is over-identification with ego at the exclusion of the transpersonal. The great lesson of this time is consciously connecting the separate self with the broader universe. As inside, so outside—our life energy and consciousness is inseparable from all of life.

Astrology too cannot be separated from consciousness, but our legacy tends to divorce the two. Many astrologers approach a chart with an "all things being equal" mindset, not fully acknowledging the uniqueness of individual experience. The reality we experience is conditioned by an infinite number of factors including gender, genetics, family, culture, religion, ancestry, and karma. These influences say nothing about the level of consciousness, the subjective orientation of a soul in question. We may understand consciousness as the prime variable that influences how an astrological chart manifests and the quality of life available for the chart owner. As we develop, our experience of astrology becomes less concrete and more subtle, reflecting the movement from Saturn to beyond. The patterns within any chart still hold true; however, the implications of how they can manifest change significantly, as an individual happens more onto life, as opposed to life happening onto the individual.

In the transpersonal approach, we don't see life in terms of "good" and "bad," for those are relative to needs at the personal level. Instead, the emphasis is on growth, which often plays out in ways that are difficult. Instead of supporting the resistance to these necessary experiences in our spiritual curriculum, we can find ways to embrace the lessons that inevitably come our way. We can trust that we reside within an intelligently orchestrated system in which we co-create all of our experiences. Without a transpersonal orientation, astrology may be prone to sabotaging growth by advocating only for what the astrologer believes to be "good" for the client.

From the transpersonal perspective, hierarchical assumptions and techniques that define astrological practice start to break down. No longer are there preferable planets, sign placements, types of aspects, etc. We begin to see everything as relative to a particular mindset and value sphere. As challenging as it may be to initially accept, there isn't a "true" or objective astrology. Each of us is like a musician composing a song, each choosing a different key and tempo; some choose a classical style, others more contemporary, others experimental. Each produces a melody, but the means of composition are not the same in each case. Some of the musicians will resonate with what has been produced by their contemporaries; others will merely appreciate the craft of their colleagues. Seven major notes, five minors, infinite ways of composing. Ten major planets, twelve signs and houses, a symphony to orchestrate.

Our role as transpersonal astrologers is ultimately to help open awareness of choices; to facilitate a more informed, less ego-based questioning; to look past the limitations of black and white dualistic thinking and ask *what purpose does this experience serve for my soul's growth*; to empower and generate hope; and to really understand what aspect of a person's life is seeking to grow during any given event or experience. If we can help someone step over that threshold, then our job as a bridge-maker is done!

With that in mind, this book is a compilation of essays by astrologers who practice from a transpersonal perspective. The chapters herein contain some of their thoughts on various issues within our celestial craft. The common consensus that unites the authors is that each believes individual consciousness connects beyond the confines of separation typified by ego, thereby into the transpersonal. Each chapter represents a unique way of understanding the transpersonal through an astrological lens—and a way of finding a path towards greater spiritual wholeness.

The book contains several "big picture" chapters that address broad philosophical issues. As we are in a time of accelerated change, this collection contains several chapters that provide us with perspective. Jessica Murray writes on the crucial spiritual opportunities and egoic challenges in this world moment. Bill Streett discusses the current Uranus–Pluto square, how our collective consciousness has an evolutionary connection with technology. Armand Diaz surveys the evolution of the collective consciousness itself and where we are at this point. Eric Meyers discusses the urgency of incorporating the transpersonal into today's astrology, offering a vision for that integration in the 21st century.

Other big-picture chapters include an exploration of our co-creative relationship with astrology by Rafael Nasser. Adam Elenbaas puts forth a philosophical piece on sacred duality, while Faye Cossar asks whether the transpersonal is becoming personal in her discussion of evolution. Margaret Gray focuses on the transpersonal in relationships, and Mark Jones addresses the connection between the personal and transpersonal planets as seen with "higher octaves."

Other authors write on the application of the transpersonal. Benjamin Bernstein introduces his version of shamanic astrology in the counseling room. Andrew Smith focuses on the relationship between time and space and explores issues relating to using locational astrology from a transpersonal angle. Sherene Schostak plumbs the depths of the shadow as a fertile ground of transformation and draws upon her experience as an analyst.

The remainder of the chapters focuses on specific and unique topics of inquiry. Adam Gainsburg looks at the transpersonal relevance of the Mars cycle. Maurice Fernandez discusses the spiritual implications of the death chart. Julene Packer-Louis clarifies the transpersonal context in which we can understand the Vertex, while Dena DeCastro discusses visionary Neptune and its role in divine inspiration. Enjoy!

Armand Diaz, Eric Meyers, Andrew Smith – Spring 2013

1

A Transpersonal Vision for Astrology

Eric Meyers

Astrology has a rich history with deep roots in its underlying methods and assumptions. For almost all of this history, Saturn was known to be the farthest orbiting planet. The transpersonal outer planets (Uranus, Neptune, Pluto) were discovered only in the last few centuries. Today, we know of many new celestial discoveries which may perplex both the astrological student and expert. Just as our understanding of the cosmos expands, so too does our capacity to explore new frontiers of consciousness.

How do we reconcile the new world we now inhabit with the far older astrology we've inherited? Evolution is widely embraced, so how can astrology evolve in meaningful and appropriate ways? At this writing, we're at the climax of the Uranus–Pluto square, which is urging us to connect the power of tradition (Pluto in Capricorn) with the courage to pioneer new directions (Uranus in Aries).

We are standing in the present, pulled between the past and the future.

A major difference between modern and ancient times is how we conceive of the human condition. With Saturn as the final authority, the world was looked at in terms of orderliness and physicality, what is most obvious and manifest. Paralleling the planet Saturn with its orchestration of rings symbolizing containment, it has been natural to see the human condition only *within* the parameters of the skin. The world outside this physical casing is understood as being separate.

Whereas Saturn pertains to the structure of the physical realm, Uranus is the organizer of the metaphysical realm, the world of energy. Since the discovery of the cool, electrical blue planet, the world has seen a scientific and technological explosion of breathtaking proportions. We have learned to harness and utilize energy in a myriad of ways, and we also know that we too are energy. Just as Uranus orbits beyond Saturn, we now know that our energy extends outwards from our physical boundaries. We can no longer define the human condition only in terms of physicality and separation.

Fire: The Transpersonal Element

Fire is energy; our source of it is the Sun, which energizes life. The fire of an individual's life force radiates into the world, just as the Sun shines. Through focus and practice, many are now learning to experience and work with the "energy body" or "light body." Some have called it the aura; some say it's the soul. It has been symbolized by the halo, and now we have the technology (Kirlian photography) to capture our radiance. Quantum science informs us that our energy reaches out and is "entangled" with the entire world!

Within the boundary of the skin are our flesh and bone (earth), emotions (water), and thoughts (air). Earth (body), water (heart), and air (mind) can be considered "personal" elements, while one facet of fire is to connect us with the transpersonal, life beyond the parameters of our separateness. The organization of life into body–heart–mind–soul is universally found— throughout many cultures and time periods—largely because it follows the template of the four astrological elements (earth–water–air–fire). Fire is associated with *inspiration*, which means to be *in Spirit*. The soul is not something otherworldly; it energetically connects our physicality with the oneness (Spirit) that envelops us.

The two main characteristics of fire are its light and heat, both of which have transpersonal implications. Light correlates with awareness. When cultivated, awareness brings us out of the darkness of unconsciousness to realize greater *awakening* or *enlightenment*, both of which have fire connotations. Many spiritual teachers discuss awareness as a universal constant, the context or field of energy in which all content arises. Sri Ramana Maharshi said, "The brain functions by light borrowed from another source."[1] It might appear to us that the awareness we experience is our own, but the spiritual view tells us otherwise. Maharshi continues, "The light within, that is, the Self, gives light to the ego, the intellect, the memory and the mind without itself being subject to processes of growth and decay."[2] (Note that his term for Spirit is "the Self.")

Heat equates to presence and vitality, the sustaining energy of life. Science informs us about the conservation of energy: the totality of energy in the universe is neither growing nor diminishing, but maintains its oneness. This is similar to the "eternal flame," a concept used in many religions and spiritual paths. Fire is the crackling, everlasting spark of spiritual creativity that is beyond us and within us, never extinguishing, and always recycling.

It would be a mistake to describe fire as being spiritual and suggest the other elements are not. Fire is creative potential, but it partners with the "lower" or "denser" vibrations of the other elements. Einstein's famous equation $E = mc^2$ tells us that matter is solidified energy. Therefore, matter is spiritual because it is actually a transformation of energy. In order to see fire as transpersonal, we must refrain from construing it only in personal, human ways, and see it as the energy that pervades all of life. Instead of a random universe separate from us, the entire world becomes ensouled when we understand the transpersonal reach of fire. Though fire is our source energy, we are rooted to the familiar dualistic state, so we tend to categorize fire as yang or masculine. Though this is undeniably true from one lens of perception, I'm suggesting that there's also a transpersonal component to its scope.

Here's a little experiment to see the transpersonal nature of fire. Notice how the experience of the body (earth), emotions (water), or thoughts (air) are only contacted through awareness (light) and the ability to be present (heat) in the moment. These personal facets of our humanness arise within this transpersonal context. Fire is eternal, while matter is temporary and a physical transformation of fire. We can understand evolution in terms of the motion of energy (fire, transpersonal) down to matter (earth) in a manifesting channel, and from matter back to the nonphysical in a path of liberation.

Evolutionary Movement

The philosophy of evolutionary movement I'm putting forth is not new at all. In fact, it seamlessly connects with what has been termed the Perennial Philosophy[3], which has enjoyed broad consensus throughout history. The manifesting channel assumes a pyramid form (see graphic below).[4] The process of evolution begins at the "top," the creative impulse of fire, where souls connect with Spirit. A soul is like an individual flame connected to the broader fire. Seen when we bring two candles together and then apart, fire can both separate and also reunite into one flame. Our souls can venture into separation while simultaneously maintaining a connection to, and identity with, the broader fire source.

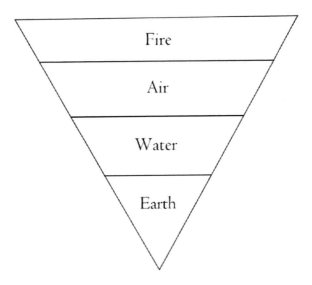

The Manifesting Pyramid

As the manifesting channel moves down the "elemental levels," there is a narrowing process that eventually leads to manifestation on the earth level. From the fiery source, souls choose to incarnate in the everyday world to evolve. Moving down to the conceptual air level, creative possibilities narrow into a specific plan, and the astrology chart depicts this plan. Next, the soul reaches embodied life at the biological water level—a fetus is incubated in the waters of the womb—which engages our humanness. We attain autonomy at birth, we arrive on the Earth, and the earth level is engaged.

We immediately begin our travels in the liberating channel. We first learn to orient to our body (earth), then we define ourselves through our emotions (water), then with the mind (air). Many believe that evolution ends with intellectual development, but spiritual realization (fire) is ours to discover.

Whereas the manifesting channel concerns the process of coming into *being,* the liberating channel concerns *growth.* We can look to nature to see the universal program of development through these elemental levels. Everything is situated on the earth, the broadest and most mundane level. Next, life (water) emerges from this foundation in the form of autonomous beings. Fittingly, life-forms require water for sustenance. The next advancement is the development of intellectual and communicative (air) skills. Membership at the air level requires some form of nervous system. The air level is more exclusive than the water level, which is more exclusive than the earth level. Each level builds upon the previous, while also moving beyond it. Evolution continues towards spiritual realization (fire), which is even more exclusive, though very much available for us to claim.

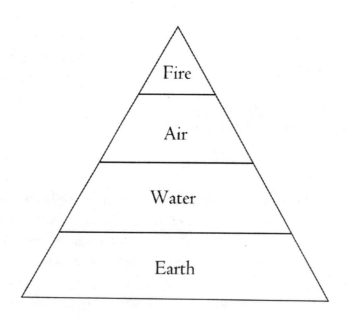

The Liberating Pyramid

At the fire level, we consciously understand and experience our energy (soul) as belonging to Source (fire). The zenith of the pyramid would be the full illumination of Spirit, or enlightenment (fire). However, notions of linear movement are from separation consciousness. When we get to the transpersonal, linearity gives way to timelessness. Spirit is not seen as a "level" since it envelops everything. Oneness eludes systems based on division.

Some tend to view what is higher as "better," a by-product of Saturn's reliance on hierarchies. Instead, we can view this movement from the physical to the nonphysical. Up is not better than down, no more so than being an adult is better than being a child. Everything, and every level, has its usefulness. We can remove value judgments and see this motion in terms of development. Also, there is a tendency to think that when we advance, we are leaving the denser levels behind. Instead, we can see this as a maturation process. We build from the earth foundation into higher levels of development, just as the child grows into an adult, or a seed into a flower. The inner child or seed remains, but one's *identification* shifts to the more mature level.

So we are in the middle of two complementary channels of evolution. Paradoxically, we are both growing (personal) and being (transpersonal). At the personal level, everything alive changes (and potentially grows) every single day as time passes. The liberation channel is from the frame of reference of our autonomy (separation consciousness). The manifesting channel is from the transpersonal reference of being, simply abiding in the timeless, eternal present moment. Here, there is no growth; everything exists eternally in its underlying interconnectedness.

Our heart foundation is within separation consciousness, growing in the liberating channel. We are emotional creatures on the clock of linear time. The Moon is our connection to our physicality and biology, our inherent humanness. The fire of Spirit is unified and transcends time and the relative world. It is transpersonal, our connection to being. The Sun is our energy and life force, our soul connection with all of life. As we'll explore, the Moon (water) and Sun (fire) play the central roles in these two very different ways of operating.

The Sun and Moon

The astrological Sun plays the crucial mediating role between the endless fire of Spirit and an individual's life force. We may think of the Sun as the singular flame of a candle that is "lit" from the universe (Spirit). This fiery spiritual connection illuminates and sustains our individual physicality (Moon)

11

in separation consciousness. We are rooted in the various hungers, needs and emotions of being human, which often occludes the underlying interconnectedness at the fire level. We are in the process of maturing towards greater spiritual realization, seeing life as broader than ego, personality and dualistic categorizations. The development of the Sun potentially leads to spiritual awakening or enlightenment—terms with solar (*soul*-ar) connotations. We may grow to identify primarily with the energy body, while the physical body would be seen as a tool to carry out creative impulses.

As we are in the process of development, the ego tends to identify with the creative energy of fire and often claims ownership of it. The universal awareness and presence of soul realization (Sun) becomes used for personal reasons, and the Sun and Leo are frequently equated only with personality and ego. We don't yet realize that we are using the vessel of our humanness to distribute Spirit. At this time in history, we are collectively reaching the point where we realize that energy is only ours to *borrow*. If we make this important shift, the Sun can be associated with awakening from ego, not the ego itself. Astrology can clarify each person's inherent light of divinity, a vast difference from the cartoonish profiles of Sun signs portrayed in pop culture. We are shifting to organizing life around soul, instead of ego, perhaps the defining lesson of this time.

For now, we have inherited the notion that the Sun is the ego. Whereas the Sun radiates outwards into all of life, the ego is contracted in pursuit of personal survival and autonomy. The ego and the Sun are actually opposites. In fact, we can see the Moon as far more relevant to the ego as it pertains to our personal attachments, identification as a physical, separate person, our defense mechanisms and imperative to survive. I call the pairing of the ego and the Sun the "egoic takeover."[5] The Moon (ego, separation) takes ownership of energy (Sun, soul) and reduces it to strictly human (rather than transpersonal) terms. The limitless creativity of the Sun serves as a projector for the more contracted Moon, radiating a dualistic and subjective orientation to life.

The tendency to see and categorize life in terms of dualistic pairings is found in the conventional understanding of the Sun and Moon as indicative of the masculine and feminine. This gender-oriented perspective parallels the pre-Copernican understanding of the Solar System. For eons, we erroneously thought the Earth was at the center of the universe. The Sun and Moon were seen as lighted orbs of similar size, taking turns encircling us. The apparent reality has become a fixture in our collective consciousness, and though it is completely inaccurate, many people continue to live in accordance with the illusion. People speak of the Sun rising or setting (instead of the Earth turning), or moonlight (instead of reflected sunlight). In the field of astrology, we maintain the illusion of the Sun and Moon being equal because of the historical pairing with gender. They are considered "the luminaries," which is irrefutably false (however persistent and pervasive the notion may be).

Today we know that the Sun is 64 million times larger than the Moon, the Moon reflects the Sun's light, and both the Earth and our Moon orbit the Sun. The Sun is a star, while the Moon is one satellite (of many) in the Solar System. No longer can we say that they are equal. My proposal is to value both the viewpoint from the Earth (personal), and also a perspective of the system not wedded to this one vantage point (transpersonal). Accepting only the personal (gender-oriented) view tethers us to a perspective we surpassed 500 years ago.

Throughout much of history, we have seen a historical imbalance between the sexes, where the masculine has asserted dominance. This parallels the enormous difference in size and power between the Sun and Moon. By complementing our paradigm to include the transpersonal, we understand that we revolve around our source energy, not the masculine value sphere. If we refuse to incorporate the transpersonal reality, astrology serves as a reflection of the broader issue on the world stage. It can be so much more. Astrology is uniquely positioned to be the premier tool of spiritual awakening, to lead us to the transpersonal. As we are healing the inequities of patriarchy, it is timely to incorporate the larger reality of the Sun as our spiritual source. The planet Uranus (transpersonal) orbits beyond Saturn (separation), portraying how the personal world is enveloped *within* the transpersonal. In the same way, the familiar personal perspective of the Sun and Moon is contained within a broader reality.

I believe it is reasonable and timely to update astrology to match what we now know about nature. However, many do not want to modernize (Uranus) the tradition they cherish (Pluto in Capricorn), and they thereby keep astrology hostage to times of less awareness, the darkest potentials of the planet relating to psychological control (Pluto) in the sign of preservation (Capricorn). As frequently stated, the planet Pluto pertains to *transformation*, and done well, the limiting forces of tradition (Capricorn) are eliminated (Pluto). If we have the courage to modernize (Uranus in Aries), astrology becomes more empowered to sculpt civilization in accordance with spiritual realization instead of patriarchal control. Instead of masculine and feminine being the primary (and only) division as reflected in the Sun and Moon, the perspective of humankind in relation to our spiritual source is added, causing a shift. The Sun is of spiritual realization, and the Moon equates to our fragile humanness in separation consciousness. Every man and woman has emotions, unconsciousness, and defense mechanisms. We all participate in families (Moon) and have attachments and particular identifications that define us as separate, physical individuals. The Moon is the foundation of every person's emotional center and locus of egoic functioning.

The spiritual view of the Sun and Moon does not replace the familiar gender-based perspective but gives us an additional angle. We can think of the Sun and Moon in terms of energy and matter, the transpersonal and the relative, soul and body, while also understanding them as signifying yang and yin *from the position of separation.* In the state of incarnation, we take on roles, and life is akin to the unfolding of a story. The Sun and Moon—and all of the planets—form a fantastic theater of characters for us to identify with and play out. Here, the Sun can go along with the ruling monarch, while the Moon is the nurturing wife. All of this is subjective and relative, only true from the projection of consciousness in the egoic state. From the transpersonal perspective, this is all gloriously made up...there are no stories, just an exchange of energy. These two very different perspectives relate to two very different types of astrology, which are based on solar and lunar orientations.

Geocentric and Heliocentric Astrology

Almost all astrology is understood from the geocentric (Earth-centered) perspective—quite understandable as we live on the Earth! Here on planet Earth, the Moon encircles us. Scientists now consider the Earth and Moon to be a unit, an interconnected system. Therefore, the Moon is not seen as a planet "out there." It is intimately connected to us—the foundation of unconsciousness that initially surrounds us (just as the Moon encircles the Earth) prior to the maturation of our awareness. A spiritual view is that we incarnate on Earth and renew the Moon's deep basin of unconsciousness, the foundation from which we grow.

Geocentric astrology is from the lunar foundation, which has an egoic focus in the realm of separation. Switch the first two letters of geocentric, and you have egocentric. Here we have the perspective that the Earth is at the center and the Sun and Moon are lighted orbs of the same size encircling us. Stationed within Saturn's orbit, we tend to see life in terms of potential benefit for our survival and happiness. We are "enrolled" within the liberating channel of evolutionary growth. The Moon is paired with the water element (biological life). As the liberating pyramid portrays, we stand on the Earth and reach up towards the heavens.

The motion is from unconsciousness to awakening, developing towards greater spiritual realization and acting on our soul intentions. We start out in unconsciousness when we are born, completely dependent on caretakers. We connect with the vulnerability of the human condition, alone and separate, needing love and support. This enables us to re-experience the familiar themes of love that are in the soul history; and what is *familiar*, plays out with *family*. The Moon is paired with Cancer, the archetype of family and nurturance, which is traditionally associated with feminine and maternal themes. Within separation consciousness, life tends to be split up dualistically.

From the broader transpersonal view, we cannot say that the Moon represents the mother or that anything in the chart can be assigned to anyone away from the chart owner. We project our subjective unconsciousness, "the ego dream," onto the external world and evaluate life in terms of the self. Seeing the Moon as "the mother" is a distancing of responsibility from *our own* unconsciousness. As we cultivate awareness, we learn to see the self in everything (including everyone) and retract our projections. We realize that we were interacting *with ourselves* through the very intimate mother/child connection. However, in the roles that are played in our stories in the unconscious state of separation, the Moon can represent one's mother (though its projection tends to be more broad).

The Moon absorbs and digests experience. When we have no issue with something, its energy cycles through our system and releases, analogous to how food is ideally processed and burned up. When we have an issue, we pause this process and form attachments. You probably remember September 11, 2001,

15

more clearly than June 11, 1998, because the former made a deeper impact (unless you are not American or the latter date has some personal significance). The Moon is our emotionally charged memory bank that helps us navigate the world's uncertainties. It molds defense mechanisms, survival tactics, and strategies all designed to attain security and love. We identify with the Moon and believe it is us. Spiritual teacher Adyashanti writes in *The Way of Liberation*:

> By identifying with a particular name that belongs to a particular body and mind, the self begins the process of creating a separate identity. Add in a complex jumble of ideas, beliefs, and opinions, along with some selective and often painful memories with which to create a past to identify with, as well as the raw emotional energy to hold it all together, and before you know it, you've got a very convincing—though divided—self.[6]

The core issue with the Moon is love. A soul with a deep, secure foundation of self-love will incarnate within an environment that reflects this. Most of us lack this foundation to some degree, so we choose family environments that reflect our status. I have asked hundreds of clients where they might place themselves on a "self-love scale" from 1 to 10 to help them make sense of their histories with love, family and relationship issues. Most place themselves between 3 and 7. This lack of unconditional self-love becomes projected out and met in the form of others. As the Moon is anchored in separation, it is all too easy to blame others for our issues, failing to recognize the self in the sacred reflection being cast back to us. The process of awakening involves the recognition of the self in all of life. Then, we can have acceptance and gratitude for all the players in our personal stories, for they were playing the roles for which we "hired" them at the soul level.

The Moon, which carries remnants of the false self, is rooted in the stories of the past. The egoic self has difficulty letting go of the past because it is convinced that it has been wronged and demands some sort of justice, apology or corrective action. Upon breaking the spell of separation, we see that the world was only reflecting back the self, and we take full responsibility for being the co-creators of these dramas. The remnants of the false self are the inaccuracies we have solidified (Moon) from operating only under the illusion of separation, motivated by concerns for survival and personal happiness.

As we accept responsibility for co-creating our prior experiences, we can learn to forgive all others for the roles they played in our stories. We no longer petition the world (especially others) to provide us with love or "positive" experiences, for those are now found within. We release the emotional impact from the past by processing the energy through our systems. The Moon is physical, while the Sun is energy. We bring in light (awareness) and heat (presence) to what has been hardened, and free it to return to Source. Energy in motion is *emotion*; we typically experience the emotional impacts from the past that we refused to feel at the time. As we are *energy processing systems*, we can replace the pain from yesteryear with self-love in the present. Adyashanti says:

> The false self is both an obstacle and a doorway through which you must pass on your way to awakening to the dimension of *being*. As you pass through the world of self, the identification with self dies, either temporarily or permanently, and you are revealed to be presence. Presence is not a self in any conventional sense. It has no shape or form, no age or gender. It is the light and radiance of consciousness in which entire worlds arise and pass away[7].... The tendency to take our thoughts to be real is what keeps the dream state intact and keeps us trapped within its domain of unconsciousness and strife.[8]

Spiritual growth involves releasing the emotional impact from the past and deconstructing our mental stories. All of it was derived in states of less maturation when we needed to secure a strong and viable ego in order to survive. When we secure our lunar foundation with love and acceptance, we are better able to expand into new, more awake, ways of being. Geocentric astrology is most appropriate for us as we address the unresolved nature of our egoic condition, but Heliocentric astrology becomes increasingly relevant as the awakening process progresses.

Heliocentric astrology relates to the creativity of the present with the Sun at the center. It conveys how the soul wishes to use the vehicle of separation to distribute Spirit. Heliocentric astrology is not about the resolution of egoic wounding. In fact, there is no Moon on a heliocentric chart! The Earth (manifestation) is on the chart, and the Moon is always in the same place from the Sun's perspective. As noted before, we can see the Earth and Moon as a unit, representing separation consciousness and manifestation in physical form.

From the solar perspective, the separate self is an illusion; it turns out to be just a collection of concretized energy. The Moon's disappearance from the heliocentric chart means that the Lunar Nodes are also absent. *The human drama and its karma is not the province of the heliocentric chart.* The soul (Sun) is guiding the journey into incarnation—it assists the ego (Moon), but it is the job of the separate self to learn greater soul realization in order to resolve the karma it has created.

Heliocentric astrology is a portrayal of our awakened selves, how we might approach the world as realized beings. Since most of us are not awakened, it can be a premature exercise to use this chart. We are prone to projecting our unconsciousness onto everything. We must resist the impulse to turn heliocentric astrology into geocentric. The difference is literally night (geocentric: Moon-focused, emerging from the dark) and day (heliocentric: Sun-focused, coming from the light).

Heliocentric astrology portrays the soul motion through the manifesting channel described earlier. Whereas the ego wants to liberate from the chains that bind, the soul is interested in crystallizing its intentions on the Earth plane. The soul wants to matter, in both meanings of the term. Matter is earthy substance, and when something "matters," there is meaning attached—it increases in significance or potency.

The geocentric chart is like the energetic magnet pulling the separate self upwards through the liberating pyramid (or channel). That is the pull of spiritual growth: heat (soul) wants to rise. The Sun becomes our life energy, continually inviting expansion and awakening. The weight of the ego (Moon) is necessary for us to be grounded and to define ourselves. However, when we *over-identify* with this definition, we claim ownership of the borrowed energy and so remain unconscious. Upon awakening, we return the energy to Source.

Heliocentric astrology has its own workings and logic. All the planets continually move in the same direction—unlike the familiar retrogrades of geocentric astrology. Retrogrades involve process, which has relevance to humans who need to absorb experiences. Mercury and Venus are not tied within a certain range to the Earth as they are to the Sun with geocentric astrology. Mercury and Venus can have any aspectual relationship with any other planet. Houses portray our orientation to life around us. There are no houses on the heliocentric chart because we don't live on the Sun! This means that there is no Ascendant (often called the mask), nor is there a Midheaven (public role). Whereas many people identify with the Ascendant in personal ways, with heliocentric astrology, there is no "person" to wear a mask. Instead, the focus is just on energy—how the planets are arranged in particular patterns in a more general way.

The heliocentric Earth always appears exactly opposite the geocentric Sun. A Taurus Sun (geocentric) will always be a Scorpio Earth (heliocentric). We see the great dance between the ego and the soul going in opposite directions, meeting in the middle as you. In the liberating channel (geocentric), the separate self (Moon) awakens into spiritual realization (Sun). We inhabit the life force (the Sun in geocentric chart) of the very thing we are *becoming*. We have already arrived, but we have to catch the past up with the present. In the opposite direction, the fire of Spirit/soul is emerging *through* us. We do not fully inhabit our heliocentric Earth until we *dissolve* everything (empty the proverbial cup) on the water level (Moon) on the manifesting channel for the energy to completely move down. Most of us have not loosened our attachments and identifications, so the water level hardens (Moon), and souls are unable to fully root in the Earth.

We can simultaneously take part in the maturation process of spiritual growth (geocentric), while also abiding in being (heliocentric). The Sun (fire level) is at the top of the liberating channel (geocentric chart), while the Earth (the bottom level in the manifesting channel) represented on the heliocentric chart is the focus. It is a grave mistake to point to the Moon on the geocentric chart as the place to rest in being. This unwittingly promotes regression, attachments, immature patterns, and further crystallization of the false self instead of deconstructing it. The Earth/Moon unit on the heliocentric chart is the appropriate astrological indicator where Spirit is manifest as *being* through us.

The Moon on the geocentric chart is resolving its very legitimate issues, needs, and requirements. Though the separate self is an illusion from the solar perspective, it is anything but that to the ego! The Moon is universally unresolved, requiring greater unconditional self-love and acceptance of the past. It is necessary for personal survival and to meet base needs, but for those who want to awaken beyond the personal, its attachments and identifications need to be released. The Moon is involved with the liberating channel, which is about growth. Once heliocentric astrology is more clarified and pervasive, the Earth/Moon unit on that chart will take on the role of manifestation and being.[9]

To work with heliocentric astrology, we must approach it from the transpersonal perspective, the exact opposite of the egoic emphasis of geocentric. For those ready to look through the transpersonal lens, an entire new world is available. What is your soul contributing to the planet through you? Are you able to identify as a soul having a human experience? If so, welcome to the next exploration at the frontier!

Towards an Awakened View

The additional perspective of the Sun (creative energy) and Moon (crystallization into matter) has found limited interest at this point. The main obstacles may be the reluctance to employ another viewing lens and some resistance to the transpersonal. Both of these issues become rectified when we learn to move beyond our reliance on Saturn and venture toward the thrilling, yet largely unknown, terrain of Uranus.

Regarding the reluctance to employ an additional viewing lens, we can look to the most Uranian of disciplines, quantum science. Here, we understand that *the observer affects the object of observation.* We do not exist in an objective, mechanistic universe. Rather, there are multiple meanings and multiple perspectives (perhaps even multiple dimensions) in how we approach life and how the world may appear. Physicist Max Planck said, "When you change the way you look at things, the things you look at change." Upon inquiry, it is difficult to find anything that has only one potential use, function or scope. Everything changes as we shift our preferred lens of perception.

It is frequent practice in astrological literature to discuss the physical characteristics of the planets as representative of their essence and functioning. Mercury is quick like our minds, Jupiter's size is indicative of its expansiveness, and the reddish hue of Mars calls to mind anger and blood. It is an irrefutable fact that the Moon is 64 million times smaller than the Sun and reflects its light. If we are to look at them *only* from the personal viewpoint of gender, how would astronomical reality portray the relationship between the masculine and the feminine? If this cannot be explained in a way that is universally agreeable, the conventional paradigm is on very shaky ground. The viewpoint I am offering is consistent with what we know about nature, while also providing a context to understand the conventional view.

The other obstacle is the resistance to the transpersonal, which can be understood in the mythology of Saturn and Uranus. In characteristic Uranian fashion, Uranus was detached from the needs of his wife and children, far more interested in the broader picture. Consistent with the less-than-affectionate form of love often called "agape," his perceived aloofness created issues with those more rooted in the personal story. Saturn castrated his father, rendering him impotent—the manifest world is severed from the transpersonal. Life is reduced to survival and the maintenance of well-being. Saturn devoured his children in fear of suffering the same fate as his father. As physical beings, survival is necessary, but not only does an over-attachment to this requirement inhibit our development, we may end up harming others as a result of our fear.

It is frequently stated that Uranus is the "higher octave" of Mercury or the "Great Awakener." To heal the Uranus/Saturn rift, we can look through the transpersonal lens, a far different perspective compared with dualistic Mercury. Uranus understands everything as part of the One, and makes no judgments or "good" and "bad" designations. Everything is *energy*, and all of it has spiritual usefulness. We can relax our attachments to our stories about this energy (benefic, malefic, etc.) and learn to exist in harmony with it. However, Uranus also has an unbalanced side. It may refuse to cooperate with the manifest world and insist on staying above it all.

Ideally, these titans can be integrated: Saturn can serve as a gateway to the transpersonal. To pass through this gate, we must learn to accept reality (Saturn)—our mortality, the events in our past, our deepest fears and vulnerabilities. We must move beyond our egoic preferences and stories. If not, then we stay perpetually confined in them. With Uranus, we learn to abide with life's natural unfolding. We can trust that it is organized in a meaningful and intelligent way. The universe may actually be doing things *for* us and *with* us, rather than *to* us.

The Uranian view sees matter as a temporary concretization of energy. We emerge from Source (metaphysical), and we are returning there. As Ram Dass says, "We're all just walking each other home." Instead of only identifying as physical, we may understand our metaphysical parts (energy, consciousness) to be our "foundation" and our physicality to be impermanent. While we are incarnated, there is a sacred relationship between energy (Sun) and matter (Moon); they are completely interdependent. *Both liberating (growth) and manifestation (being) are equally valid for us in the state of separation.* And also, in the final analysis, all energy does recycle back to Source. This recycling brings the idea of reincarnation forward. For astrology to truly be a transpersonal discipline, spiritual growth must play a central role. If not, then everything becomes reduced to serving egoic needs, trapped in the limitations of matter and separation consciousness.

From the Uranian perspective, everything can be seen as teeming fields of energetic potential that interact with consciousness. We have a *co-creative* relationship with the universe. Many times people look to astrology to find answers, but perhaps it asks us questions. How are we going to approach life and live it consciously? It is up to us whether transits or particular natal configurations bring "positive" or "negative" experiences. Just as Saturn orbits within Uranus, every experience in the mundane world brings opportunities for us to awaken (Uranus).

The transpersonal holds our interdependence. Chief Seattle said, "Man did not weave the web of life, he is merely a strand in it. Whatever he does to the web, he does to himself." This collectivity has been historically feared, as it requires some degree of release of egoic preoccupation. We have seen the struggle between "rugged individualism" and systems that ask each individual to yield to the welfare of the whole. The shift to incorporating the transpersonal is not about sacrificing the self for the collective but to forge an alliance between them. Aries, the will of the self, is as equally valid an archetype as Pisces, in which we dissolve the personal story in our interconnectedness. We are not dissolving the relative world of separation consciousness but learning to navigate within it consciously.

Arriving in the 21st Century

In order to develop the transpersonal in astrology, we have to fully integrate the advancements that have led us to this moment. In the 16th century, we learned of the heliocentric reality in our solar system. Yet the implications have not been fully brought in. It serves us well to understand the central significance of the Sun, as well as the Moon's role as a far smaller reflector. The 17th century brought the scientific revolution. Among other things, this signaled a revolt from adhering to orthodox doctrine and brought open-minded inquiry and modernization forward. Yet the field of astrology has been reluctant to entertain new ideas, and the most traditional forms of astrology are in vogue. The 18th century brought the discovery of Uranus, which correlates with a surge of technology and democracy and the accompanying fall of monarchies. It signals the conscious movement towards the transpersonal and paradigm shifts. Yet astrology has predominantly maintained a Saturnian approach and value system, hierarchal judgments of its various facets and the continued marginalization of the transpersonal. During the 19th century, Neptune was discovered. We made tremendous strides understanding spirituality and consciousness, and the theory of evolution proliferated at this time. Yet astrology still has deterministic underpinnings and tends not to be seen in terms of spiritual evolution.

Pluto was discovered in the 20th century. During this time, we saw major advancements with the field of psychology and the quantum revolution. Yet astrology is lagging in understanding the chart in terms of a developmental process in which we co-create our reality. The young 21st century has brought us a striking expansion of our understanding of our Solar System. For most of history, we have understood Saturn as the farthest orbiting planet, and we believed it orbited around the Earth. Now we know of Sedna, which (as the other planets) orbits our Sun, reaching out 100 times further than Saturn. We are in a time of incredible expansion and possibilities. Staying within Saturn's confines is like using one room in a mansion. In order to see the rest of Spirit's "house" in the 21st century, we will need to integrate with the advancements of the last several. One of the greatest strengths of astrology is its rich history, but we must not allow that to inhibit the richness of what is available in the present.

Endnotes

1. Sri Ramana Maharshi, *Be As You Are: The Teachings of Sri Ramana Maharshi*, ed. David Godman (England: Arkana, 1985) 142.

2. Ibid. 14.

3. The Perennial Philosophy is an idea that crosses many cultures and time periods. It posits a universal thread of evolutionary progression: oneness divides into separation then realizes the underlying oneness. The term was first used by Agostino Steuco in the 16th Century, and expanded upon by Gottfried Leibniz in the latter part of the 17th Century. Aldous Huxley helped to popularize the term for a 20th Century audience. He wrote, "Rudiments of the Perennial Philosophy may be found among the traditionary lore of primitive peoples in every region of the world, and in its fully developed forms it has a place in every one of the higher religions." For more, see: http://en.wikipedia.org/wiki/Perennial_philosophy

4. The Manifesting / Liberating Pyramid(s) from Eric Meyers, *Elements & Evolution: The Spiritual Landscape of Astrology* (North Carolina: Astrology Sight Publishing, 2010).

5. Eric Meyers, *The Astrology of Awakening, Vol 1: Eclipse of the Ego* (North Carolina: Astrology Sight Publishing, 2012) (for more discussion on the egoic takeover).

6. Adyashanti, *The Way of Liberation: A Practical Guide to Spiritual Enlightenment* (Campbell, California: Open Gate Sangha, 2013) 12.

7. Ibid. 13-14.

8. Ibid. 15.

9. I plan to make Heliocentric astrology the focus of subsequent work and will feature it prominently in *The Astrology of Awakening* series.

2

The World Moment

Jessica Murray

It was a bold move of ours, being born into this particular epoch. Our soul-selves deserve every credit for incarnating into an era this intense. This era has been singled out by a remarkable number of ancient traditions, among them the Mayan calendar and the Sanskrit scriptures, as a crossroads in human evolution. Many Western astrologers see it as the end of the precessional Great Year: the dawning of not only a new zodiacal age—the Age of Aquarius—but a new 26,000-year-long cycle.

Within this epochal transition—and as of this writing—the Uranus–Pluto square is peaking, its symbolism explicitly expressing the radical necessity of the times. In Capricorn until 2023, transiting Pluto is forcing an upsurge of awareness of the patriarchal assumptions and destructive practices of the industrial world, and of the plutocratic imbalances that exist even in putative democracies. All over the globe, old certitudes are splintering and crashing down. A lot is happening, and in exact parallel with the urgency of the times, the potential exists for a spike in human consciousness.

The whole human race, as a collective soul, can be seen as possessing its own growth arc, one which is making an extraordinary leap right now. To do justice to this unusual time, it feels very important to be psycho-spiritually awake—that is, to stay grounded in our deep selves while opening up to consciousness expansion at every turn, accessing all our internal resources and chipping away at denial wherever we find it. Astrologically speaking, this is "living through the center of the chart." In this state we are fully alive, utterly present, and using everything we've got.

Historically, visionaries of every stripe arise to match the world's need for them. We can say the same about tools of consciousness, such as astrology. There is a sense among spiritually oriented astrologers that the highest reaches

25

of human capability are spelled out, in potential form, in every birth chart; but that they cannot be grasped from the personal perspective alone. To crack this code we need to encompass the transpersonal.

Inner and Outer

It is a fundamental premise of astrology that the internal and external realms are mirrors of each other. This idea has compelling implications in times like these. If our natal charts—the portraits of our inside worlds—are inextricably connected to the outside world, then the challenges upon the Earth right now must be exactly what our souls need to evolve. The dramas in our environment, including those in the world at large, must be part of each person's singular drama—and every bit as cosmically ordained.

In this view, even extremely disturbing global crises are here to help us integrate our unused potential and to inspire us to develop wisdom. And it must be no less true that each and every one of us, by virtue of having been born when we were, is exactly what the world needs at this moment in its evolution.

Popular astrology has tended to give far less attention to the generational or epochal dimension of the birth chart than to its personal dimension. Certainly a practitioner is far more often asked to parse a client's relationship to her boyfriend than her relationship to the era into which she was born. But this may be changing.

Many of my clients these days express a strong desire to understand the roles they play in this tumultuous era. It occurs to me that the urgency of the times is putting pressure on our old definitions of identity, stretching our notions of what a human lifetime means. At this moment in history, the age-old question *Who am I?* seems to require a broader context than it once did.

Consider the case of a client whose chart features a world-altering transit such as the current Uranus–Pluto square hitting his Ascendant and MC. It would seem quite incomplete to try to explain what he is experiencing in purely personal terms. The changes upon him are about more than just himself. The transit is revealing him as a child of his age.

26

Outer-Planet Thinking

In *The Astrology of Awakening*, Eric Meyers talks about the way the modern mind has become habituated to a perspective that limits our collective consciousness growth. We are stuck in what he calls the *relative level* of existence, symbolized by the planets within Saturn's orbit. In this realm, bounded and defined by time, separation reigns supreme. This is the world we consider real. The whole construct of "reality"—consensually-agreed-upon, 3-D, cause-and-effect reality—is associated with Saturn.

Meyers suggests that humanity is only just beginning to open up to the mysteries symbolized by the planets that reach beyond Saturn, into the vastness of the galaxy. The outer planets, which describe not the personal but the transpersonal self, represent the realm beyond time. From their point of view, everything is connected in a timeless unity.

Mercury, within Saturn's orbit, has to do with the everyday thinking that allows us to analyze and categorize life in the relative realm. By contrast, Uranus, the first planet beyond Saturn, is considered the "higher octave" of Mercury. Its more abstract vision allows us to grasp holistic systems like astrology. Mercurial intelligence can inform us, but it cannot make quantum leaps; it cannot think outside of the box. Uranian intelligence, by contrast, prompts paradigm shifts. It beckons humanity towards our collective future, inspiring social change by ushering in ideas whose time has come.

It would seem that the urgent realities of our epoch impel a running leap into outer-planet thinking. The human race is at a point in its growth arc where our infatuation with material and technological knowledge has outstripped our connection to deep wisdom, throwing us out of whack. From a lack of transpersonal understanding, our stewardship of the Earth has gone derelict. Our spiritual capacities are languishing in arrested development.

Of the many tiers of symbols that make up the astrological pantheon, it is the tier beyond the personal planets that compels our attention here. The high- frequency intelligence of Uranus, the all-inclusive vision of Neptune and the purgative power of Pluto are perfectly designed to match the crises of our post-millennial world. It is outer-planet perception that we need if we are going to transform our guardianship of the Earth to something rather more life-affirming than what we're doing now.

We are all born with a functioning set of outer planets. Each of us knows what it feels like to be nudged, occasionally, beyond separation consciousness. But it is time to put a new degree of focus upon the transpersonal way of seeing, which so far has been the exception, not the norm, in human experience.

It is the Saturnine conception of reality and the Mercurial linear mind that have monopolized the conventional worldview and its institutions. They cannot, by themselves, take us where we need to go.

Good and Bad

But lest we risk making Mercury and Saturn the bad guys here, let us remember that they are perfectly suited to their functions in the relative realm. Separation consciousness is a function of Saturn being Saturn. Its job is to put boundaries around things so they are perceivable in our material world.

Mercury, which is traditionally linked with Gemini (dualism) and Virgo (mechanism, analysis), separates by dividing things into parts, allowing us to understand and assimilate them. This gives rise to the dualistic worldview, which the modern human mind has applied to just about everything in our collective experience.

This is asking Mercury to do too much. We have gotten a lot of mileage out of Mercurial thinking, especially during the Machine Age. But when we start applying it even to numinous symbols—for example, labeling planetary archetypes as malefic or benefic—we ought to realize we have taken dualism out of its league.

Simplistic, quick and easy, the dualistic approach seems especially well suited to assessing the offerings of pop culture, for which it has become the *lingua franca*. Labeling everything in terms of *good* or *bad* has become the default in public discourse. But this asks very little of our intelligence. To settle at this conceptual level is to stay stuck on the very first rung of the intellectual ladder.[1]

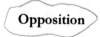 Opposition

As a concept, dualism is a value-neutral archetype: the simplest way of dividing a circle (or an experience) in two. The archetype of the Pythagorean dyad does not imply inherent antagonism any more than two planets in opposition imply mutual exclusion. The essentially neutral valence of dualism is illustrated by the varying expressions of the 180-degree aspect in a natal or transit chart.

Depending on how it is used, an opposition can manifest either as a pitched battle or as a sublime revelation. With Mercurial perception, alone, fueling its expression, an opposition looks like nothing more than two energies contradicting each other: enemies in a zero-sum game. With Uranian intelligence applied, however, the two halves are seen to be parts of the same whole.[2] A person experiencing an opposition through the transpersonal lens may feel a light bulb of truth appear over her head, with the tension suddenly snapping into resolution. The polarized energies reveal themselves to be flip sides of the same coin, giving rise to a previously unseen third meaning.

The Moon and Neptune

Most modern astrologers believe that all the planets can manifest either well or poorly, depending on the native's awareness. But if our focus is the spiritual potential of the birth chart, we must concede that even the most optimal use of the personal planets cannot bestow transpersonal understanding. To the extent that a native fails to integrate his outer planets, he confines himself to a well-worn zone of consciousness that is relatively primitive compared to the wisdom of which he is capable.

Consider the Moon, whose job it is to assess our surroundings for comfort and security but is ill-equipped, all by itself, to usher us into more sublime emotional states. Just as the Moon is associated with literal infancy, the feeling range represented by the Moon is associated with spiritual infancy, i.e., with those primal needs for nurture and safety that dominate the early stages of human psychological development. Moreover, as a reservoir of unresolved hurts and emotional habits, the Moon specializes in the past. But there is a whole universe of emotional–spiritual experience available to us when we get beyond the past and partake fully of the boundless Now.

Consider the difference between the Moon and its corresponding number among the outer planets: Neptune. The transpersonal receptivity of Neptune accepts any and all feelings without the dilution of personal need. Its sensitivities are not dictated by the child-mind's impulse to survive, but by the awareness—often hauntingly inchoate, but nonetheless fundamental—that everything in existence is connected and made of the same divine raw material.

When confined to the personal, our lunar impulses stay on the first rung of the emotional ladder. But when supported and amplified by Neptune, our instincts comingle with what our soul knows.

Venus and Mars

Or consider Venus, which is most commonly known by the ego-driven forms of the two signs she is said to govern: Taurus (material resources) and Libra (relationships).[3]

In her earthy guise, unenlightened Venus can manifest as an enslavement to matter through the illusionary concept of ownership, a malady for which the modern Western world would surely win the prize over any other era in the annals of history. Venus is also the seat of our creative capacity. But when driven by ego, she cannot perceive the flawless beauty of Nature nor appreciate the honoring of its patterns that gives rise to great art. A collective manifestation of stunted Venus is the thumbs-up/-down trope popularized by movie critics Ebert and Siskel—surely the most primitive rung of the aesthetic ladder.

In her social function, too, Venus expresses a mere shadow of her potential unless she is inspired by the trans-egoic. In this case, the law of attraction brings us not love but an objectification of the love object. When we are relating through a strictly personal lens, we are incapable of seeing that the other person is merely reflecting back to us what is in our own hearts.

As for Mars, when confined to its egoic expression, the blowback is especially obvious—and can be brutal. Mars's impulses spring from the most primitive regions of the psyche, where short-term goals are generated from the will to survive. Distorted Mars usually acts out on the event level, with behaviors that serve the ego (or try to).

The uninspired use of Martial energy is everywhere visible in our troubled world, from hurtful acts in the personal sphere to collective violence in the form of war. To express Mars with transpersonal awareness would mean unleashing its vitality into righteous acts of courage, which arise—by cosmic appointment—from the world moment.

Ethics and Belief

The majesty of Jupiter, too, has been constrained by egoic purposes. Symbolic of the human desire to learn and to believe, Jupiter can lead us into the *Right-vs.-Wrong* trap when it is cut off from the transpersonal. Thus estranged, our Jupiterian instincts atrophy; we risk forgetting the purpose of a moral core. We may slip into blind, rote belief, the first rung on the ideological ladder.

Fundamentalism can be found in all three of the dominant sky-god religions (Judaism, Christianity and Islam) and in any other system where a narrowly defined viewpoint is rigidly held.[4] Jupiter's expansive impulses are used here to feed the ego rather than to satisfy our hunger for truth.

In collective life, distorted Jupiter shows up as the designated moral or religious stance identified by the dominant power structure to shore up its power (e.g., Henry VIII's creation of the Church of England), with whole countries being demonized as "evil" if they stand in the way of governmental policy (e.g., Ronald Reagan referring to the USSR as "the evil Empire").[5]

Throughout the ages, human beings have deferred to moral authorities, allowing ourselves to be dictated to, as if we were credulous children. But at this point in Earth's history, we can no longer afford this kind of moral laziness. We may still follow worthy role models, leaders and teachers; but we must hold onto our own inner vision in the process.

Spiritual versus Secular

Freeing ourselves from the limitations of group thought requires disabusing ourselves of many conventions that run very deep. Of particular interest to the meaning-seeker is the idea of a divide between the spiritual (or psychological) and the secular.

The supposed struggle between self-search and work-in-the-world is an old construct, revamped in every age. In an earlier epoch, it might have been expressed as the requirement to either marry or join a nunnery. A modern version might be the belief that being a social activist means disdaining the rarified arena of spiritual search—and that, conversely, being a spiritual searcher means declaring oneself too sensitive to follow the news.[6] The pressure exists to view personal growth and worldly activity as cordoned off from each other.

It is true that some individuals may be specialists in one area or the other. A person's inner drives may lead them to emphasize the professional realm, exemplified astrologically by a grouping of planets at the MC. By contrast, a double Pisces native with a stellium in the twelfth house would probably be happier in some modern version of the nunnery: an ashram or yoga retreat. But the existence in every natal chart of all twelve houses tells us that all of these fields of activity exist, at least in potential form, for every one of us. The existence in every chart of both hemispheres, whether occupied by planets or not, indicates the promise of a fully lived life.

We need to be wary of this conceptual tradition whereby inner life and outer life seem to comprise an *either/or* scenario. It has done a great deal of violence over the ages to the complexity of human aspiration.

Disensouled

The primary problem we are grappling with here has been centuries in the making. The spiritual–secular split has its roots in an epistemological trend seen as modern, and therefore superior, in the evolution of contemporary thought: the notion that spiritual impulses are not really *real*.[7]

In the secular West, the outer world is the *sine qua non* of realness. This is where we cultivate a recognizable identity and a cultural niche, through our outward behavior, professional roles and material circumstances. Explorations into the mysteries of consciousness, by contrast, cannot be measured as such and are barely on the collective radar. Being invisible and subjective, how can they be proven even to exist?

The subtle intuitions of the private inner self evoke confusion and suspicion from many quarters, sometimes even from ourselves. This is an indication of how deeply ingrained in our thinking is the belief that spiritual search is, at best, tangential to the serious pursuits of life. Non-egoic pursuits tend to be seen as a luxury, attended to only when there is extra time. They are tacked onto our workweek, like a hobby. Or an app. When things get hard in "real life," the first thing to be dropped is yoga class.

Spiritual Apartheid

Astrologically, we can chalk up this bias against the transpersonal to the fact that the dominant global paradigm—positivistic mechanistic materialism—is governed by Saturn, which holds physical reality to be the be-all and end-all of reality and cause-and-effect to be the only game in town. The revelations inspired by the outer planets do not fit into Saturn's definition of legitimacy.[8]

It speaks volumes about Saturn's hegemony in consensual reality that what is surely the most profound impulse in human experience—the yearning to return to an awareness of Oneness (Neptune)—is so often walled off from the rest of our identity by means of a kind of psychic apartheid. "Being spiritual" (for example, to pray, to meditate, to experience compassion, to explore non-ordinary states of consciousness) is not seen as a human universal but is spoken of as a personality trait, a kind of idiosyncrasy, as if it were a feature that some people have and some people don't (as when a client confides to an astrologer, "I'm a very spiritual person").

Were we to recognize our spirituality *not* as an adjunct to, but as the essence of, our true nature, our self-image would be very differently constituted. We would know that the divinity at the core of our being is there at every moment; all we have to do is get in touch with it. We would know that this spiritual core is in fact the constant, which all the other layers of our identity are there to serve. As it is, the way most of us have been taught to approach the mystery of identity is upside down.

The modern world's allegiance to mechanistic materialism is deeper than a mere belief (Jupiter); it is a bone-deep assumption about the nature of reality (Saturn). (Compared to this assumption, a belief system is more conscious. We may say, "I'm an Episcopalian," but we probably would not say, "I am a mechanistic materialist".) If our goal is to integrate every part of our psyches—not just the parts that conform to Saturn's standard of credibility—it is important to ask ourselves how we might have internalized our society's biases. We astrologers should not exempt ourselves from this exercise, despite the fact that our work is premised upon principles that fly in the face of physicalism and causality.

Consider the way we put our faith in the over-riding realness of money. This is especially striking in the case of aficionados of metaphysics because of the theoretical exceptionalism involved. We astrologers, although we tend to agree in every other respect with the idea that we create our own reality, often unthinkingly exempt the financial arena from this law. As with everyone else in modern society, we are conditioned to see our financial lives as *über*-real: taking place in a realm that is so Saturnine it is out of reach of our reality-creating capacity.

As Rob Hand has pointed out, many of us think like astrologers when we're doing astrology, and like modern people when we do everything else.[9]

Essential Saturn

But the All-That-Is did not create Saturn to thwart our exploration of the transpersonal. Every member of the astrological pantheon, if used with awareness, supports the overall evolution of the soul. Saturn's value-neutral essence is what we should be aiming for, not its expressions when misused.

What might it look like to use Saturn as a support for, not an inhibitor of, our spiritual evolution? To use this archetype with consciousness, we need to remember its core meaning: maturity and responsibility. This is the planet that teaches through experience, conferring upon us the ability to respond rather than react.

A reaction is automatic and unconscious of consequences. Very young children do not know, until they experience it, that if they drop a glass on the floor, it will break. Moreover, they do not realize, until they are acculturated, that they must clean up the mess.[10] The ability to take responsibility for the results of our actions divides children from adults (from the transpersonal point of view, this extends to words and thoughts as well as actions)—although being grown up in terms of calendar age does not, as we know, guarantee being grown up in other ways.

Saturnine law socializes the singular ego, accommodating it to life in a collective. This aspect of Saturn's meaning is suggested by its spatial role in the solar system. The planets closest to the Sun (the personal planets) deal with the construction of the individual identity; Jupiter and Saturn (the social planets) extend to group membership; and the trans-Saturnians—the outer planets— stretch the definition of selfhood even further, to the point of identifying with, ultimately, everything in Creation. The developmental arc of a human lifetime follows the same logic: once someone is old enough to have had a Saturn return, she is a card-carrying adult with new responsibilities.

It is hazardous to take on the outer planets without factoring in Saturnine responsibilities. This is a point often missed by adherents of the transpersonal realm, which can lure us with the glamour of the exotic.

Global Grown-Up

I speak as a member of a generation whose collective mind was blown by a newly fashionable infatuation with drugs, resulting in a roster of notorious casualties.[11] To take acid and then jump off a roof because you believe the law of gravity (Saturn) is an illusion (Neptune) is an example of experimenting with the outer planets without having incorporated the laws of Saturn. If we are not grounded in spiritual maturity, we end up in dangerous terrain. Consider the activist in a street demonstration (Uranus) who thinks he's changing society by smashing store windows.

As for Pluto, the utmost ethical and spiritual maturity (Saturn) needs to be brought to bear, or we end up with mass destruction. The misapplied Pluto principle is quintessentially exemplified by our era's modern nuclear and chemical weaponry, with their potential to extend mass homicide and ecocide to their ultimate conclusions. These nightmarish concoctions have arisen at this point in humanity's growth arc to jolt us awake unambiguously.

Similarly symptomatic of a profound collective imbalance is the dystopian imagery that has become *de rigueur* in the popular entertainments of the United States which, for good or ill, set the trends globally. The movies we watch that feature post-apocalyptic landscapes in which lone mercenaries seek bloody revenge, the exaggeratedly violent video games that we peddle to children— these are the *cris de coeur* of a world in desperate dis-ease. Where does the healing lie for dysfunction this profound?

If it is true, as the great teachers tell us, that awareness comes into the world through individual consciousness, then changing the world begins with us.

When read through a transpersonal lens, the astrological chart describes our unique role as life-affirmers in a destructive age. Outer-planet vision is, by definition, transformational enough to change the world; and how handy it is that each of us has access to it by birthright.

Distorted Saturn

But true Saturnine maturity—not just the chronological kind—is the prerequisite to the fully integrated use of Uranus, Neptune and Pluto. To cultivate this maturity, we need to be clear about the distortions to which the Saturn archetype has been subjected in cultural expression.

A ready example is the way the phrase "taking responsibility" has come to mean *being at fault* (as in, "It's not my responsibility that my Smartphone was manufactured with slave labor!"). The fact that in American English this connotation has become the dominant one reveals just how far the true meaning of responsibility has fallen out of favor as a cultural value. Consider the compulsion—so strong in the United States—to hire a lawyer and sue. The convention of paying someone to legally relieve us of accountability has all but wiped out the old-fashioned value of taking responsibility as a means of building character.[12]

Part of Saturn's social function is to sensitize us to *what other people think*, which, unless we are grounded in the centers of our charts, can tempt us to betray our individual instincts and follow the crowd. It takes considerable self-discipline to resist the herd mentality when, for example, people around us are gripped by fear.

Instances of the power of group hysteria are legion throughout history. In Tudor England, rumors of invasion provoked the lynching of Catholics every few years; in many places and epochs, "witches" and Jews were blamed when crops failed or cattle died. The ease with which we can find examples of this shameful pattern is testimony to the power of conformity.

Crowd Control

It would be naïve to overlook the role played by human agencies in the provocation and maintenance of group fear. In every age, unscrupulous authorities (negative Saturn) have understood that fear makes for effective crowd control. We see this in the slew of civil rights-abrogating measures that the American government has foisted upon a citizenry traumatized by 9/11. These include wars against peoples who had nothing to do with the destruction of the twin towers, the Patriot Act and HR 347 (the "anti-Occupy bill"), and a multi-trillion dollar "homeland security" apparatus—all of which have served to undermine some of the nation's most cherished values (for example, the loathing of torture and of extrajudicial assassination).[13] In troubled times we need to revisit, again and again, our own core values, while being especially discerning about what we allow into our minds and hearts.

When used with maturity, Saturn does not kowtow to fear, for that would be an abrogation of responsibility, as would be refusing to follow the news because it is unpleasant. The most unsentimental of planets, Saturn confers the kind of clear-eyed understanding that knows, for instance, that in the face of profound social change, the bastions of the Old Guard will probably not assent good-naturedly to retirement. Saturn knows such things and accommodates them as it moves forward with the urgency of the world moment.

We need to be vigilant in our critiques of our society. But if we want to find our roles as responsible citizens of the world moment, we cannot keep blaming our culture's puerility, or our president's perfidy, or even—dare I say it?—an unhappy childhood. Nor can we use them as an excuse, for though these limitations can slow us down, they cannot keep us from growing. For the spiritual seeker, they are part of the roster of life lessons.

I do not mean to trivialize these trials of life, just to say that if we want our world to express real maturity, it is going to have to start with us. We will have to model it, using the planet of karma not in the service of the ego but in its full transpersonal capacity.

Earth Changes

In the material sense, taking responsibility on the most basic level means acknowledging ourselves as having incarnated into a limited, physical world. We take up space on the planet and require certain resources in order to survive. The burgeoning world population—seven billion and counting—is creating crises of the most explicitly tangible kind, everywhere in the world.

Unprecedented in Earth's history, the crises related to environmental degradation and overpopulation are forcing us to use our Uranian potential. Answers to the question of how, for example, we will power our machines when the oil runs out will have to be ingeniously inventive. But even to know what questions to ask, the depth of self-examination we must undertake has to be more radical (in the classic sense; from *radix*: root) than ever before—that is, Plutonian.

Now in Capricorn—the sign traditionally associated with Saturn—Pluto is offering us lessons in radical maturity, and they are offers we cannot refuse. Humanity is being forced to concede which of the fundamental structures of our material lives have run out of viability, to the point of having turned against us.[14]

At the same time, Neptune, in Pisces at this writing, is nudging us outside the bubble of our provincialisms, as more and more people are seeing the world in terms of interconnected systems. As it becomes common knowledge that, say, a polluted Danube in Germany means the befouling of the rivers in Poland, and then in the Balkans, and so on, our thinking can lead to only one place: the realization that any measures to heal the environment must be tackled internationally because we are all in this together.

Neptune is undermining traditional notions of exclusivity and separation both explicitly and implicitly. The rapid erosion of coastlines around the world, as global warming causes sea levels to rise, is quite literally threatening national borders, as land merges with ocean. Sociologically, age-old conceptions of separateness are being undermined by demographics, as in once relatively homogenous regions such as Scandinavia, where massive immigration is creating what demographers are calling "super diversity."[15]

We are being coached in the realization that Earth's myriad living beings and systems constitute an interconnected Whole. We are being made to see that whatever separates us is not as fundamental as that which unites us. We are being forced into the transpersonal wisdom because nothing less will do.

Crack between the Ages

The idea that the Earth is in the throes of unprecedented crises has taken up residence in the postmillennial imagination. From the sober scientific warnings of ecological crisis to the pop phobias about the "world ending" that circulated around December of 2012, a sense of fatal peril is afoot. But emergency has power in it. If we can avoid shutting down in fear, we can use this sense of urgency to fuel our passage over a threshold of consciousness. The transpersonal approach to astrology seems extraordinarily well suited to guide us in this passage.

All by themselves, the inner planets are not enough to allow us to creatively explore, let alone resolve, the fraught issues of our culture and greater world. But when explored from the vantage point of the soul's evolution, the symbols of the birth chart hint at not just what we are like, but why we were born. They offer a blueprint for each of us to cultivate the holistic vision necessary to pull humanity into a healthy future.

In this essay, we have discussed freeing our minds from dualistic groupthink by pressing into service the full intelligence of Mercury, Jupiter and Uranus, combining our inborn common sense with our native moral instincts and iconoclastic genius. We have explored using the Moon, Venus and Mars for the sake of our transpersonal purpose, rather than in service to the ego. We have considered what it might look like to put the personality at the behest of our soul work, difficult though this may be in a culture where this priority is reversed. We described Saturn as the planet of social and spiritual adulthood, without which we cannot step up to the plate in times like these.

To be a true adult is to be able to walk the fine line between individuality and group role, between realism and idealism, between staying informed and becoming overwhelmed. Thus grounded, we are safely positioned to undertake the challenges of the outer planets, which open the conduits of spiritual growth full throttle.

Uranus, Neptune and Pluto are deservedly notorious when exercised within the confines of ego, but they inspire veritable leaps of consciousness when channeled with understanding. Their natal placements show us what it would feel like to live life fully awake, acting as agents for the genius of our era. Their transits give us a sense of when we will be supported in letting go to the unknown. We are in the eye of the storm, then: the only place to be. We are in the center of our chart, merged with the world moment.

Endnotes

1. In the case of the American government, dualism has reached its logical extremity: politics-as-duopoly. A policymaker's party affiliation—Democrat or Republican—trumps all other considerations. States are labeled "blue" or "red." A person is presumed to be a Democrat if he criticizes the military-industrial complex, a Republican if she abhors the Democratic president's drone policy.

2. In the counseling arena, an example of a Uranized approach to dualism is the technique certain mediators and communications experts use to find common ground between a pair of antagonist parties: they recommend substituting "both–and" thinking for the "either–or" kind.

3. The term *ego* in this context refers to the part of a person's psyche that identifies exclusively with the relative realm (which the dominant paradigm calls "reality"), described by the planets within Saturn's orbit. The trans-egoic part of the psyche identifies with the realm of the unbounded universe, accessed by the transpersonal planets.

4. Global fundamentalism has become especially obvious since Pluto's transit through Sagittarius 1995-2008, at which point the *geopolitical* merged with the *religious* in the mass mind.

5. In a presidential address immediately after 9/11, then-president Bush pronounced the words "bad guys" with a trace of ironic ambivalence, as if he knew the locution would remind his listeners of kindergarten. Since then, the frequent use of this and other juvenile word choices to refer to violent official acts—e.g., Obama's "kill list"—seem to have dulled the public's ethical sensibilities, preempting the kind of moral alarm that might have been expected from concerned citizens.

6. Especially in the media-saturated USA, where big-money politics has become so grotesque, it is tempting to buy into the spiritual-versus-political trope. Why should we take seriously the turf wars of a crowd of plutocratic politicians? But this dismissive attitude takes on an added dimension when we consider that, in vernacular usage, "politics" often seems a catch-all term, intended to mean not just the workings of governments but any and all arenas beyond the speaker's personal domain, as in, "What do you think of global warming?" "Oh, I'm not political." Thus do many Americans justify ignoring some of the most significant universal issues of our times.

7. In *The Passion of the Western Mind*, Rick Tarnas discusses the modern world's gradual shift away from the numinous and its embrace of mechanistic materialism, and how we have become disensouled as a result.

8. Stan Grof has written that, as modern rationalism took root in consensus thinking, intellectuals began to look upon spirituality as the refuge of the uneducated. Experiences of the divine came to be diagnosed either as eruptions from an infantile part of the mind that projects deific qualities onto a parent (and vice versa) or as pathological illusions to be cured with pharmaceuticals.

9. Remark in a lecture.

10. A modern spin on karmic law was made famous by former general Colin Powell, who referred to the U.S. invasion of Iraq with a phrase from Pottery Barn: "You break it, you own it."

11. Many of these overdoses took place at the Saturn return: Hendrix, Joplin and Morrison all died at 27. This suggests that the non-ordinary states of consciousness (Stan Grof's phrase) promised by the outer planets came crashing against the Saturnine deadline, when we must come to grips with the limitations of a physical lifetime.

12. The natal Sun–Saturn square in the U.S. (Sibly) chart bears witness to the difficulty this group entity has with the notion of maturity—both physically (aging) and in terms of taking responsibility.

13. The peculiar power of the World Trade Center episode can be understood from an analysis of the Sibly chart, discussed in detail in my book *Soul-Sick Nation*. The national mood of bellicose defensiveness since 9/11/01 corresponds with the alignment of transits over the U.S. horizon line and the opposition thereafter of transiting Pluto to the Sun cluster, which has triggered the country's potential for self-protective reactivity (Cancer).

14. There was a major spike in this consciousness trajectory under the Saturn–Neptune opposition of 2005–2008, which coincided with the appearance of Al Gore's 2006 documentary "An Inconvenient Truth." Saturn (consensus reality) encountered Neptune (fantasy), and climate change morphed from an eccentric Neptunian opinion into something most people consider real.

15. The populations of Africa and Eastern Europe are among those most destabilized by globalization, habitat destruction, war and climate change. In the host countries where these refugees seek succor, today's "majority" populations will soon be numerical majorities no longer.

3

Tracking the Evolution of Collective Consciousness

Armand Diaz

The evolution of consciousness is accelerating, and this has significant implications for astrology. Of the seven or eight major stages of human development recognized by most evolutionary theorists, the first two extend far back into human prehistory. Early on, humans had not yet developed self-reflective consciousness and had not fully differentiated themselves from their clan or group. Following these long early stages, the Iron Age (the Age of Aries) saw the formation of isolated egos, initially in the person of the king and eventually extending to almost everyone. At the Axial Age (roughly the beginning of the Piscean Age), abstract principles began to emerge, and traditional society, based on belief in a universal *way* or truth, was born. The Renaissance and European Enlightenment began the modern era, with its cardinal virtue of progress. Each of these stages—clan, egoic, traditional, and modern—represents not only an advance in skills and technology but also a more inclusive, complex, and comprehensive way of seeing the world than those that came before.

So far we can see that thousands of years—or longer—passed between the first evolutionary stages. But once the modern era was reached, the transitions began to accelerate. By the 19th century, the seeds of the humanistic consciousness that would become prominent in the 1960s were already being planted. Although this is the last wave of consciousness to have shown significant influence thus far, further evolutionary steps have been recognized—steps into what has been described as self-actualizing or *integral* consciousness and then on to *transcendent* or global consciousness.[1] As the population increases dramatically and the entire planet becomes connected both digitally and physically, new structures of consciousness are emerging rapidly to deal with a dynamic environment: we need new ways to see, experience, and act upon a constantly changing world.

Evolution, Awakening, and Emergence

When faced with crises, individuals can move in several different directions. One option is to manage the crisis more or less without significant change to who they are: if a woman loses her job when the company closes, she can find a similar, or even better, job. Another option is regression, a return to a simpler, emotionally and cognitively limited state of being: if a man loses his relationship partner, he might relive childhood abandonment feelings, throw a tantrum, and declare that he will never again love another. Regressions like that can be temporary and even healing, but they can also be permanent and scarring. A third possibility for individuals in crisis is to qualitatively and quantitatively expand understanding, redefine themselves, and operate from a more complex yet also more cohesive perspective—that is, they may *evolve*.

Evolution is a controversial term. Outside of fundamentalist religious groups, there is not much question about biological evolution, but there are questions aplenty within the community of those who accept evolutionary change. One controversy centers on whether biological evolution represents any kind of progress. Many evolutionary theorists, such as the late Stephen Jay Gould, maintain that organisms are simply better or worse adapted to their environments and that no value other than survival can be placed on any adaptation. By this logic, humans and horseshoe crabs are equivalent—and in fact, in terms of temporal success, crabs may have the advantage (they certainly have a longer history). Human social and economic structure, music and art, and other hallmarks of progress are seen as nothing more than successful or unsuccessful responses to environmental conditions. Increased complexity, including the cognitive ability to reflect on such issues, is given no value beyond its biological relevance.

The biological evolutionaries' reticence to recognize value or progress in the process is in part a result of their mechanistic approach to nature: it is all a vast machine lacking any substantial consciousness and so must be ultimately valueless. But this reluctance may also be a response to a more controversial interpretation of the concept of evolution: social evolution. Darwin's ideas about evolution of species were used (in part with his encouragement[2]) to justify social stratification. *Social Darwinism* is an ugly term, suggesting that those who claw their way to the top of the social ladder are naturally more fit and healthier. Social Darwinism was the high-water mark of hubris within secular scientific society—it fell to natural law to make billionaires and czars, who thus had little responsibility to those below. The views of Social Darwinists have given us reason to pause when ideas about collective evolution are raised.

In fact, some feel it preferable to move away from the term *evolution* entirely. Alternatives include *awakening* and *emergence*, although these terms have slightly different meanings. *Awakening* implies a kind of enlightenment; the Buddha described himself as "awake." It is therefore a *state of being*, a kind of awareness, usually described as being in accordance with the present moment and having an acceptance of, or even identification with, all that is. Awakening is a shift in awareness of the conditions of existence, an ontological revelation. In *The Astrology of Awakening*, Eric Meyers defines awakening as "*the transcendence of the ego as the primary orientation and identification*" (italics in the original).[3]

Emergence is a term that has a slightly different connotation, implying a movement *through* or *from* something. Spiritual emergence can be seen as a movement of awareness through the boundaries of biology, the personal ego, or the social constructs of society, culture, language or history. In their book *The Stormy Search for the Self*, Christina and Stanislav Grof define *spiritual emergence* as "the movement of an individual to a more expanded way of being that involves enhanced emotional and psychosomatic health, greater sense of personal choices, and a deeper connection with other people, nature, and the cosmos."[4]

Evolution does not correspond to either of these two terms in any exact way, although it overlaps with each of them in certain respects. As applied to consciousness, evolution is usually seen as the linear or stepwise progression through a series of stages, each of which is in some way a more or less enduring *structure* that represents a movement in the direction of greater complexity and inclusiveness. It is the ability to understand a wider variety of perspectives as well as to expand one's limits of compassion and caring. Consciousness evolution is a dynamic and ongoing process, and implicit in the concept as it applies to human consciousness is a kind of progress. The specific end point of that progress is necessarily open and uncertain because each successive evolutionary stage is unknowable at the prior stage: individuals traverse the known evolutionary landscape in a predictable order until they get to the edge of the process, where they individually and collectively forge the next step forward. That next step is made based upon the awareness that has been achieved in concert with the conditions that currently prevail; consciousness interacting with the environment produces a new consciousness, and perhaps eventually a new environment.

Awakening may involve temporary peak experiences, or may be the beginning of a lasting change in personality, worldview, and sense of identity. In other words, awakening may lead to evolution. It also seems at least plausible that consciousness evolution is the process of creating stable structures that may eventually resemble or be identical to the states experienced in awakening, just as repeated visits to advanced states of awakening may lead to consciousness evolution. Separating the processes of evolution and awakening seems particularly useful when we consider large groups of people, although it may be the case, as Arjuna Ardagh has suggested in *The Translucent Revolution*, that individuals are becoming enlightened in large numbers to form a kind of mass movement.[5]

Among those with a spiritual orientation, the concept of individual evolution is not particularly controversial, although it has often been conflated with awakening or enlightenment. Applied to the collective, however, evolution does indeed become controversial, and that is true whether we define the collective as a particular culture, a segment of a culture, or all of humanity. It is not hard to look at the technological advances of modern society and see that they have often been applied to less-than-enlightened ends: degradation of the environment, exploitation of less technologically sophisticated cultures, the persistence of warfare, and selective access to the benefits of modern society (healthcare, justice system, education, and so on). It is certainly possible to question whether the movement into modernity (just one stage on the evolutionary journey) really represents any kind of progressive evolution or merely the acquisition of a new set of tools with which to apply the lowest impulses of our species.

Each evolutionary step forward contains both light and dark elements. Just as a child reaching the terrible twos has greater independence of thought and action while also potentially becoming something of a tyrant, so at every other stage of consciousness we can find constructive and destructive qualities. Common problems as each evolutionary level is reached include a negative attitude towards prior levels (hence, exploitation of them) and failure to see the shadow side of the new level. Until relatively high in the developmental spectrum, it is also very common to fail to see the value of the entire evolutionary scheme, and instead to focus on the glories of one's present level.[6]

Finally, we need to acknowledge that for both individuals and cultures we may speak of an average level of development, but the actual situation is far more complex. A person may be quite well developed with regard to career and place in the world while lagging in terms of personal relationships, or vice versa. Societies are composed of such complex individuals and so reflect a diverse mosaic of evolutionary stages. We may note that a culture holds very conservative, traditional views towards family structure, while a more progressive, open-ended attitude towards business and commerce prevails. Different groups within societies will tend towards value structures that are in accord with the development of the individuals that comprise those groups, and these may be at odds with other groups of individuals. American society, for example, contains a prominent egocentric "outlaw" segment; a more traditional segment; a dynamic scientific–business community; and an influential postmodern, humanistic minority concerned with social justice and individual development. All of these groups reflect different developmental stages and coexist (often uneasily) with each other within the larger society. Add in that each evolutionary stage also has its shadow side and that the entire process is in constant flux, and a very high degree of complexity becomes apparent.

The introduction of a new developmental stage in consciousness does not mean that prior stages disappear or are replaced, nor does it mean that we begin to approximate a utopian society on earth. Rather, new stages are added on to existing structures of consciousness. Those people who participate in the new structures continue to have access to and experience aspects of earlier stages, something that is apparent enough when one encounters threatening situations. Another consideration is that the movement to a new evolutionary stage does not involve all members of a group or society—in fact, initially only a very small minority participate in the advance in consciousness. Witch hunts

46

continued even as the Renaissance and Enlightenment produced high art and progressive philosophy.

Astrological Timing of Consciousness Evolution

The pace of evolution is speeding up: at first, new structures of consciousness emerged over millennia, then centuries, and now they are appearing within decades. Remember that each successive stage of consciousness represents not only something new and different but also a more complex, inclusive, and cohesive way of viewing the cosmos. As such, we can expect the next stage to be more adaptive to present conditions than previous ones; thus its influence may be strong despite relatively small numbers of people participating in it.

Until very recently, astrological understanding of cultural change, and evolution, has largely been centered on the large astrological ages, based on the precession of the poles.[7] The slow unfolding of the earliest stages of human evolution may have spanned many of these astrological ages. However, as the pace of evolution accelerates, astrologers may require a different tool for measuring evolutionary change. One such tool would be the emergence of the outer planets.[8] Significantly, around the time of the discovery of Uranus we made a leap in our collective understanding of evolution itself. It can be hard for contemporary people to imagine that until recently it was assumed that most of the universe was in a kind of steady state. Classical understanding of the cosmos, for example in Plato, assumed that the earth, sky, and perhaps even humans were all part of an eternal sameness—things changed locally, but the grand scheme had always been and would always be more or less the same. That's why philosophy and religion from the traditional era highlighted discovering and living in accord with eternal, universal principles. The Judeo–Christian belief system was one of the few that countered the steady-state cosmos with an alternative: specifically, the addition of definitive beginning and end points in time.

Around the time that Uranus came into view, our understanding of evolution itself began to evolve. Geologists discovered changes in the earth that suggested things had been very different on the planet in the past. Fossils found within the layers of rock suggested biological evolution. Astronomers

47

began to postulate the universe's expansion from a unique starting point, suggesting an evolving cosmos. With our minds opened to the possibility of so many kinds of evolution, psychologists began to consider whether consciousness itself might not be in a process of evolution. Western psychologists such as Freud and Piaget described a kind of evolution from birth through adulthood, while those who looked towards the East found that models for the evolution of consciousness (and in fact of the cosmos) already existed—and extended far beyond well-adjusted adulthood in the Western world. More recent work by theorists of consciousness evolution such as Clare Graves, Don Beck, Christopher Cowan, Ken Wilber, Allan Combs, and Jenny Wade has created a series of deep and detailed maps of the process.

The discovery of Uranus, Neptune, and Pluto may correspond with the emergence of new structures of consciousness. After a point, however, it becomes somewhat unreasonable to expect a planet to show up each time we are ready for an evolutionary leap, especially if the process is accelerating, so perhaps a different approach is called for. For example, in recent years astrologers have been inundated with new planetoids and asteroids, the latter now numbering over 13,000. Asteroids are named for individuals, objects, and even popular cultural icons (there's a *Monty Python* asteroid). Clearly, each does not represent a unique level of consciousness that we all will pass through (that would be the equivalent of 13,000 chakras). While planets and/or zodiac signs may have had a one-to-one correspondence with evolutionary stages in the past, the sheer number of asteroids suggests that kind of symbolism is itself evolving into something new. Perhaps as a reflection of the Age of Aquarius, we are developing the ability to choose our own symbols from a large array. As we go forward, we may develop heliocentric and even galactocentric astrologies to express our evolving consciousness of the cosmos.

An Active Role in Evolution

In his book *Evolutionary Enlightenment*,[9] Andrew Cohen takes the accelerating pace of evolution a step further. As the title suggests, Cohen acknowledges both evolution and enlightenment. As enlightenment involves a transcendence of identification with the ego, and evolution involves the creation of ever more inclusive structures of consciousness, *it becomes possible to identify with the process of evolution itself.* At a fundamental level, we *are* the evolutionary process. Now that we, as sentient beings, are aware of evolution, we have the opportunity to actually *direct* the process, to create the cosmos consciously. No longer restricted to playing in a universe in which the rules are already written (albeit obscurely), we can begin to take part in the formation not only of ourselves as individuals but of our collective reality. Not only is our consciousness of ourselves and the cosmos evolving, our *consciousness of evolution* is taking on a new level of self-reflective understanding and power. As applied to astrology, we start to recognize our own creative role in astrological symbolism; we begin to realize that we do not discover the meaning of a planet, a sign, or anything else—we actually collectively create that meaning.

Psychiatrist and psychologist Stanislav Grof has noted that on the individual level personal change and growth are often correlated with both the timing and type of astrological transits. In his work in the area of transpersonal psychology, Grof noted that during intense therapeutic work—at first with psychedelics and later with holotropic breathwork—the character of the experience tends to relate to the relevant astrological transit the person is having. Of course, astrologers are well aware that transits and progressions correlate with both internal states and external circumstances, but the emphasis on deep experiential work represents a shift in perspective, and the implication is that one can see a significant transit coming and use it as an opportunity for engaging in experiential therapy. Astrologers could encourage clients to truly take a proactive approach to transits—actually intensifying their effects through techniques that can bring out the most challenging sides of an astrological configuration. Undertaken with awareness and self-compassion, this approach may help individuals to maximize the inherent potential in transits and so further their individual evolutionary progress. It is interesting to consider whether this same pattern could have any meaning when applied to the level of cultural evolution.

When we consider a significant mundane transit, such as the Uranus–Pluto square in the years 2012–2015 or the passage of one of the outer planets through a sign, we see that pressures develop around personal and cultural areas that are described by the relevant symbolism. Pluto's transit through the sign of Libra in the 1970s, for example, coincided with significant changes in relationship patterns, while his move into Capricorn in 2008 coincided with major pressures on the structures of government, business, and economics. The development of new stages of consciousness evolution, as well as the move from lower to higher structures already in existence, is precipitated in part by cognitive–emotional and psychospiritual readiness, but it is frequently triggered by changes in what Beck and Cowan call "life conditions."[10] Powerful mundane transits seem to provide at least a partial description of changing life conditions; they may therefore be useful in identifying opportunities for the advancement (or possibly regression) of consciousness in the collective. Just as warming and cooling of the planet are changes that can effect biological evolution—creating a change in the environment that calls for physical adaptation—the transits of the outer planets may describe changes in the environment of the collective consciousness that require evolution.

Knowing when we are approaching an opening for collective evolutionary change is important for several reasons. Such pivot points are often highly disruptive for both societies and the individuals within them, as the movement towards change often meets with strong resistance. Those who are in the process of creating a new mode of consciousness (relatively new within a given society, if not entirely new on the planet) are often misunderstood and alienated at first. Perhaps most importantly for the consulting astrologer, individuals who are deeply involved in collective evolution often fail to recognize it as such; while they are focused on the issues in front of them, they may have little time or inclination to reflect on the larger process. As with personal transits, we may anticipate and resolve to work with mundane transits consciously and actively.

An Example of Astrological Timing of Evolutionary Change

The discovery of Neptune in 1846 signaled a shift in consciousness. Neptune is associated with the dissolution of boundaries, a kind of porous relationship to alternative realities, as well as illusions, delusions, and confusion; and we can see that in the West, this energy went in several directions.

Neptune certainly corresponds with the humanistic worldview. Transcendentalists of the 19th century such as Emerson and Whitman represent a significant step in the development of this worldview. A feeling of oneness with the natural world and all people was a hallmark of their writings.

50

The spiritualist movement, peaking in the late 19th century, opened up the possibility of communication with departed souls, a clear example of the porous quality of Neptune. Spiritualism coincided with and was followed by theosophy and anthroposophy, the Order of the Golden Dawn, and other movements in the late 19th and early 20th centuries that would serve as the foundation of the New Age in the latter part of the 20th century. In all of these, we see an inclusive spiritual perspective that counters the isolationist tendencies of traditional religion and which honors individual experience above accepted dogma. This aspect of the Neptunian/humanistic worldview incorporated a spiritual perspective that not only ran counter to the strong materialistic bias of the times but also challenged established religion.

On a more earthly level, the modern, material-leaning worldview also adopted Neptunian porousness. Lincoln and Darwin—born on the same day, a Uranus station—both challenged divisions and separateness. Lincoln is known for his stand against slavery, one of the harshest divisions among people ever to pollute our planet. Darwin dissolved the very boundaries between species, placing all of life on a continuum. This more secular strain of the humanistic perspective infused a variety of social and political movements, including those focusing on labor and women's suffrage in the late 19th and early 20th centuries.

As the humanistic value set began to really gain influence in the 1960s and 1970s, the Civil Rights, Women's, Gay Rights, and other movements advocated for social and political inclusiveness and respect for diversity—much the way the New Age advocates for the same values in the area of spirituality. We can see that the discovery of Neptune corresponded with the emergence, slowly at first, of a new way of viewing the world that was neither traditional (relying on external authority) nor modern (obsessed with progress and development). This new worldview is inclusive, it seeks to tear down boundaries between people and even between species, and it honors diversity while recognizing an underlying unity. It may be hard for many readers to accept that this is truly a new way of viewing the world and an evolutionary leap in consciousness, but not only is it a recent development, it is still comparatively rare.

Yet Neptune did not only energize those who were ready for an evolutionary leap. For those who held fast to the modern, materialistic worldview, Neptune represented an intensifying of those values. Communism and the many varieties of totalitarianism are examples of Neptunian energy mired within a modern worldview. Traditional societies also received a dose of Neptunian energy, with fundamentalism as the result. Of course, totalitarianism and fundamentalism continue to exist, to the extent that Neptune pushes on modern and traditional societies that are not ready to move to a more inclusive humanistic perspective. What then is the requisite for evolutionary change?

If we look at the three most prominent current Western worldviews, we see that traditional is followed by modern, which is followed by humanistic. Evolutionary steps must be made in sequence, so it is not possible to move directly from traditional to humanistic. The humanistic worldview therefore can only take root in a society where a sufficient number of people are already seeing the world through modern eyes (although Neptune encountered modernism with only modest effect until the 1960s).

Pluto's discovery in 1930 is seen by astrologers as the start of a new epoch in our understanding of change on both a personal and global level. Pluto represents radical, fundamental processes of transformation: death and rebirth, and the excavation and processing of forgotten and repressed psychic material. On an individual level, Plutonian processes may lead to a more core or soul orientation, although whether to associate this planet with a particular evolutionary stage is an open question. Pluto's role in transformation, however, is not in doubt.

Pluto's entry into Virgo and the Uranus–Pluto conjunction of the 1960s energized the move from modern to humanistic worldviews for many people. Although the number of people who have truly evolved to the humanistic level remains rather modest—perhaps 10 percent of the population[6]—this small segment of the population has a degree of influence that is out of proportion to its numbers, an indication that its time has arrived; the humanistic worldview is in many ways more adaptive to our times than the traditional or modern. Virgo is the sign of service, and Pluto's time in Virgo deeply transformed attitudes towards service. For example, not only had African Americans been slaves in the past, the dominant 1950s *image* of a black person in the United States was still a service position—a maid, a Pullman porter, or a chauffeur. The Civil Rights Movement was largely the uprising of what was at least *perceived* to be a servant class. Military conscription was another prominent *service* issue (the military is often referred to as "the service"). As millions of educated, modern young men faced the prospect of going to war, they began to question the authority that claimed power over their lives. Unlike their more traditional parents, this generation was unlikely to accept the call to duty without assessing the situation for themselves. Virgo is also a sign with a strong feminine energy; in fact, it may be considered the sign of feminine strength. During Pluto's time in this sign, women entered college at unprecedented levels, on the way to claiming an equal place in the workforce.

We can see that Pluto's transit of Virgo corresponded with pressures that, when combined with a progressive, individualistic modern worldview, could result in sufficient force to move large numbers of individuals towards a humanistic perspective—collective evolution. (Pluto in Virgo was no guarantee of cultural evolution; in traditionalist China, it coincided with the disastrous Great Leap Forward.)

Following the story a bit forward from the 1960s, we can further see that Pluto's time in Libra had a transformative effect on relationships in the Western world. While Pluto/Virgo had political and social themes, Pluto/Libra extended the transformation to relationships as women became more engaged in the workforce, and relationship patterns began to change. For those who had made the leap to the humanistic worldview, the values that had been applied to work and social standing were extended to partnership, creating a variety of new ways of relating that valued inclusiveness and equality in relationships. The area of relationship thus "caught up" with the humanistic worldview that had established itself elsewhere.

On the other hand, Pluto in Libra, applied to more traditional societies and individuals, coincided with a move towards modernism; liberalization of divorce laws, the prevalence of living together before or without marriage, and living single all signaled a new autonomy for individuals, allowing them to chart their own course in relationship.

The discovery of Neptune coincided with the opening of potential for a move to humanistic consciousness, although initially very few people adopted the new worldview. During the transit of Pluto through the sign of Virgo, sufficient tensions and changes were created to attract many people towards the humanistic worldview, at least in those societies that had reached a peak of modernism. The following transit of Pluto through Libra helped to bring the area of relationship—often a laggard in personal development—into the humanistic orbit. We can also see that, although relatively few people have

53

become established in the humanistic consciousness, this worldview has had increasing influence over the past five decades and can be expected to attract greater numbers as time goes forward. The process of consciousness change in the collective takes place in steps; each significant transit opens up the possibility of further expansion of newer worldviews, although the end result is always up to the individuals affected.

Towards a New Era

Looking forward, we are confronted with a unique situation. Recognizing that we are part of the evolutionary process—that we *are* the evolutionary process—we are in a position to guide it consciously for the first time. Rather than waiting for or reacting to change, we have the potential to move in the direction that we choose. Consciousness evolution always moves towards more inclusive, compassionate, and complex ways of viewing and acting in the world, and astrology is perfectly suited for showing us what areas of life are going to be ripe with potential for change. Given the information, it is up to us to decide how we will respond, individually and collectively. We can sit and wait with anxiety or hope, or we can recognize our potential to engage and actively participate in the evolutionary process.

Endnotes

1. For a comprehensive description of the stages of development, see Jenny Wade's *Changes of Mind: A Holonomic Theory of the Evolution of Consciousness*. State University of New York Press, 1996.
2. Chap 3, Religion, *The Autobiography of Charles Darwin*. Barnes & Noble, 2005.
3. Eric Meyers, *The Astrology of Awakening, Volume 1: The Eclipse of the Ego*. Astrology Sight Publishing, 2012.
4. Christina Grof and Stanislav Grof, *The Stormy Search for the Self*. Penguin, 1990.
5. Arjuna Ardagh, *The Translucent Revolution*. New World Library, 2005.
6. Ken Wilber's *Integral Psychology* (Shambhala, 2000) has a good section on this.
7. Alice O. Howell, *Jungian Synchronicity in Astrological Signs and Ages*. Quest Books, 1990.
8. See the chapters by Faye Cossar and Rafael Nasser in this book.
9. Andrew Cohen, *Evolutionary Enlightenment*. EnlightenNext, 2011.
10. Don Beck and Christopher Cowen, *Spiral Dynamics*, Blackwell Publishing, 2006

4

The Telos of Techne:

Technological Development and the Uranus-Pluto Cycle

Bill Streett

Upon first glance, it may appear odd and even perplexing to focus on technology in a volume dedicated to transpersonal astrology. In an age of nuclear weapons, predator drones, and the vapid clutter that constitutes the majority of cyberspace, it would appear that technology is more of a hindrance to the evolution of consciousness than a catalyst for its advancement. More dubiously, as the byproduct and henchman of the scientific–mechanistic worldview, technology has put us on the precipice of collective annihilation with its conception of the earth as a dead object and its treatment of our planet as an infinitely renewable resource for our benefit. Aldous Huxley, considered by many to be one of the inspirational forerunners of the entire transpersonal movement, poignantly and presciently warned of technology's darker potentials in his dystopian *Brave New World.*

Given this view of technology as the instrumental and applied knowledge of a dying worldview, it would be shortsighted to focus on technology within the scope of transpersonal thought. However, if we broaden our view and treat technology in its more general and essential form, we can see technology as being the external manifestation of the collective consciousness. Technologist Kevin Kelly puts this view in sharp relief as he writes, "Technology is the visible extension of an archaic force which runs up in time while the universe runs down. Technology is the latest chapter in the continuous story that builds up order, structure, freedom, possibilities and good against the inescapable black drain of entropy... Technology is a cosmic force."[1] While Kelly may overemphasize the positive aspects of technology at the expense of its shadow potentials, he perfectly captures the meaning and basis of technology in its most general form.

"Technology" derives from the Greek *techne*; the early Greek philosophers believed not just that technology was the practical application of thought necessary to build tools but also that technology had moral, aesthetic, political, and even epistemological dimensions. Although we are prone to see technology as the sum total of gadgets created to make our lives easier, the Greeks admonished that technology does not exist in a vacuum but reflects a society's values, judgments, and desires. Martin Heidegger, concerned as he was with the essences of things, expanded and elaborated upon the Greek definition of technology to suggest that technology is, at its root, a "revealing" (or "un-concealing") of truth. Taking our cue from Heidegger, just as a sculptor liberates an artwork that lies in potential in a slab of stone, humanity's collective technological development is poised to reveal and liberate ever-increasingly complex forms of consciousness. Given this broad view, technology is an externalization of consciousness, an outer reflection of social goals, values, and desires. Thus, from a transpersonal perspective, we can see technology not just as an accrual of contraptions and cultural ephemera over time but as artifacts, or footprints, if you will, of Spirit as it makes its arduous climb up the Great Chain of Being.[2]

The Evolutionary Framework: The Uranus–Pluto Cycle

This is a pivotal moment in our collective technological development. By most accounts, we are leaving the Age of Industry behind and entering into the Age of Information. Far from just representing a shift in economic modes of production, this epochal change symbolizes a shift in worldview—a shift in consciousness—with its concomitant transformations in values, motivators, priorities, and orientations. The movement from one epoch to the next—whether it be the transition from the Age of Agriculture to the Age of Industry or this current transition—is not a linear, smooth shift, but one characterized by pivot points in time in which the leaps of advancement are accelerated. These quantum leaps—these great periods of revolutionary progress—can be likened to the hypothesis of punctuated equilibrium within evolutionary biology, whereby the evolution of species takes place suddenly within relatively short periods of time. Put succinctly, evolution—whether biological or technological—occurs in bursts.

From the vantage point of astrology, these punctuated bursts of accelerated development correlate with the cyclical alignments of the outer planets: Uranus, Neptune, and Pluto. That is, alignments of the outer planets, most notably the "hard" aspects of the conjunction, opposition, and square (or quadrature alignments) strikingly and synchronistically correlate with periods of rapid evolutionary advance. Restricting our view to technological development, the cycle that most profoundly correlates with technological advancement is the Uranus–Pluto cycle.[3] When Uranus and Pluto form hard alignments, we observe great quantum leaps forward in technological development. However, beyond just being markers in the sky that correlate with these periods of rapid advancement, the *quality* of these periods of progress markedly resonates with the archetypal meanings and associations attributed to these planets.

To better appreciate the Uranus–Pluto cycle, it is important to understand the archetypal qualities of Uranus and Pluto in isolation, particularly those qualities that are most concerned with technological advancements. As the planet of inspiration, insight, genius, and creative breakthrough, Uranus is the planet most associated with the "Eureka" effect or the "Aha" experience that has been so well documented in scientific discoveries and technological breakthroughs. While it may be true, as Thomas Edison said, that "genius is one percent inspiration, ninety-nine percent perspiration," Uranus is the archetype most associated with the lightning strikes of visionary insight that catapult societies into new technological landscapes. Thus, as we shall see, when Uranus is in major alignment with Pluto, these creative breakthroughs are particularly intensified, leading to rapid technological advancements within relatively short periods of time.

Technical wizardry and strokes of creative genius are arguably the signature manifestations of Uranus. However, when understanding technology in terms of the evolution of consciousness, Uranus' most important quality is its association with the drive to liberate oneself beyond constraints and the urge to transcend limitations. This quality of Uranus is perfectly captured in the quest for flight, for well before air flight (and space flight, for that matter) had any practical purposes and utilitarian import, the extraordinary energy and sheer economic resources devoted to these endeavors were compelled by the need literally to transcend our initial earth-bound limitations.[4] While we often see technology as simply an economic reality aimed at improving the quality of our lives, perhaps the greatest motivation for technological progress is the deep-seated desire to transcend and aspire to greater levels of consciousness and to break through the often insufferable limitations placed upon our mortal condition. This sentiment is perhaps most beautifully and poetically captured by the novelist Jonathan Franzen, as he writes, "The ultimate goal of technology, the telos of techne, is to replace a natural world that's indifferent to our wishes—a world of hurricanes and hardships and breakable hearts, a world of resistance—with a world so responsive to our wishes as to be, effectively, a mere extension of the self."[5] Thus, while it is beyond the scope of this article to attribute any final meaning, or teleological vector, to either technology itself or the archetype of Uranus, certainly the profound desire to transcend limitations may be considered one of the prevailing motivations in the story that is technology's unfolding.

Inspiration, genius and creative breakthroughs are not enough to account for the extraordinary and massive technological shifts that we are undergoing as we transition from the Age of Industry to the Age of Information. The archetype of Pluto is the other planet that must be addressed. As an entry point, Pluto is the "archaic force," the "cosmic force" that Kevin Kelly refers to when discussing the heart of the meaning of technology. Pluto is the archetype arguably most associated with the unfolding of evolution itself, as Pluto is the prime mover, the transformational engine, that destroys, transforms, regenerates, and metamorphoses one form of being into something utterly new. When discussing our current transition from the Age of Industry to the Age of Information, Pluto can be best expressed as both the extraordinary pain associated with the death of outmoded socioeconomic models while, at the same time, the profound ecstasy that comes with the emergence of new modes of being. Not unlike the concept of *kundalini* or *shakti*, Pluto is akin to a titanic libidinal life force that drives—often with unrepentant willful force and extreme intensity—anything with which it connects.

The current technological landscape often conjures up images of feeble, ineffectual Silicon Valley "geeks"—hardly a symbol that resonates with the powerful, libidinal, and titanic forces associated with the astrological Pluto.

However, with more careful consideration, we realize that these same individuals run corporations that are global in scope, that affect worldwide political policy, and that have economic revenues larger than many countries' gross domestic product. These seemingly nerdish individuals are the current titans of industry, and, in a somewhat ironic twist of fate, do on some level symbolize the Plutonian archetype.

Taken together, Uranus and Pluto symbolize the twin engines of technological advancement, and when these planets align, they reinforce and activate their archetypal principles. With this in mind, we can see that the conjunction of Uranus and Pluto in the 1960s and the current square alignment (in orb from 2007 through 2019) as critical periods of time, ushering in the Age of Information.[6] If, as technologist Andrew McAfee suggests, the Industrial Revolution was aimed at overcoming the limitations of our individual muscles, then the Technological Revolution is the attempt to overcome the limitations of our own brains.[7] With this in mind, we see the affect of the activation of both the archetypes of Uranus and Pluto during pivotal alignments. Uranus symbolizes the motivation and divine spark to overcome the limitations of the physical, the earth-bound, the mortal, and the transitory state of life. Pluto, on the other hand, symbolizes the titanic life force, or collective self-overcoming, needed to impel such a desire into manifestation.

With these factors in mind, we can now turn to specific correlations of the current Uranus–Pluto square alignment. It is beyond the scope of this article to present even a moderate cataloguing of important technological advances and discoveries that have occurred under the current Uranus–Pluto square. Rather, the correlations presented below best represent those areas of technological progress that can be seen not only as externalizations of the current development of collective consciousness but also as representing areas of life in which the technological interpenetrates the social, moral, political, and indeed spiritual dimensions of life.

Rise of Mobile Computing and the Proliferation of Social Networking

Without question, the computer is the device that best symbolizes the emerging Age of Information and is at the nexus of the great shift away from the Age of Industry. While computing as we know it could not have been possible without the invention of the transistor in the 1940s, it was during the Uranus–Pluto conjunction of the 1960s that computing—with the manufacturing of mainframes and the initial production of microprocessors— truly emerged as an economic reality and social force.

During the current Uranus–Pluto square, several developments in technology have both increased and expanded the importance of computing and the internet. The release of Apple's iPhone in mid-2007 initiated a veritable explosion of new mobile computing devices, including tablet computers, smart phones, and personal digital assistants. Seen as the logical heir apparent of the first telephone (invented by Alexander Graham Bell under the last Uranus– Pluto square of the nineteenth century) and adumbrated by the high-tech devices envisioned in television shows such as *Star Trek* under the last Uranus– Pluto conjunction, smart phones and other mobile devices have represented a major advancement in computing. So revolutionary has been the rise of smart phones and other mobile devices that it represents not just the exponential growth of the internet's reach, but a qualitative shift in the way technology affects daily life. As the name implies, mobile devices have allowed individuals constant access to each other and to the internet—to information at any time and any place. Mobile devices have also represented a major shift in way we interact with computers. With the integration of touch screens and speech recognition software, mobile devices, many analysts suggest, represent the third major revolution in computer user interface design, taking individuals beyond text and graphical user interfaces that dominated computing in the last quarter century.

Concurrent with the rise of mobile technologies, and in some sense facilitated by these devices, has been the advance of social media and networking sites on the internet, best represented by Twitter, Facebook, and YouTube. While many social media sites such as Facebook were founded slightly before the current Uranus–Pluto square, their exponential growth and establishment as worldwide phenomena occurred during the alignment. From mid-2008 through mid-2011, the number of Facebook users skyrocketed— from 100 million users to just under 800 million users worldwide.[8] Microblogging site Twitter demonstrates a similar pattern of staggering growth in roughly the same time period. While it took approximately eighteen months for Twitter to add its first 500,000 accounts, by 2011, Twitter was adding

500,000 accounts daily.[9] Correspondingly, to achieve a sense of how popular the video-sharing website YouTube has become, at the time of this writing (2012), in an average month, more video content is uploaded to the site than has been generated by the three major U.S. television networks in the past sixty years.[10] Put another way, by the end of 2012 there was so much content on YouTube that it would take over 1,700 years—or over twenty average lifetimes—to view it all.[11]

We can see the exponential rise of social media and networking as an expression of the sharply accelerated technological shifts that accompany Uranus–Pluto alignments. In addition, the nature of these sites, which rely almost exclusively upon user-generated content, can also be seen as the radical empowerment of individual expression, a hallmark characteristic of Pluto empowering and intensifying the archetype of Uranus.

Although social networks are bogged down with mindless clutter, in their most positive, life-affirming expression, these networks allow for thousands of otherwise disenfranchised individuals to find each other through online groups, creating a haven in a virtual world where new ideas and new modes of expression can be articulated. Rapid interaction through social networks gave protestors information about how best to counteract security forces during uprisings in Tunisia and Egypt, and as the Arab Spring revolutions rose, social media carried, as one researcher put it, "a cascade of messages about freedom and democracy across North Africa and the Middle East."[12] While many commentators suggest that no technology is inherently either positive or negative, the framework of social media networks does appear to facilitate the open exchange of ideas that past technologies could not promote. The many-to-many format of social media networks is unique among broadcast media, and this arrangement—in conjunction with near-instantaneous transmission of messages—makes social media a potent agent of change and distinctive in its ability to act as a forum for democratic ideas.

Social networks are unintentionally facilitating, and reflective of, a major advance in the evolution of consciousness. Because of the medium's many-to-many nature, the variety of opinions, voices, and viewpoints that are not only disseminated but also assimilated has created a radical plurality of truths—not just one monolithic, dogmatic form of truth. Consciousness researchers such as Don Beck suggest that a hallmark of increasing forms of consciousness is the ability to hold and respect differing, if not paradoxical, viewpoints simultaneously. Certainly, social networks hold the promise of increasing one's cognitive dissonance "load capacity" exponentially, and while some will regress and retreat into dogmatic extremism as a result, far greater numbers will likely leap into greater tolerance and acceptance of differing viewpoints.[13]

Social and Economic Repercussions of Technological Advancements

As with the major Uranus–Pluto alignments that punctuated the Industrial Revolution (namely, the 1787–1798 opposition, 1816–1824 square, and 1845–56 conjunction), the most recent conjunction and square of these two planets have birthed extreme socioeconomic changes and marked epochal shifts in society and commerce. While ecommerce may have been birthed during the recent Uranus–Neptune conjunction, the development of ecommerce during the current Uranus–Pluto square has seen a shift from ecommerce as an innovation and novelty to ecommerce as a necessity in today's retail landscape. The several advantages afforded by ecommerce—twenty-four hour convenience, instantaneous comparison shopping, and an extraordinarily large selection of products—have changed shopping dynamics worldwide, simultaneously birthing new patterns of commerce while destroying older modes of business. Online ecommerce giants such as Amazon and eBay have revolutionized retail shopping and, in their ascent, have inadvertently destroyed brick and mortar competitors.

Technology has not only transformed retail but has changed the dynamics of the workplace and patterns within the workforce. During the current Uranus–Pluto square, the rise of cloud computing (in which software, databases, and platforms exist in remote networks shared by multiple companies) has, in essence, uprooted the traditional office space. An older model of business—whereby employees arrive in one location during set time intervals—is being steadily replaced by a decentralized workforce run by telecommuters, data centers, contractors, and outsourced virtual employees. Just as mobile devices have liberated the computer user, who is no longer restricted to accessing information at a particular time and place, technologies such as cloud computing are emancipating workers and companies from traditional geographic and time-bound constraints.

While corporations focus on the advantages and freedoms that these virtual solutions can provide, the risks of these technologies are often minimized or ignored. The more workforces build infrastructures unbound to time or place—literal "castles in the air" of data—the more susceptible businesses are to computer viruses, cyberattacks, blackouts, and simple computer failure. The more commerce moves from tangible "earth-bound" modes of production to ephemeral clouds of information, the more vulnerable these enterprises become. Like a tumbling house of cards, whole corporations can potentially be destroyed as a result of the fragile nature of networks and data.

Beyond decentralizing the workplace, computers and technology are also significantly changing the workforce. Robots and automated machines are quickly replacing manual labor in many service sectors such as motor vehicle, metal, and food production. Even in the heart of the most recent recession, shipments for robots increased in every region of the world.[14] For several decades now, the public's imagination has been gripped by images of robots replacing humans in jobs that entail menial, repetitive tasks. However, with the increase in computing speed and power, lower cost of memory and storage, and ever-increasing complexity of computer programming, robots and computers are no longer just taking over simple, unskilled jobs but also labor requiring some degree of advanced skill and specialization. For instance, simple news articles, such as briefs and financial reports, are now being "written" in large part by sophisticated computer programs that mimic human reasoning and intelligence.[15]

While 3D printers—machines that are able to create virtually any solid object from digital models—are just becoming an economic viability, they represent a fundamental shift in the manufacturing process that so dominated the centuries since the Industrial Revolution. The factory model of mass production, replete with assembly lines and vertical integration, has become so ubiquitous over the last century as to be taken for granted. However, 3D printers represent a threat to the centralized factory, whereby anyone can create any product he needs without the reliance upon large factories, distributors, and corporations. With the advent of 3D printers (and other "DIY" manufacturing technologies that are sure to emerge in the years ahead), we witness not only the signature of Uranus, with its democratizing, liberating qualities, but also Pluto, with its capacity to destroy old structures while simultaneously engendering new ones.

Genetics and Evolution

The Human Genome Project achieved the entire mapping of the human genome—an immense endeavor spanning over thirteen years (1990–2003) and costing nearly four billion U.S. dollars.[16] If ever a technology best captured the Promethean qualities of the Uranus archetype, it is the harnessing of the very spark of life, as the field of genetics promises. However, so expensive and time-consuming was the initial sequencing of human DNA that we might compare it to a caveman spending weeks with two flint stones to generate one single spark of fire. Recently, though, as geneticist Richard Resnick notes, a veritable revolution in genomics has occurred. Spurred by advances in both computer speed and analyzing techniques, the cost of analyzing the human genome has dropped one hundred millionfold since the initial sequencing, and analyzing a human genome now takes only a few weeks.[17] Under the current Uranus–Pluto square, the pragmatic possibilities of genetics—some undoubtedly positive, others debatably dangerous and with unknown consequences—have arrived.

Recent advances in genomics allow us to reach into the far distant past as well as catapult us into an unknown future. Although it was long suspected that some humans have Neanderthal DNA, the first hard genetic evidence for this interspecies breeding was found in 2010.[18] This discovery constitutes a new awareness of the co-mingling of the "ape-like" Neanderthal with the modern *Homo Sapien*. This portrait of a "hybrid human" perfectly captures the juxtaposition of the Pluto archetype, with its emphasis on the biological and primordial, and Uranus, with its characteristic quantum leaps into new and original forms. The discovery also fits into the diachronic pattern of Uranus–Pluto alignments with what Richard Tarnas calls the "motif of chthonic awakening."[19] During Uranus–Pluto alignments, we often witness revelations and heightened interest in the primal, instinctual and biological side of human nature. Arguably the most famous example is Darwin's beginning to write *The Origin of Species* during the Uranus–Pluto conjunction of the mid-nineteenth century.

Beyond allowing for greater understanding of humanity's origins, the current genomic revolution is also generating far-reaching consequences in medicine. With the cost of genome mapping now affordable for the average family, far more people can take advantage of the technology's medical benefits. A personalized genome portrait allows one to determine with far greater accuracy than ever before statistical probabilities for diseases: certain forms of cancer, Alzheimer's, diabetes, heart disease, and hundreds of other conditions. This powerful prognostic tool is lowering the need for invasive surgeries, extending lifespans and permitting more targeted diagnostic interventions. Genetic portraits are the cornerstone of a larger revolution within healthcare called "personalized medicine" in which, as the name implies, healthcare decisions and interventions are customized and tailored to the individual versus large populations.

During the current alignment, the archetype of Pluto is intensifying the creative, emancipatory qualities associated with Uranus; thus it is fitting that the present configuration is a square between these two planets, bringing about the more problematic, complicated implications of these archetypes. Perhaps the most startling, and potentially dangerous, ramification of the current genomic revolution lies in the possibility of self-directed evolution, or what medical ethicist Harvey Fineberg calls "Neo-evolution."[20] By tampering with our DNA, we can now remake ourselves smarter, faster, better. Nearly two hundred years after Mary Shelley published *Frankenstein,* the hypothetical moral dilemmas inherent in her cautionary tale have been realized. The allure of such technology is obvious: Who wouldn't want to have improved memory, a longer lifespan, and greater athletic ability? However, the pitfalls of such technology are catastrophic, as a totalitarian eugenic state could emerge if genetic manipulation were to land in the wrong hands. While the ethical quandaries surrounding bioengineering are complex and varied, perhaps at the root of these arguments is the same conundrum that Shelley so masterfully articulated: tampering with nature can bring about unforeseen consequences.

Subatomic Research

In perhaps no other technological field is it easier to witness the mutual activation of Uranus and Pluto than in subatomic research. Uranus' emancipation of and effect on Pluto can be observed in the sudden awakening of nature's hidden depths and the probing into the unseen and elemental. Concurrently, Pluto's stimulation of Uranus is easily discerned in profound breakthroughs and radical leaps of insight and understanding. Fittingly, major advances in physics have occurred under Uranus–Pluto alignments, and the current square alignment is no exception.

On July 4, 2012, CERN (the European Organization for Nuclear Research) scientists found a particle that was consistent with the predicted existence of the Higgs boson particle (often casually referred to as the "God Particle"). While there are at least 36 confirmed subatomic particles, the Higgs boson has taken on special significance in the pantheon of tiny, elementary stuff. The discovery of the boson is not profound in isolation; however, the particle is assumed to be the producer of the Higgs Field—a quantum field responsible for giving all elementary particles their masses. Not only is such a groundbreaking discovery an example of scientific breakthroughs that typically occur under Uranus–Pluto alignments, but the search for the Higgs boson itself is also representative of Uranus–Pluto dynamics. The machine used to discover the Higgs boson, the Large Hadron Collider, is a $9 billion dollar behemoth that lies deep underground beneath the border of France and Switzerland. The cost, the size (it is the largest machine in existence), and its underground, hidden existence perfectly encapsulates the titanic, colossal, and subterranean qualities of Uranus–Pluto phenomena. Moreover, while there were certainly some dangers associated with operating the Large Hadron Collider, there were some rumors—some humorous, others to be taken seriously—that the machine could destroy the planet in a cataclysmic nuclear meltdown. The sense of threat—either real or imagined—captures the monumental elemental forces that can be unleashed during Uranus–Pluto alignments.

The discovery of the Higgs boson is not only the culmination of over forty years of research. According to science popularizers like Sean Carroll, this finding concludes the search for knowledge of particles initiated by the Greeks 2,500 years ago and completes what is known as the Standard Model of particle physics.[21] In essence, the discovery of the Higgs boson is in many ways the summation and culmination of the materialistic–mechanistic project and worldview. While more hubristic scientists have declared that such a discovery completes the entire quest for knowledge, most researchers realize that the Higgs boson discovery closes one door as another one opens. Thus, it is fitting that this discovery occurs under the current Uranus–Pluto square, symbolic as it is of a transition to a new Age of Information and a new worldview.

The current Uranus–Pluto square symbolizes an exciting turning point in the spiral of the evolution of consciousness, as the alignment is pregnant with both extraordinary life-affirming and positive qualities, as well as problematic shadow expressions. While technology represents the externalization of consciousness, we are also in constant relationship with our technological creations, forcing us either to advance forward along the evolutionary arc or to regress. This potent moment in time posits many developmental possibilities: How will we handle computing devices that weren't even a figment of our collective imagination a few decades ago? With the mechanistic–materialistic worldview seemingly concluding, what will emerge in its place? With the ability to direct our own evolutionary fates, will this most Promethean of technologies catalyze new and dynamic horizons, or plunge us in a truly dystopian nightmare?

These questions open us up to the possibilities being activated during this current Uranus–Pluto square. Further, as Pluto moves through Aquarius in the 2020s and 2030s, the darker side of technology will be up for collective review. Whether technology's darker or more life-affirming potentials manifest over time remains to be seen. However, Alan Watts gives us a good prescription of how to engage our technology, regardless of the era: "Technology is destructive only in the hands of people who do not realize that they are one and the same process as the universe."[22]

Endnotes

1. Kevin Kelly, "Cosmic Origins of Extropy," November 12, 2004, http://www.kk.org/thetechnium/archives/2004/11/cosmic_origins.php.

2. Ken Wilber's four-quadrant model of reality recognizes both an interiority and an exteriority of experience. According to Wilber, technology would fit within the right side, or exterior side, of his quadrant model of reality. See, for example, *Sex, Ecology, and Spirituality: The Spirit of Evolution* (London: Shambhala, 1995).

3. A broad overview of the Uranus–Pluto cycle in all its manifestations, not just technological, is outlined in *Cosmos and Psyche: Intimations of a New World View* by Richard Tarnas (New York: Viking, 2006).

4. Major breakthroughs in aviation and space exploration correlate with the cyclical alignments of Jupiter and Uranus; the first hot air balloon ride, Lindbergh's transatlantic flight, John Glenn's orbiting of earth, and Sally Ride's initial missions (the first woman in space) occurred under major Jupiter–Uranus alignments. Perhaps the greatest exploration project in human history—the Apollo 11 mission to the moon in 1969—occurred under a rare triple conjunction of Uranus, Pluto, and Jupiter. With the moon landing, we see an event that perfectly captures the archetypal qualities of the three planets involved: the creative genius and urge to transcend limitations associated with Uranus, successful expansion and the penchant for new horizons affiliated with Jupiter, and the power and massive scale of the endeavor connected with Pluto.

5. Jonathan Franzen, "Liking Is for Cowards. Go for What Hurts," *The New York Times*, Opinion Pages, May 29, 2011,

    http://www.nytimes.com/2011/05/29/opinion/29franzen.html?pagewanted =all&_r=0.

6. Using a 10-degree orb of influence.

7. Andrew McAfee, "Are droids taking our jobs?" TED: Ideas Worth Spreading, June 2012,

    http://www.ted.com/talks/andrew_mcafee_are_droids_taking_our_jobs.htm l.

8. Inqbation: Digital Marketing Agency, "Facebook Timeline of Events - A History of Introductions," February 3, 2012, http://www.inqbation.com/facebook-timeline-of-events-a-history-introductions/.

9. Visual.ly, "The Growth Of Twitter," http://visual.ly/growth-twitter.

10. David Hill, "Now Serving the Latest In Exponential Growth: Youtube," SingularityHUB, May 25, 2012, http://singularityhub.com/2012/05/25/now-serving-the-latest-in-exponential-growth-youtube/.

11. Jeff Bullas.com, "48 Significant Social Media Facts, Figures and Statistics Plus 7 Infographics," April 23, 2012, http://www.jeffbullas.com/2012/04/23/48-significant-social-media-facts-figures-and-statistics-plus-7-infographics/.

12. Andrew Couts, "Study Confirms social media's revolutionary role in Arab Spring," Digital Trends, September 13, 2011,

    http://www.digitaltrends.com/social-media/study-confirms-social-medias-revolutionary-role-in-arab-spring/.

13. Don Beck's Spiral Dynamics theory of human development posits that the later stages of human development (what he calls late "First Tier" and "Second Tier" development) are characterized by the ability to tolerate and respect a variety of differing viewpoints. See, for example, *Spiral Dynamics* (Oxford: Blackwell, 1996).

14. Aaron Saenz, "Robotic Labor Taking over the World? You Bet – Here Are the Details," SingularityHUB, September 12, 2011,

    http://singularityhub.com/2011/09/12/robotic-labor-taking-over-the-world-you-bet-here-are-the-details/.

15. Steve Lohr, "In Case You Wondered, a Real Human Wrote This Column," *The New York Times*, September 9, 2011,

    http://www.nytimes.com/2011/09/11/business/computer-generated-articles-are-gaining-traction.html?pagewanted=all&_r=0.

16. Richard Resnick, "Welcome to the genomic revolution," TED: Ideas Worth Spreading, July 2011,

    http://www.ted.com/talks/richard_resnick_welcome_to_the_genomic_revolution.html.

17. Ibid.

18. Ker Than, "Neanderthals, Humans Interbred-First Solid DNA Evidence," *National Geographic*, May 6, 2010,

    http://news.nationalgeographic.com/news/2010/05/100506-science-neanderthals-humans-mated-interbred-dna-gene/.

19. Richard Tarnas, *Cosmos and Psyche: Intimations of a New World View* (New York: Viking, 2006), 180.

20. Harvey Fineberg, "Are we ready for neo-evolution?" March 2011, http://www.ted.com/talks/harvey_fineberg_are_we_ready_for_neo_evolutio n.html.

21. Sean Carroll website, "The Particle at the End of the Universe: How the Hunt for the Higgs Boson Leads Us to the Edge of a New World" (audio) http://preposterousuniverse.com/particle/.

22. Laurence Boldt, *Zen and the Art of Making A Living: A Practical Guide to Creative Career Design* (New York: Arkana, 1992), 22.

Special thanks to Keiron Le Grice and Grant Maxwell, editors of *Archai Journal,* for the initial foundation and preparation they provided for this article.

5

Neptune and Opening to Creativity

Dena DeCastro

Although I consider myself to be a writer, as I sat down to write this chapter, I confronted the same struggles I always do at the beginning of a creative project. I worry about my ability to complete the task. I want to jump up, run around the house, and clean everything. I am scared to death of failing. I feel like a fraud, imagining that I've only been able to fool people into thinking I'm a writer. The voices come in: "What if such-and-such reads this? What if nobody reads this at all?"

What I've learned so far, however, is that my life without creativity might as well be a life unlived. If I'm not creating, life becomes flat and boring. The rewards of creativity come when I am able to let go of those familiar ego-centered concerns: Will I look good to others? Will this be a success? Will I get the applause? In order to let go, I find myself calling on my ability to surrender, to trust, and to allow creativity to flow through me. This is a practice I've learned over time—and that I am continuing to learn. I certainly have not mastered it. But this place where I can relax my fears enough to let a creative project come through me is my natal Neptune at work.

By accessing the Neptune within us, we are able to open up to unseen forces, those which reside in the world of ideas and the imagination. In order to do this, we need to be able to move beyond the ego's fears. Since everyone *has* a Neptune, each of us can learn to use this function to bring forth our own creative expression. Yet while we are all born with the ability to be creative, so many of us shy away from—and even fear—using our creativity. Instead, we project these abilities upon the Artists, as if they have something special that we do not.

The Artist Mystique

I believe that *everyone* is creative and that our lives are enhanced greatly when we actively engage our creative talents. So it has been an enigma to me as a counseling astrologer that the majority of my clients almost flinch at the word "creativity" when it comes up in a reading. Some shuffle their feet apologetically, saying, "Oh, I'm just not very creative." Where does this attitude come from? We have come to see creativity as something that only the "gifted" possess, something that is solely conferred by the gods upon the artists. It may very well be that creativity is an energy that comes from *outside of us*, and we are only a channel for it. But what, then, allows the working artist to easily access that flow, while most people shun their own inherent ability to do the same? What makes people who define themselves as artists, and who make creativity the centerpiece of their lives, any different from the rest of us?

It might appear that creative artists have special access to their creativity, access that the majority of people, the "non-artists," don't share. However, we might come to understand artists in terms of certain skills they have, skills that we may also acquire with awareness and practice. From an astrological perspective, we can view the skill set of the creative artist as an attunement to natal Neptune. As Liz Greene writes, "...a dominant Neptune in the birth horoscope reflects a special receptivity to certain feelings and images arising from the deeper and more universal levels of the psyche."[1] In the charts of many famous artists, a prominently placed Neptune can often be found. I define *prominent* as being in aspect to the Sun or Moon, on an angle, or in multiple aspects with other planets. I would also include planets in Pisces (Neptune's sign) or the twelfth house (naturally ruled by Neptune) as synonymous with a prominent Neptune. Because of the close connection with Neptune, perhaps the artist is able to move the ego's fears aside more readily in order to let creative energy flow.

When we are overly attached to egoic concerns, such as looking good to others, getting applause, or receiving credit for the work, we can get in our own way, unable to freely express what is inside of us. Fears arise in response to the ego's agenda. These fears are a survival mechanism, the ego's way of keeping itself intact. We might hear those voices: "You'll look foolish if you put yourself out there," or, "You'll never be as good as such-and-such," or, "You can't control what will happen next, and that isn't good!" These are the voices that prevent most of us from taking the risks required in order to create. In response, we clamp down on the channel and close off the creative flow. When we do so, we close ourselves off to other things as well. The artist, attuned to Neptune, is somehow able to open up to inspiration, "the breath of spirit," even in the face of the ego's objections. Neptune holds a key for each of us in moving past the ego's need for security and approval so that we can receive the gifts of creative expression.

Why Creativity Matters

When we access the Neptune archetype, we can become more connected to the transcendent, moving beyond the concerns of everyday life. Creativity is a means of spiritual connection, but this is only one of the gifts that creative expression can bring us. The wheel of the birth chart represents the life areas that come together to create wholeness; without creativity (represented in the fifth house of the birth chart), we would be missing one of the crucial ingredients of an integrated, fulfilling life. We may each channel and express our creativity in different ways, but each of us has the ability to experience the joy that comes from engaging our innate talents. The fifth house of the birth chart is known as the house of Creativity, Play, Recreation, Romance, and Children (or the Inner Child). We might also simply consider it to be the house of all things enjoyable. The fifth house is naturally ruled by the Sun, which is itself is the creative spiritual source. This is the area of life in which we are rejuvenated and energized. We can "fall in love with life" when we are engaged with a creative activity. Creativity isn't just art—experimental cooking, rearranging drawers, gardening, and decorating a room are all creative acts that can energize us, if they are things we enjoy. When we let the creative force flow through us, we are connected to life in an almost romantic way.

Neptune allows the artist to open to inspiration, and the fifth house is where we can manifest the product of that meeting between heaven and earth. Only through consciously working with our Neptune can we empower ourselves to bring joy into our own lives through creative expression. We might begin by observing how creative artists move past the obstacles that stop most of us in our tracks.

Merely a Channel

Creative artists throughout the ages—musicians, writers, painters, poets, actors—have expressed the idea that a creative work came *through* them, as opposed to believing themselves to be its source. They often see themselves as a channel for the art, which itself seems to come from *somewhere else*. In a 2009 interview, Bob Dylan expresses the idea that his songs were written *through* him:

> Over more than four decades, Bob Dylan has produced 500 songs and more than 40 albums. Does he ever look back at the music he's written with surprise?
>
> "I used to. I don't do that anymore. I don't know how I got to write those songs. Those early songs were almost magically written," says Dylan, who quotes from his 1964 classic, "It's Alright, Ma." "Try to sit down and write something like that. There's a magic to that, and it's not Siegfried and Roy kind of magic, you know? It's a different kind of a penetrating magic."[2]

Dylan's chart reflects a very prominent Neptune placement. His Neptune makes major aspects to five of his planets: it trines the Moon, Jupiter, Saturn, and Uranus, and squares Mercury.[3] Neptune is also conjunct his North Node, indicating the evolutionary need to move toward the lessons of Neptune in this lifetime. Neptune as it sits on the North Node is an ally for Dylan; when he surrenders, opens, and trusts, he is able to align with his soul's path of growth. Each of the planets that Neptune aspects functions in relationship to Neptune. For example, with Neptune trine his Moon, Dylan can easily find emotional security and sustenance (Moon) when spending time in the world of symbols and dreams. Neptune square his Mercury, on the other hand, shows that Dylan may struggle with clear communication. This has been evident in his speaking style during interviews, in which he speaks softly, even mumbles, and comes off as rather enigmatic. The work of a Neptune–Mercury square is in balancing the psychic and intuitive input of Neptune with Mercury's need for understanding. Yet his Neptune and Mercury are both in Mercury-ruled signs, so perhaps this accounts for his ability to convey material from Neptune's realm with some amount of ease, despite the tension usually indicated by a square.

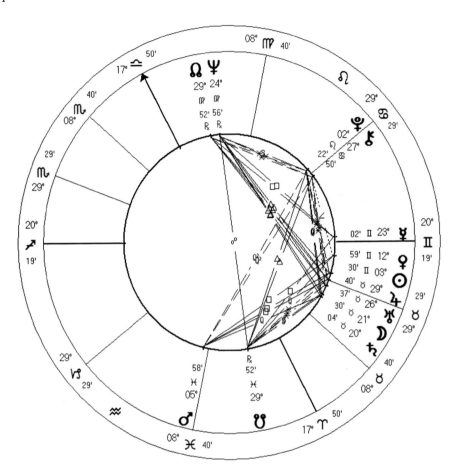

Figure 1 - Bob Dylan

Dylan's attunement to Neptune ultimately seems to grant him a strong ability to stand outside of ego-consciousness. His lack of need to claim credit for the work may seem, on the one hand, merely humble; in the above interview, he effectively dismisses his own role in the writing of his songs. But he seems truly mystified as to the source of the work. When we can move out of the way, in a sense, seeing ourselves as a channel through which creative energy is expressed, the ego doesn't need to generate fears to protect itself—because the creative work isn't coming from the ego. We become caretakers,

75

ushers, midwives—we are not the Source itself. We are able to engage the creative energy, as long as we do not fall into the illusion that our egos are defined by the work that comes through.

Jeff Buckley

Another musician with a prominent Neptune, Jeff Buckley, is an example of someone whose musical expression was often described by his devoted fans as ethereal, otherworldly, spiritual—in other words, Neptunian. In an interview about Buckley's work after his death, fan Brad Pitt stated, "He tapped into something and he was the conduit. And it makes me think of this: where does art come from? Where does a true genius come from?"[4] While Buckley had an odd kind of fame (his name, spoken in a crowd, often goes unrecognized), he is seen by many—particularly fellow musicians—as one of the bright lights of creative talent in the modern era of music. He is known for his body of work in the '90s, particularly his album *Grace*, which is both critically acclaimed and dear to fans and musicians alike. Unfortunately, he passed away at the young age of 30, victim to an accidental drowning. He left the world with much of his potential still unexpressed, but during his short life, he made a huge impact upon the musical community. Bono of U2 once called Buckley "a pure drop in an ocean of noise."[5]

The oceanic metaphor is an apt one, for the prominence of Neptune and the element of water in Buckley's natal chart is undeniable. Neptune is conjunct his Sun, Venus, and Mercury in water sign Scorpio, trines his Saturn in Pisces, and sextiles his Mars and Uranus in Virgo, making a grand total of six major aspects in his chart. Buckley felt that his lyrics came from poems: "Songs come out of poems, and poems come out of dreams...or reality."[6] The lyrics of the title song from the album *Grace* embody the Neptunian concept of complete and ultimate surrender, even to death. Of the song, Buckley said, "'Grace' is basically a death prayer. Not something of sorrow but just casting away any fear of death. No relief will come; you'll really just have to stew in your life until it's time to go. But sometimes, somebody else's faith in you can do wonders."[7]

Buckley seemed to be in touch with a level of surrender that allowed him to create from a somewhat fearless place. He saw himself as a servant to the work.

When asked how he'd like to be remembered, Buckley answered, "As a good friend. I don't really need to be remembered; I hope the music's remembered."[8] As did Dylan (whom he greatly admired), Buckley expressed a lack of need to take credit for the end result of the creativity, hoping instead only that the music would serve as a gift to others.

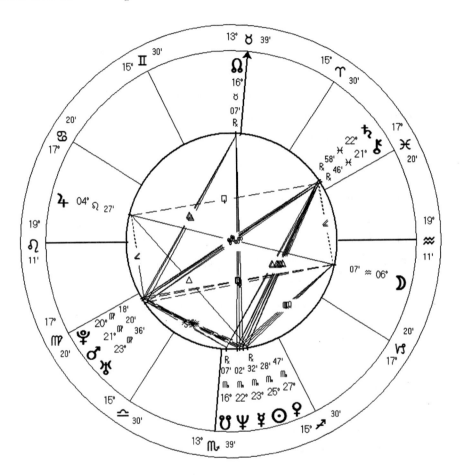

Figure 2 - Jeff Buckley

Confronting Shadow Neptune

Along with the gifts that a pronounced Neptune in the chart may bring the creative artist, there are also potential shadow expressions: addiction, escapism, and mental or emotional instability. It is possible to go so far in the direction of

77

negating the ego that there is a loss of healthy ego function. The stories of creatively talented individuals who abuse alcohol and drugs, or who have suffered from mental breakdowns, are commonplace. There is strong evidence for a correlation between creative talent and the tendency toward these behaviors. So what is it about being an artist that opens the door to Neptune's shadow expression?

The artist's life is by necessity filled with risk and vulnerability. The creative artist must constantly face the fear of rejection, the fear of not measuring up to other artists, the fear of not meeting one's own high expectations. Additionally, creative artists are often sensitive, a quality that enables them to be gifted in their crafts. But those who are most sensitive can find the harsh world and its suffering to be overwhelming. It is the very gift of sensitivity, then, which may often cause the artist to want to shut down. In order to numb himself to these overwhelming feelings, the artist may choose any number of available numbing substances; or perhaps he experiences a mental break, a split from reality.

The archetype of the "Suffering Artist" is pronounced in our culture. Edgar Allan Poe, Vincent Van Gogh, Ernest Hemingway, Billy Holliday…. These are just a few of the hundreds of famous names that may at first bring to mind their creative achievements and impacts, but might also readily evoke thoughts of suffering, mental illness, and addiction. Each of these artists has a prominent Neptune in the birth chart as well.[9] We see the starving artist, the self-sacrificing artist, the mentally ill artist, the alcoholic artist. And who of us would want to go there willingly? We fear opening ourselves to the very gifts that allow the artist to create.

But when we do not engage our Neptune in life-affirming ways—creative expression, spiritual practice, service to a higher ideal or vision—we find ourselves searching for connection via shortcuts. Denied Neptune leads down the same shadow road as an over-functioning Neptune: pointless escapism that serves to take us further and further from the very sense of connection we long for. By activating our Neptune proactively in healthy ways, we move off the shadow road. We can regain a feeling of belonging, to the universe and to ourselves.

Creating with Neptune

I'd like to offer some practical activities that can help us to exercise our Neptune function. By opening the door to Neptune's associations with dreams, the otherworld, and spiritual practice, we can access our own creative gifts.

Dream Work

Neptune is connected to the dream world through its association with the unconscious, the liminal, and the unseen. Dreams do not occupy the physical world we experience as objective reality, residing instead in the domain of sleep, where our conscious mind—with its egocentric orientation—is subdued. When dreaming, we experience an altered state of consciousness that, from the vantage point of waking life, seems unreal. But the dream state can inform our waking lives in ways that enhance our ability to connect with our creativity.

Dreams have often been a resource for the creative artist. Paul McCartney, for example, famously received the melody for the song "Yesterday" complete in a dream.[10]

McCartney's chart features several Neptunian signatures. He has Neptune in late Virgo conjunct the Ascendant, with Neptune squaring the Sun and Mercury in Gemini, and Jupiter in early Cancer. As with Dylan's chart, Neptune and Mercury are both in signs ruled by Mercury. This configuration points to some ease, despite the square, in transmitting information from the dream world (Neptune) to the conscious mind (Mercury). Neptune in square to McCartney's Sun also indicates the challenge between needing a rational explanation (Sun in Gemini) and surrendering to the invitation into more mysterious waters via the dream state. In fact, it took McCartney some time to come to terms with the fact that he could have received something directly from a dream. He questioned it in good Gemini fashion, asking around to see if perhaps he'd unconsciously stolen the melody from another song. Still, he went directly to the piano and played the tune from his dream upon waking, as if taking dictation directly from Neptune.

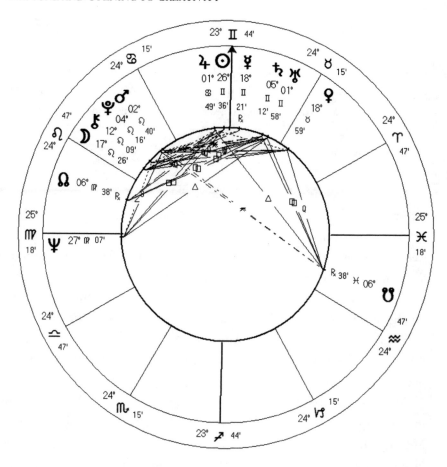

Figure 3 - Paul McCartney

There are ways to further develop our ability to connect with our dreams, thereby enhancing our creativity. The practice of lucid dreaming in particular can lead to creative breakthroughs. In her article "The Lucid Artist: Lucid Dreaming as a Transformative Element of the Artistic Process," author Clare Johnson, Ph.D., writes: "My research has shown that while asleep and dreaming, the artist can work uninhibitedly with new techniques and mediums, consciously seek ideas for paintings or stories, enter into dialogue with fictional characters, sidestep the inner critic, and work on current creative projects."[11] Johnson is herself an artist as well as a scientist who has focused her research on lucid dreams. She also states that, for those who find lucid dreaming difficult, an alternate set of techniques designed to induce a "creative trance" can also induce a similar effect of being able to access creative ideas more readily as dream imagery infiltrates the imagination.[12]

Robert Moss, dream expert and author of several books on the topic, has written of dreams as a way to enhance every aspect of our lives, including our creativity. In *Dreaming True,* he states that dreams "...deliver both the *big* creative breakthroughs and the flow state in which we can follow through and bring them into full manifestation."[13] The "flow state" might also be understood as that Neptunian place where we can release our identification with the day world of the ego, and the symbols and images can emerge from the deep waters of the unconscious. Working with our dreams can allow us to let the rules of waking life dissolve, because in a dream, anything can happen. When we spend time working consciously with our dreams, these rules can be seen from a different perspective and therefore become more malleable.

Besides journaling, drawing, and lucid dreaming, a practice called "incubating a dream" has become well-known with those who regularly look to their dreams for guidance and creative inspiration. This practice can be used to actively call in creative ideas or to ask for advice on a creative project. As Moss writes in *Conscious Dreaming:* "You can incubate a dream to solve problems or provide creative inspiration in an intentional way."[14] Incubating a dream is a simple process. You need only think of a problem, question, or project as you are falling asleep, then set the intention for your dreams to offer guidance. It is also helpful to set an intention to remember your dreams. Although the dreams that occur may not always seem directly related to the intention put forth by the dreamer, the unconscious has had time to process it during sleep. This is perhaps where we get the concept of "sleeping on it," referring to letting a situation that has been troubling us rest overnight before dealing with it. In the same way, we can "sleep on," or more accurately, "dream on" our creative intentions. Dreams open us up to messages from our own unconscious that the conscious mind, ruled by the ego, filters out. Through dreams, we can receive messages from a place beyond the ego's reach.

Unseen Helpers

Neptune, in its association with the otherworld and the invisible realms, may also connect us to what some artists have referred to as "The Muse." The

Muse is a Greek term referring to the daughters of Zeus, goddesses who reside over the arts. It has been the belief of many creative artists that they must call upon, invoke, or pray to the Muse in order to receive guidance and inspiration. In an interview with Elizabeth Gilbert, author of *Eat, Pray, Love*, she describes the process of negotiating with the Muse: "The world is being constantly circled as though by gulf stream forces, ideas and creativity that want to be made manifest, and they're looking for portals to come through in people. And if you don't do it, they'll go find someone else. So you have to convince it that you're serious, you have to show it respect and you have to talk to it and let it know that you're there."[15] The "it" she is referring to is the Muse. She goes on to tell the story of how she prayed to the Muse for the title of *Eat, Pray, Love*, and it arrived the next morning.

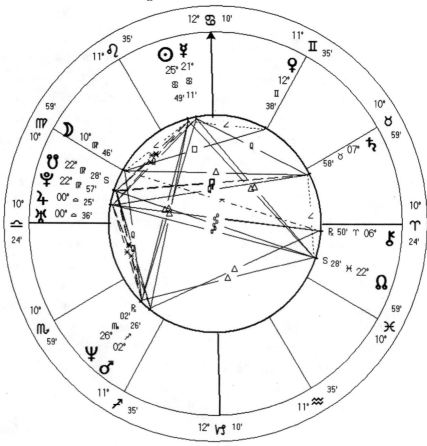

Figure 4 - Elizabeth Gilbert

Gilbert's own Neptune in late Scorpio is conjunct Mars in early Sagittarius and trine her Sun and Mercury in Cancer. There is an easeful exchange between Neptune and her Mercury–Sun conjunction, all in water signs. Her willingness to relax into the flow of information that comes through Neptune is encouraged by this connection. Mars in Sagittarius in its conjunction with Neptune directs the passionate pursuit of adventure toward a palpable engagement with Neptune's mysteries—such as unseen helpers.

Angels may also offer creative assistance. In his motivational book, *The War of Art*, Steven Pressfield asserts that to do anything creative, we must continually fight what he calls "Resistance," which arrives wearing the faces of fear, doubt, and the usual list of ego-related concerns. He writes of angels as our allies in the war against Resistance: "I think angels make their home in the Self, while Resistance has its seat in the Ego. The fight is between the two. The Self wishes to create, to evolve. The Ego likes things just the way they are."[16] When the artist forms the intention to create, Pressfield believes angels, the Muse, and other unseen helpers show up to assist. However, the artist must submit, in a sense, to become the servant to the idea that wants to be born: "The artist is the servant of that intention, those angels, that Muse."[17] Whether or not we believe in the Muse or in angels, perhaps when we simply humble ourselves enough to ask for help, we are reminded that creative ideas do not actually come from us, but *through us*. By placing ourselves in the position of "servant" to the work, the pressure to come up with something unique, spectacular, earth-shattering…dissolves and is released.

Creativity and Spiritual Practice

Our creativity can be aided by engaging in what some might call a spiritual practice. Whether we feel drawn to contemplation, meditation, or prayer, we are opening ourselves up to connection with something beyond our ego consciousness. Through contemplation, we might sit quietly and turn over an idea in our heads, allowing images and words to float through our minds. In the Eastern practice of meditation, we can use breath and body awareness to turn down the volume on the active mind, thus strengthening our ability to receive inspiration and creative ideas. Through prayer, we may actively request assistance with our creativity. Perhaps we connect with a deity, or perhaps we make the request of a personified guide or angel. But through each of these practices, we place ourselves in the position of surrender, humility, and receptivity. When we are able to move the ego out of the driver's seat for a time, we are more receptive to what comes.

We might also see the creative process itself as a spiritual practice. Expressing your creativity, and doing the work of a creative project, is yet another path to inner peace.

Conclusion

More people are "non-artists" than artists. There are fewer who consider themselves to be creative than who create. We continue to be fascinated by watching the artist from afar, playing at the edge where ego dissolves into Neptune's all-consuming waters. We project upon the artist the ability to take us into these waters vicariously. But we are afraid to swim there ourselves. Neptune asks us to surrender the ego's need for a clearly defined map of reality and to trustingly walk into a terrain where dreams are as real as waking life, where the angels and the Muse reside.

But while Neptune is often associated with gentleness, the path of Neptune is not always an easeful one. When we begin a creative endeavor, we must confront uncertainty and self-doubt, and that overwhelming feeling that "all of this may be for nothing." We know that the path of the creative artist has its joys and sorrows, its triumphs and sacrifices. But when we own the artist within ourselves, our lives can become infused with magic. And magic is something that I, for one, would not want to live without.

Chart Data:

Bob Dylan, Rodden Rating AA. May 24, 1941, 9:05 PM, Duluth, MN

Jeff Buckley, Rodden Rating C. November 17, 1966, 10:49 PM, Anaheim, CA. (Note: Although the Rodden Rating is currently C, I have confirmed this birth time with a source close to Jeff Buckley's mother.).

Paul McCartney, Rodden Rating B. June 18, 1942, 2:00 PM, Liverpool, England.

Elizabeth Gilbert, birth time unknown. July 18, 1969, noon chart, Waterbury, CT.

Endnotes

1. Liz Greene, *The Astrological Neptune and the Quest for Redemption* (Weiser Books, 1996) 319.

2. Bob Dylan, interview with Ed Bradley, *CBS News*, February 18, 2009, http://www.cbsnews.com/2100-18560_162-658799.html.

3. Major aspects are defined as the Ptolemaic aspects: conjunction, sextile, square, trine and opposition.

4. "Jeff Buckley: Everybody Here Wants You," from Memorable Quotes (television show), 2002, http://www.imdb.com/title/tt0351127/quotes, accessed January 10, 2013.

5. Jeff Apter, *A Pure Drop: The Life of Jeff Buckley* (Omnibus Press, 2008) 223.

6. Jeff Buckley, personal interview, YouTube,

   http://www.youtube.com/watch?v=toE8YoMtcRE.

7. "Jeff Buckley: Everybody Here Wants You," from Memorable Quotes (television show), 2002, http://www.imdb.com/title/tt0351127/quotes, accessed January 10, 2013.

8. Ibid.

9. Shadow Neptune: artists with prominent Neptune in the chart.

10. Billie Holiday: Neptune opposed Moon, trine Mars and Mercury; stellium (Mercury, Venus, Mars, and Jupiter) in Pisces

11. Edgar Allen Poe: Neptune conjunct Saturn, square Moon, Venus, and Pluto; stellium (Moon, Venus, Jupiter, Pluto) in Pisces

12. Ernest Hemingway: Neptune square Mars, opposed Saturn, sextile Mercury, conjunct Pluto, conjunct South Node

13. Vincent van Gogh: Neptune in Pisces square Moon; Neptune, Mars and Venus in Pisces

14. McCartney composed the entire melody in a dream one night in his room at the Wimpole Street home of his then girlfriend Jane Asher and her family. Upon waking, he hurried to a piano and played the tune to avoid forgetting it. Turner, Steve, *A Hard Day's Write: The Stories Behind Every Beatles Song* (New York: Harper Paperbacks, 2005) 83.

15. Clare Johnson, "The Lucid Artist: Lucid Dreaming as a Transformative Element of the Artistic Process," *Dream Time: A Publication for the Study of Dreams* vol. 29, no. 3 (Fall 2012), 9.

16. Ibid, 11.

17. Robert Moss, *Dreaming True: How to Dream Your Future and Change Your Life for the Better* (New York: Pocket Books, 2000) xxxii.

18. Robert Moss, *Conscious Dreaming* (New York: Three Rivers Press, 1996) 315.

19. Elizabeth Gilbert, "Me, Myself and Muse," Radiolab (audio, begins at 8 mins 10 secs) http://www.radiolab.org/2011/mar/08/me-myself-and-muse/, accessed December 15, 2012.

20. Steven Pressfield, *The War of Art* (Black Irish Entertainment, LLC, 2002, Kindle version) 134.

21. Ibid, 162.

6

The Transpersonal Dimension:

The Higher Octave of the Personal Planets

Mark Jones

The outer planets—Uranus, Pluto and Neptune—have long been seen as the *higher octaves* of the three inner, or personal, planets: Mercury, Mars and Venus. Thinkers as diverse as Pythagoras and the authors of the Rigveda have emphasized the music of the spheres, and astrology itself has emphasized its similarity to music. Continuing with this analogy, a relationship can be drawn between the personal planets and the transpersonal planets in terms of the music that they make. This chapter explores this association and how it can contribute to a transpersonal understanding of astrology in the form of three core sections expressing the planetary pairs: Mercury with Uranus, Mars with Pluto, and Venus with Neptune.

Before beginning the core analysis, it is worth saying something about the nature of the octave in music, where the term originated. In essence, the octave is an expression of measurement: the interval that exists between the pitch of notes. So if a note exists with a pitch of 400 hertz (Hz), then the higher octave of that note would exist at 800 Hz...and so on in intervals of 400 Hz. The key to change, then, is the change in pitch, i.e. frequency. The form is changed by the speed at which it vibrates—the hertz represents the number of cycles per second within the sound wave—so the higher octave is the same form but vibrating at double (or triple, etc.) the speed to produce a higher pitch.

So if we extend the analogy into the astrology, using of the idea of the octave, we would say that somehow Uranus, for instance, is like Mercury but operating at a much faster rate. We will see that, suggestive though this idea is, especially in highlighting the importance and depth of relationship between these planetary pairs, it ultimately falls short of describing the shift in quality and dimension when moving from the inner, or personal, planets to the outer, or transpersonal, planets.

Ultimately this is a transition that involves a movement from the linear to the non-linear realms where, in some key way, the very nature of the pre-existing identity, planetary function and corresponding aspect of the personality or identity must be fundamentally transformed or left behind in order to make the leap.

Mercury with Uranus

Mercury represents the nature and function of our mental capacities: language, communication and basic organization of one's relationship to one's environment. Mercury traditionally rules both Gemini and Virgo. Exploring the symbolism of rulerships, Mercury is in a yang role as ruler of Gemini and the third house, where it corresponds to curiosity, the inquisitiveness of children learning to name and label their environment and mimic those around them in order to become facile and effortless in their relationship to language and social codes. Gemini corresponds to that same spirit in adulthood that wishes to read everything and engage in the environment in a curious and open-minded fashion.

In its more inward or yin expression as ruler of Virgo and the sixth house, Mercury begins a vital process of discrimination: "Of all this information that I have taken on board through the curious, restless and expansive phase of Gemini, what best suits my real needs and my evolutionary goals?" There is a crisis to the extent that some of the information taken on is contradictory and other feedback from the environment may include problematic or critical messages. The individual is left with an internal mental dialogue for which the intention is self-improvement and the discovery of what is most useful, but which can become a problematic tape loop, endlessly recycling the same thoughts and associated reactions to those thoughts. Even the most focused and constructive person will discover elements of this internal dialogue if he or she, for example, undertakes a silent retreat.

Uranus, Aquarius and the eleventh house represent a quality of what we might call subtle mind, what the theosophists called higher mind. Whereas Mercury corresponds to the conscious memory that one would use to cram for a test or to remember what happened last summer, Uranus corresponds to what we might call far or deep memory. This quality of subtle mind, of deep memory, has a relationship to aspects of the energy field that, in many people, will operate primarily unconsciously...and yet these aspects can emerge into awareness through dream states, hypnotic regression, meditation, an intense therapy session or spontaneously in very receptive states of mind. In such a state of receptivity, people are able to recall early childhood incidents in enormous clarity; people may experience memories of birth, or being within the womb, or prior lives. People refer to this as a non-ordinary state of consciousness, and yet as I do more and more work as a transpersonal therapist, hypnotherapist and astrologer, I find that such experiences are perfectly ordinary if one creates the space in which they can be allowed to emerge.

The simple metaphor of the octave, neat though it is, implies that the higher octave is just the same quality enhanced, i.e., moving at a faster rate. This fails to do justice to the transition involved from the linear rational mind (Mercury) and awareness (Uranus). In its pure form, the level of awareness originating from Uranus, Aquarius and the eleventh house is experienced as memory or a mental awareness arising from the Soul: a blueprint of the energy field of the individual's whole life experienced on a subtle mental level. This includes information as to the nature of past lives or states of existence in the womb; the impact of this level can be likened to that of a morphogenetic field, an energetic shape identified by the evolutionary biologist Rupert Sheldrake that allows forms to grow to their full potential.[1] Sheldrake's work conveys the biological capacity of a species to learn systemically across the generations. This perspective on the archetype of Uranus, Aquarius and the eleventh house sees the individual learning systemically from their own generations, i.e., their own experiences from other realms (prior lives, bardo states, the many mansions within the Soul).

The individual and collective energy fields accessible from the vantage point of the Uranus archetype contain memories, images and energy that can feed the individual in his or her growth. The contrast with the linear mind is enormous: the rational mind can merely label and identify such processes as concepts or part of a self-image or constructed self. The Uranus level of experience, when it intrudes on that constructed self or rational mental apparatus, can shock it out of its normal operating procedures, as it is part of the deeper level of the mind that has an impact upon the normal linear functioning of Mercury:

> But the essential fact is that the activities of Uranus, Neptune and Pluto **run counter** to the normal functions of Mercury, Venus and Mars. The former are not just personal activities of a "higher" kind; they are activities meant to disturb and transform—indeed, utterly to repolarize and reorient those of Mercury, Venus and Mars. The source of Uranus' power is basically different from that of Mercury's power.[2]

From my experience, Rudhyar is referring to something of critical importance when discussing the shift from the personal to the transpersonal in both astrological and personal evolutionary terms. The term "higher" is useful only in that it alludes to a different order of experience, for which the octave metaphor is only partially appropriate; for the shift from the personal to the transpersonal dimension involves a shift from the constructed, or conditioned, realm of the personality to the essential life of the Soul—a shift in which the previous understanding of life is completely transformed, a process that could be likened to waking from a dream.

Uranus symbolizes a quality of awareness from within the soul nature that can then be experienced on a subtle mental level. It is in a different category of experience than indicated by the conceptual powers of the mind: When approaching the Uranian level of awareness—say, through intense therapy— the experience is the complete opposite of "normal" mental functioning (Mercury), sometimes silencing the mind altogether.

A long-term client of mine recently underwent a shift of this nature. The client has a very senior position within a media company. In coming straight from work one evening, she was able to acknowledge the contrast between her prior state of being overwhelmed, having had a devastating personal crisis at work, and the feeling of self-confidence and being understood that she experienced in the therapy room. She was courageous enough to stay with that contrast and, in placing the two different selves on two different chairs within

90

the room, she was able to approach the overwhelmed self as a direct experience. In that state, she felt as though she had no history, that she was a raw being in a brown wasteland, left alone to pick up the pieces. The moment was completely experiential and shocking; her normal mental functioning was suspended.

She was able to reflect only afterwards, with my assistance, on how the space included the young, pre-verbal child who was left alone with a sense of the young child in a dysfunctional family—one left to fend for herself with only a pre-verbal sense of how much was wrong in her surroundings. Her childhood sowed the seeds for an excessive sensitivity to bearing responsibility. She had intellectually understood this before, but in that process, she had fully seen/felt it as a truth. I have found this level of experience especially transformative therapeutically. While she will need to cover the same emotional ground again and again, this lady has an immediate clarity about the issue that will never leave her, as a subsequent session has shown. This can be likened to the flash of comprehensive knowing symbolized by Uranus, in contrast to the mental understanding and verbal communication of Mercury.

Challenging aspects from Uranus to Mercury and the other personal planets can indicate a difficulty, or even a core shock, adjusting the life of the personality to the energy of the Soul experienced on the subtle mental level. The nature of the aspects between Uranus and Mercury will refer to the individual's capacity to integrate or communicate about (Mercury) the more essential states of direct knowing symbolized by Uranus.

Challenging aspects from Uranus, planets in Aquarius, and planets in the eleventh house to any other planets, nodes or angles also refer to what I have explained as *Trauma Signatures* in *Healing the Soul: Pluto, Uranus and the Lunar Nodes*.[3] These aspects symbolize difficult prior-life, inter-uterine or very early childhood experiences that continue to affect the subtle mind through creating energetic templates, or what Stanislav Grof calls systems of condensed experience,[4] that go on to shape the individual's life experience on a core level.

Mars with Pluto

Mars represents the nature and function of the personal will: that abiding sense of instinctual power within us. Operating on a primarily instinctual level,

Mars can be experienced as a gut feeling about another (whether attraction or repulsion), as the need to leave a confining space, or even a predilection for certain foods. Mars represents the quality of out-going expression of our instinctual desires. At the core of Mars, Aries and the first house is the primal need for a basic level of freedom, allowing the organism to experience itself and the fulfillment of its core desires. Restriction of this freedom becomes the basis of anger or rage in defense of self. If freedom is restricted and the anger also suppressed, then there is the potential for depression, a sense of futility, as the feeling becomes that of lack of permission for the core desires to be realized.

Pluto represents the Soul's primary orientation, emotionally and psychologically, towards evolutionary concerns of the deepest kind. Often unconscious (at least in part), this level of experience represents the source of a primary-level sense of security, as felt through a core filter or the individual's orientation towards the world and his or her life. This deepest level of Soul interest can be experienced as desire: the attraction towards certain kinds of experiences that enable the Soul to experience itself and evolve.

Mars and Pluto then can be compared and contrasted on the level of Will—Pluto as the Will of the Soul, Mars as that of the personality—both desiring the freedom to be and to become. This level of will is symbolized within the dual rulership of Scorpio, ruled by both Mars (traditional) and Pluto (modern). The nature of the Will's dual experience is further illustrated by the quincunx or inconjunct (150 degrees) between Aries, ruled by Mars, and Scorpio, now ruled by Pluto, revealing the tension and potential crisis implicit between the Will of the Soul and that of the personality.

As I have explored in an essay on the Pluto in Virgo Generation,[5] the quincunx or inconjunct (150 degrees) is an aspect that symbolizes the nature of a crisis—the nature of the crisis being that of the personal self before the individual other (Virgo) or of the self before the social world, or the collective body of humanity (Scorpio). Through the archetypal inconjunct between Aries and Scorpio, we see that the experience of the dual nature of desire, that of the personality and the Soul, is fraught with an inherent crisis. This is because frequently the personality has no conscious inclination towards a life event or personal expression that the Soul wishes to experience. The crisis is then between the personal self and the needs of the Soul.

92

We return now to the core point made by Rudhyar: the energies of the outer planets "run counter" to those of the personal planets. We can compare Mars and Pluto on the level of desire—but we must take note that those desires stem from a different order of experience. Compare Mars and Pluto on the level of the Will: Mars is the personal Will, the energy you draw on in a tennis match, the effort to learn guitar or tidy your office; Pluto represents the higher Will. To this extent, the metaphor of the octaves is useful. It focuses us on this key relationship. Yet we must bear in mind Rudhyar's critique (above) if we are to get the most from our analysis: the activities of the outer planets are meant to "disturb and transform." So at times higher will (Pluto) "disturbs and transforms" the personal will (Mars) to serve the evolution of the whole being.

This process can be likened to insights that have emerged from the twelve-step movement: when dealing with addiction and significant loss of power and control, the personal will is often not enough to rescue or transform the situation. When the personality is overwhelmed by a self-destructive pattern of behavior, the first step to genuine change is to recognize that loss of control and to admit the possibility of a higher power. In Pluto terms, only by allowing the energy of the higher will to emerge and function can certain states of personal negativity be understood and overcome. Higher or deeper will operates on a different level of power; to extend the metaphor of the octaves, if personal will is 400 Hz, then Higher Will is more like 4,000 Hz than 800 Hz[6].

This increase in power can save even the most abandoned and degraded beings from the throes of addiction if they sincerely surrender their control to that higher power. Yet the introduction of this higher power initially does disturb the individual from his or her own selfish plight, and the transformation emerges from this process of being disturbed from the previous way of going about things. So we see that in operation, the intrusion of the higher Will is rarely experienced as a harmonious introduction to the individual life.

We could say that on-going soul work, commitment to the truth regardless of its impact on the personal life, is what enables increasing harmony to emerge between Mars and Pluto, between the personal desires and the intentions of the Soul. Significant aspects between Mars and Pluto indicate that the current life is one in which that Soul-work is emphasized, as Pluto (the Will of the Soul) has an impact by aspect on the personal Will (Mars) to bring about

93

transformation; the nature of the aspect, and the position of Mars and Pluto by house and sign, will then comment more specifically on the nature of this work.

Venus with Neptune

Venus represents the nature and function of the relationship with ourselves (Taurus) and with other people (Libra). In its inward (yin) form in Taurus, Venus symbolizes our capacity to understand and meet our own essential needs; and then in its outgoing (yang) form in Libra, Venus symbolizes how we project what we feel is missing inside ourselves onto other people in the form of projections and attractions to what the other represents.

Most healthy relationships with others (Libra) emerge from a basic maturity in the way we commit to meeting our own needs (Taurus) so that we are not over-burdening other people with core unresolved feelings about ourselves. Conversely, we can observe that most relationship problems stem from unresolved personal feelings that block or distort the capacity to meet the inner needs of the self (Taurus). Relationships with others (Libra) are then colored with the disappointments of the self-relationship or with unrealistic projections of how the other (Libra) can save the individual from him/herself (Taurus).

We can note that the core influence on the way we relate to ourselves (Taurus) is the nature of relationships (Libra) in the early home life (Cancer–Capricorn). Understand this process, and you can understand the way that most people recreate unresolved issues from their early home lives in their marriages and long-term relationships[7].

The nature of Neptune is that of transpersonal love, the nature of spirit itself. This is an unconditional love that arises as an experience of total immersion and that leads to the understanding that something fundamental about the nature of creation is found in the nature of love:

> To understand the nature of God, it is necessary only to know the nature of love itself. To truly know love is to know and understand God; and to know God is to understand love.
> - Dr. David Hawkins, *The Eye of the I*[8]

We see truly that our self-love, evidenced in meeting our own needs (Taurus), and our love for others (Libra) arise from this field of love that interpenetrates the nature of the Cosmos. When we are lost in personal vanity (Taurus) or projecting our displaced childhood emotions (Cancer) onto others (Libra), it may seem that we have shut ourselves off from this higher love. Yet when one expresses the all-inclusive nature of the love at the heart of creation, one recognizes that all states of being, no matter how selfish or narrow, are included within the unconditional nature of its field.

So personal regard and the need for others to do what we ask or fulfill our unmet needs are of a fundamentally different category of being than the nature of love, which arises as a felt experience in response to the totality of another's being, or in response to the nature of the experience of Being itself. Yet real love can embrace more self-involved states of being effortlessly. In the radical opening created by an experience of real love, we can see that personal regard, or the very nature of personality and "ego," only arise as a defense against the overwhelming inclusivity of the all. The world itself would not, could not, exist without the love that pervades it and keeps reality itself buoyant. One way (of many) of viewing the myth of the Fall is to see it as relating to the part of our own nature that cannot bear the love and, through ignorance, fear and hurt, turns against it to form a personality. The personality as a separate, isolated unit of experience is found not to exist independently when one experiences the Neptune level of surrender to the all, the core nature of which is love.

Once again, Rudhyar's recognition that the nature of the outer planets is to "disturb and transform" the nature of the corresponding inner planets—those of which the outer planets are the higher octaves—rings true, from the side of the personality, at least. From our attachment to personality, we rightly fear the incursion of divinity, of love or a revelation of the sacredness of all of life…for those experiences threaten to topple the dominance of the ego, as ego is found not to truly exist in those states; rather, it is an expression of a lack, a hardening of true nature around a perceived threat. So the personality level (Venus) fears the transpersonal love, agape (Neptune), as this love ultimately exposes the lack of inherent existence to the ego itself.

From the perspective of the Soul, however, there is nothing to disturb. Our true nature, exposed by the brilliance of real love, is found to comprise numerous core elements of which joy, dedication to truth, wisdom, infinite love and gratitude are key. We realize then, as these essential Soul states begin to unfold within us, that the apparent loss that the ego projects onto the reality of the deep self is no real loss at all. In fact, the brilliance of what arises in place of what we dreamed was our "selves" reveals an all-embracing inclusive presence—one in which we are cared for so completely by the infinite field of divinity that all previous notions of what constituted contentment or satisfaction are found to be mere shadows compared to the radiance of the truth.

Conclusion

The notion of the higher octaves is important, as it allows us to analyze the important relationships between Mercury and Uranus, Mars and Pluto, and Venus and Neptune. The metaphor needs to be expanded, though, to include the fundamental shift in perspective involved in understanding the personal planets through their higher octaves, which represent a truly transpersonal perspective that can appear truly radical from the perspective of the personality.

Neptune represents a shift from personal love and love of other from how they relate to us and fulfill (Venus ruling Taurus and Libra) towards a universal love that spontaneously arises when the true nature of experience is seen. Pluto represents the shift from the personal will instinctively acting on behalf of the self (Mars) to a higher will that represents the desire of the Soul to fulfill its evolutionary potential in ways that may run counter to the personality's ideas of its next steps. Uranus represents the shift from the mental labeling of experience (Mercury) towards a direct encounter with the nature of the experience itself, beyond concepts or positions.

When we combine the archetypes of Uranus, Pluto and Neptune, we realize that the transpersonal dimension of experience completely alters the more conventional experience of the personality. From the transpersonal perspective, all that exists can be seen to be an expression of its own true nature and therefore just how it is meant to be:

> In reality, everything occurs of its own, with no exterior cause. Everything and every event is a manifestation of the totality of All That Is Once seen in its totality, everything is

96

perfect at all times and nothing needs an external cause to change it in any way. From the viewpoint of the ego's positionality and limited scope, the world seems to need endless fixing and correction. This illusion collapses as a vanity.

In reality, everything is automatically manifesting the inherent destiny of its existence; it doesn't need external help to do this. With humility, one can relinquish the ego's self-appointed role as savior of the world and surrender it straight to God. The world that the ego pictures is a projection of its own illusions and arbitrary positionalities. No such world exists.

— Dr. David Hawkins, *The Eye of the I*, p.151-2

By "positionalities," Dr. Hawkins means what I have referred as mental labeling, or concepts of the Mercury function, which the transpersonal dimension transcends as there is then no observer, no subject looking at a distant world. Rather, then, there is a co-present emergence of reality in all directions at once, and one is rather part of that world as it is born anew every moment. In that sense, we can see that the great project to achieve, to do something productive, is primarily the activity of the ego or personality wanting to assert itself. Our deepest being participates directly and from our essential nature; there is no need to "do" anything; from our own true nature, being spontaneously arises. From true nature, we act in accordance with the emergent needs of the situation, not from the fantasy that the world needs saving or fixing in some way.

The personal planets indicate powerful inner potentials within the individual that come together to form what can be termed the personality of the individual. The personality on its own tends to see the world as a split between self and other, between subject and object. The transpersonal dimension of experience, symbolized astrologically through the outer planets of Uranus, Pluto and Neptune, shows that truth is non-dual. That there is no split between self and other or between self and the world "out there"; the world is revealed to be also "in here," and we are a part of it. This is the change of perspective symbolized by the idea of the higher octaves. An analogy is of some use, but one that requires the understanding that to move from the level of the personal to the transpersonal is to undertake a giant step. This giant step is revealed through surrender to the transpersonal nature of life itself, to actually return, like the prodigal child, to a world transformed through the love shining forth from every face, every sentient form: the same world, but different—transfigured by the recognition of our true potential as we are living witnesses and expressions of the beauty of the one life.

Endnotes

1. Rupert Sheldrake, *The Presence of the Past: Morphic Resonance and the Habits of Nature* (Collins, UK, 1998), p. 159. "Patterns of morphogenesis are organized by nested hierarchies of morphogenetic fields... Behavior is not determined only by the 'wiring' of the nervous system...but depends on the organizing activities of these fields." Mercury can be likened to the nervous system "wiring" and Uranus to the organizing influence of the morphic fields. "Memory need not be stored in material memory traces if it results from morphic resonance; the past can exert a direct influence on the present" (p. 160).

2. Dane Rudhyar, *Planetary Octaves and Rulership*, http://www.khaldea.com/rudhyar/astroarticles/planetaryoctaves.php.

3. Mark Jones, *Healing the Soul: Pluto, Uranus and the Lunar Nodes*, ed. Tony Howard (Raven Dreams Press, 2011), pp. 183–228.

4. Stanislav Grof, *The Holotropic Mind: The Three Levels of Human Consciousness and How They Shape Our Lives* (New York: HarperCollins, 1993), pp. 188–189.

5. "The Devil in the Detail," from *Astrology: The New Generation* (Flare Publications, London School of Astrology, 2012), 115–131.

6. A great book describing the way that the higher will (along with other higher states of consciousness) affects the personal will is *Transcending the Levels of Consciousness*, by Dr. David Hawkins (Veritas Publishing, 2006)

7. Two great books on the process of projecting our value onto other people are the Jungian analyst Robert Johnson's *Inner Gold* (Koa Books, 2010) and *The Psychology of Romantic Love* (Arkana, 1990). A great book on the way the individual is conditioned by the early environment is *The Pearl Beyond Price: Integration of Personality into Being*, by A. H. Almaas (Shambhala Publications, 1996)

8. Dr. David Hawkins, *The Eye of the I* (Veritas Publishing, 2001), p. 129.

7

Is the Transpersonal Becoming Personal?

The Planets as a Guide to Consciousness Evolution

Faye Cossar

When I first encountered astrology, I learnt that Uranus, Neptune and Pluto were called the transpersonal planets. I always had a sort of love/hate relationship with the term "transpersonal," similar to my reaction to the word "ego." What did these words mean? They are both described in so many different ways that I gave up on them and moved on. Not that I forgot about the principles, just the words. But as I am now using one of these words in my title, it may be time to look at the meaning of "transpersonal" in more depth.

Dane Rudhyar was a very important writer on this topic and, if my understanding is correct, the first to use the term "transpersonal astrology." In his *From Humanistic to Transpersonal Astrology* from 1975,[1] he writes:

> The word "transpersonal," which I began to use in articles for a small magazine **The Glass Hive** in 1930, can be confusing, for the prefix "trans" has a double meaning. It can mean "beyond"; but its more essential meaning is "through." A transpersonal attitude may be one involving a reaching **beyond** the personal—an "ascent" of consciousness and will seeking to attain greater heights and "peak experiences." It is mostly in this sense that the word is used by the transpersonal movement in psychology. But a transpersonal process may also imply a "descent" of spiritual power focusing itself **through** a person, as diffused solar light is focused through a clear lens; and it is in this sense that I have always used it in the past.

Later he writes:

> What I have presented, whether at the humanistic or the transpersonal level, can evidently be called a "spiritual" approach to astrology.[2]

Spiritual is also a word that is used in many ways. Rudhyar is mainly concerned with transformation when he is talking of transpersonal astrology, meaning a process that should lead to a higher and more inclusive level of consciousness affecting the way we act. Interestingly, Rudhyar does not refer to Uranus, Neptune and Pluto as transpersonal planets but as the trans-Saturnian planets, ones that offer information on how we can transform.[3] They indicate timing—showing when transformation can take place. Many refer only to the outer planets as being transpersonal; however, according to Rudhyar, for every planet there is a transpersonal approach.

My own understanding of the outer planets used to be more like Jung's collective unconscious. I saw them as planetary archetypes that are above the social level of Jupiter and Saturn—ones that reflect the greater level of connection that mankind shares. I could understand them best as fields, so I was delighted when I realized that Rupert Sheldrake's morphic field model[4] could be applied to planets. The basic premise is that memory is not in the brain but in fields that we can tap into or rather resonate with. There can be hierarchies of memory—your own, your family, your country—but Sheldrake also refers to fields such as cultures or professions. Nature, he suggests, is not fixed but has habits that may change over time. It is this model that I want to expand on here to show how astrology can be used as a model for consciousness development, one I think that also embraces Rudhyar's idea of transformation.

When I was studying for my master's degree in cultural astronomy and astrology, I wrote a paper titled *Three Histories of Uranus*.[5] I began with a wonderful quote from Sheldrake:[6]

> Our minds reach out to touch everything we see. If we look at distant stars, then our minds stretch out over

astronomical distances to touch these heavenly bodies. Subject and object are indeed confused. Through our perceptions, the environment is brought within us, but we also extend outwards into the environment.

I took this to mean that when we become aware of something, such as a new planet, it will affect us, but we will also have an effect on what we are observing, in this case a planet.

I studied how our understanding of Uranus has changed since its discovery. I looked at Uranus as I made the assumption that the planetary fields from Mercury to Saturn (including the Sun and the Moon) were stable, as we had been conscious of these planets for a long time. As with any planet, I took Uranus to be a morphic field, but one that was, at its discovery in 1781, at first unstable. I feel this archetype is becoming stabilized as we interact with this field and become more conscious of it. When Rudhyar referred to the discovery of the outer planets, he suggested that mankind was not ready to develop the "super-physical" faculties, or the archetypal mind characterized by Uranus, Neptune and Pluto, until these planets were discovered.

On this note, I find it interesting that many astrologers draw a line between planets visible to the naked eye and the others, usually referring to those from Uranus outwards. When researching the Uranus paper, I discovered some references to the fact that Uranus can in fact be seen with the naked eye in some places. To my mind, the fact that we can view all the outer planets now through telescopes, or various other fantastic scientific means, makes this difference less important. We are conscious of the fact that they exist. Sheldrake's other work, written up in his book *The Sense of Being Stared At*, clearly shows an effect on subjects whether they are being stared at by someone in the same location or through a camera. Perhaps looking at planets with or without a telescope works in the same way, making the division between visible and invisible planets less relevant.

Combining these principles, I suggest that since 1781 we have been involved in a consciousness leap. As we have become aware of these outer planets, our consciousness has extended outwards from the earth literally, but perhaps also symbolically. When Uranus was discovered, the size of the known universe more than doubled, so this is a jump in consciousness that, in my view, needs time to stabilize. The planetary system may be seen as a model for the development of consciousness. As we become aware of objects further away from the earth, we are developing a different kind of consciousness relating to the holon[7] in question.

At this point I wish to introduce another concept, one that I wrote about in an article for the Astrological Association of Great Britain[8] and one to which Armand Diaz also refers in his book *Integral Astrology*.[9] Diaz is concerned with the question of people being at different consciousness levels, particularly within astrological consulting. Astrology has no way of identifying these levels. If we look at a chart, we have no idea about where someone is in terms of what might be called spiritual development. This is why I found the model known as *Spiral Dynamics* very exciting for astrologers. It was named by Don Beck,[10] who used an original idea from Clare Graves. In his book *Boomeritis*, Ken Wilber expands on the model, sometimes very humorously, to explain these levels of consciousness.[11] There are colors for the levels that, unfortunately, do not seem to have any particular significance. The model itself, however, is very interesting. Although at the moment it is used mostly for business purposes, it could also be applied to any group, such as families or countries. I think that Spiral Dynamics can be taken as a metaphor for our solar system with the planets related to levels of consciousness.

The table below matches Spiral Dynamics (SD) levels and colors, with my suggestion for an associated planet. The SD model suggests we are now approaching a development of consciousness with a large jump—hence the need for a second tier. Others also suggest this is the case, often related to ideas about a consciousness jump, heavily publicized in the 2012 predictions of the ending of a cycle.

The table dates from 1996, but here I have used Don Beck's 2002 updates for the estimated percentages. Below is an explanation of how to interpret the table. Note: This is a very basic description. I refer you to the book *Spiral Dynamics*[12] or the copious information on the web for a deeper understanding. Neil Crofts' *Spiral Dynamics – a map of the evolution of human consciousness*,[13] which can be found on the web, is one article I like; I find it particularly clear on the colors.

Beige describes a level of consciousness that relates to people who either rely on instinct to survive or have little ability to communicate. They make up

102

an estimated 0.4 percent of the population. According to SD, this holon has existed for about 100,000 years. In other words, in my terms, the Moon is a very old morphic field relating to instinctual capacities that everyone has; however, only a few people cannot operate above this level.

1st Tier	Population	Years	Planet
Beige – Survival Sense Instinctual	0.4 %	100,000	Moon
Purple – Kin Spirits Harmony and Safety	12 %	50,000	Venus
Red – Power Gods Egocentric	18 %	10,000	Mars
Blue – Truth Force Order and Purpose	30 %	5,000	Saturn
Orange – Strive Drive Strategize	27 %	1,000	Jupiter
Green – Human Bond Communitarian	9 %	150 (around year 1850)	Uranus

2nd Tier			
Yellow – Flex Flow Integrative	3 %	50 (around year 1950)	Neptune
Turquoise – Whole View Holistic	0.6 %	30 (around year 1970)	Chiron (?)

Table 1 - Spiral Dynamic Levels and Associated Planets

I have related Purple to Venus as it is about people who function from what SD calls a tribal mind—harmony and safety are important. The Red level is a very good match for Mars and is the right color! After communities were formed, there was a need to defend them. Red was needed for hunting too, but it can be hedonistic and selfish. It operates in the now and often shows no regard for the consequences. Blue is a perfect match for Saturn, and Orange has a lot of Jupiterian qualities, but I suspect these two would have developed in tandem and would be roughly the same age. As Blue became too restrictive, Orange wanted to expand, take risks and have adventures, causing Blue to seek order and laws. And so it continues up to Green, which has been around, according to SD, since about 1850—nearer the discovery of Ceres or Neptune.

Green could relate to either of these, but it has a very Uranian flavor. Only an estimated 9 percent of people can operate at this level.

We need all levels, and the suggestion is that the system is open-ended and will keep developing as human consciousness develops. Although I think the SD model could be adjusted to better suit a planetary model, the idea of being able to live at a particular planetary level is interesting.

I will use an example to make this clearer. Planetary fields contain both positive and negative ways of working. If we take the SD Blue level, which is a very good match for Saturn, then I would read this chart as saying that 30 percent of people can make use of a positive Saturn. They take responsibility for their actions, can work towards goals, can be good managers and can develop their own expertise or be good teachers. Saturn is an old established field, so we can "do" Saturn reasonably well on a global scale. However, there are people who cannot rise above the negative version of Saturn or to higher levels, and we still see this operating in austere regimes, harsh rules or strict religions, with many acting out of fear.

Another example: If we cannot rise above Orange, then we get the over-speculation and greed of Jupiter instead of the vision and strategy that a conscious Jupiter can offer, and we cannot reach the community level of Green.

As already mentioned, only an estimated 9 percent of the population are at what I view as a Uranian consciousness level. In *Boomeritis*, Ken Wilber summarizes Green: "Promote a sense of community and caring; promote gender equality, children's rights and animal welfare; basis of value communities."[14] I suggest that this represents the large jump we are now making from the old materialistic Saturnian view to the first stage of Rudhyar's transpersonal transformation. Many people are integrating a positive way of using Uranus. My generation fought hard for freedom to be themselves. To my mind, children now are more authentic, more independent and more "themselves" than we were. They are comfortable with technology and are (perhaps too) ready to say what they think. They can "do" Uranus. However, we see many examples of non-conscious Uranian activities, such as rebelliousness that is cruel, mental fixity, dishonesty and lack of concern for the needs of others.

I agree with the suggestion in the table that not many can incorporate Neptunian consciousness. Children are given the task of developing this field but are suffering from our inability to deal with Neptunian issues. Addictions of all kinds, attention deficit disorder, autism and allergies are very prevalent Neptunian problems for young people (and many others). Both on a personal and social level, this generation will have to learn to deal with these problems, along with the rising number of people suffering from eating disorders and Alzheimer's disease. All we seem to be able to do is throw Saturnian measures at these problems: prison, schools with more rules or, if we manage to reach a Uranian level, we leave young people to their own devices too much. With a negative Neptune, we simply use drugs to bury the problem and stop the chaos, but that also limits the imagination and compassionate ways of connecting. On the plus side, in my view, these problems are giving us the opportunity to learn how to integrate Neptune, although we have a long way to go. A good Pluto integration is even further away, with power still being abused in many ways.

Some years back, I heard a lecture given by the well-respected astrologer Lynn Bell. She remarked that when the transpersonal planets make an aspect to personal planets, particularly the Sun or the Moon, we will be called upon, even have a responsibility, to use the energies of Pluto, Neptune or Uranus in the world. Although this was many years ago, this idea stuck with me. People with these aspects "know" these planets. They meet them often in their lives in both positive and negative ways. This comes back to Rudhyar's idea of "trans" meaning operating *through* a person. Perhaps people who strongly resonate with these planets have a role in leading the evolution in these fields. Astrologers, with their knowledge of planetary energies, can play a role here.

Barbara Marx Hubbard is a heroine of mine. Her work spans many decades, and currently she heads the Foundation for Conscious Evolution,[15] where she advocates working together to co-create a planetary shift with a positive future. She is cooperating with many of the world's leaders in spiritual awareness. My favorite term of hers is "vocational arousal," meaning that when you love your work, it is fulfilling and authentic for you. You can get up every day ready to go to work and help the world towards a fertile future. "Supra-sex" is another term she uses to describe how you can be aroused by the hearts and minds of other people to birth creativity and co-create a new world. I like to think of myself as a co-creative astrologer in two ways. One is that I co-create with my clients to help them find what they love to do in their lives. My book *Using Astrology to Create a Vocational Profile*[16] is based on this principle. The other way is that I try to co-create with planets, both for myself and for my clients, by trying to understand how planetary energies could be used to advantage.

Co-creation with planets means interacting with their fields. As we discover a planet, the field changes. As scientists visit a planet, such as the current research on Mars, the field evolves. Each planetary field evolves with every interaction. Science now recognizes that observation and focus have an effect on the thing or person being observed. Astrologers can see that individuals resonate with particular planetary fields. Someone with a Sun conjunct Uranus will resonate with the Uranian field. As time has gone on, we have co-created the Uranian field. What we write, say and think about Uranus has an effect. What Uranian people do with this energy has an effect. The more we can help co-create a positive version of the field, the better. For me, this is both conscious evolution—choosing our future—and the evolution of consciousness as a whole. If enough people can "do" a positive Uranus, then we will reach a tipping point, and everyone who resonates with that field will be changed. As astrologers, we are well-placed to help raise consciousness levels because we have a wonderful model for explaining these energies. If we want to create positive fields, and I believe we have choice in this, we can give advice on how to use planetary qualities. We need to stop judging planets as good or bad. We need to stop scaring clients by saying some transits are difficult. This does not mean we negate the fact that they can be tricky, but we need to remember that we are affecting the field.

On a personal note, I think we tune into these fields all the time as we work with these archetypes. During my research for my paper on Uranus, several of my electrical appliances broke down. I had to change nearly all the light bulbs in the house. My washing machine needed to be repaired, and when the serviceman came to repair it, he broke the new part. Two days after it was finally fixed, the dryer broke down. The transformer for the light in the kitchen fused. While writing the details of what astrologers had written about Uranus over the years, there was a storm raging outside, and as I did the final edit the oven stopped working. However, I have had many flashes of insight. Is this just coincidence? Or synchronicity? Or have I, by tapping into this morphic field, invoked Uranus, as the ancients would have said, into my life? As my mind touches this heavenly body, I have yet to decide if it is a comforting thought that he is also listening to my ideas and beliefs or whether it feels more like "Big Brother."

Every planet has a transpersonal nature. If, for example, we understand what Mars represents and are aware of our Mars patterns, we are on the road to being able to transform his energy into exuberant, pioneering, daring acts. The other planets can also be used this way, but here I want to focus on the transpersonal planets and one other planetary discovery that occurred after 1781.

We were given an assignment from the cosmos in 1781 to stabilize a whole new field, archetype, holon, planet—choose your name for it. But that necessitated a big leap of consciousness. The change required to incorporate Uranus is huge and takes time. To have a world where everyone is treated as special, where everyone has a say, where independence is available to all, is what Uranus demands. Many astrologers have said we need a bridge to get to this level, and for many that takes the form of Chiron. I agree, and we probably need the wisdom of Pholus and Nessus to get us to Neptune and Pluto too. However, the Centaurs are outside the scope of this chapter, as I wish to discuss only planets, and there is one lady we often forget: Ceres.

Considering the "As above, so below" principle, something major happened in 2006. Although not every astronomer agreed with the decision, Pluto is now a dwarf planet. The Pluto field is of course still there, so the effect he has does not alter. He received a lot of attention in 2006, and scientists will visit him in the near future, so his field will be affected. But to me something more important came into awareness—again. Ceres was also reclassified—and at the same level as Pluto. These two are combined in the mythology in many different ways, so what might this mean for consciousness evolution now that they are on an equal footing?

Ceres was originally discovered on January 1, 1801. Until 1850 she was known as a planet, but due to the number of celestial bodies being discovered around that time in what is now known as the asteroid belt, she was reclassified as an asteroid—until 2006, when she was reinstated to a planet, albeit a dwarf one. Ceres (Demeter) was a major goddess in days gone by. However, it has taken until now for her field to start stabilizing. She is the first of the female children of Cronus (Saturn) and Rhea to be given a planet. Of her brothers, Zeus (Jupiter) was the first, and Poseidon (Neptune) was actually given a planet after Ceres, but she was demoted not long after he became a planet. Then came Hades (Pluto). Ceres' sisters Hera and Hestia are still waiting. Although Venus (Aphrodite) had given her name to a planet centuries ago, she is the grandchild of Saturn; hence she is a generation down and is a "young woman" archetype.

To me, this means that what is coming into consciousness again (after a trial run between 1801 and 1850) is the older wise-woman archetype. It is an energy that can match Neptune, Pluto and Jupiter. And in the mythology, Ceres does. Although she is overruled by her brothers, she fights back and negotiates with them to get what she wants. Ceres is a complex archetype, and her field has been very active since 2006. Food, genetically modified produce, fertility, the environment, democracy, women's rights, climate change and natural cycles—all part of her remit—have all become very important globally. I also think she has knowledge of the elements (periodic table) and DNA.

If we look at the discovery dates, it would seem that we need to first develop a positive Ceres field before we can reach Neptune and Pluto, as Ceres was discovered before they were. This means developing respect for older women and using the wisdom of the older feminine principle. It means looking at how we produce and consume food, and as both Archbishop Tutu and the Dalai Lama have said, allowing western women to save the world. Of course, Ceres is active in men as well, but women have an assignment here. Ceres needs to take on the negative aspects of Jupiter, or Orange in SD—greed. She needs to stand up to Pluto's misuse of power. We need her to enable us to develop Neptune and to reach the SD second tier, thus raising the consciousness level in the world.

Good examples of Ceres women who are helping do this (and who both have Ceres aspecting the Sun, making this archetype part of their vocation) are Hillary Clinton[17] and Aung San Suu Kyi.[18] They are active in many of Ceres' areas mentioned above. They are examples where a planetary energy is working through one person. Although both these women are consciously working for the world, it *is* personal. We can all play a role in creating a positive future by becoming aware of how all the planetary fields could be used positively, by acting on this knowledge ourselves and passing it on to others.

I have heard it said that, in some people, new aura layers are developing. A well-respected aura reading teacher in the Netherlands, works with a system of twelve layers rather than the frequently used seven. This is an interesting number astrologically, of course, but more fascinating is the fact that she can clearly see more layers around some people than others. Her idea is that more layers occur in people doing more spiritual work. Are there more planetary morphic fields close to them? Perhaps transpersonal planets are indeed becoming personal.

Bibliography

Beck, Don Edward and Christopher C. Cowan. *Spiral Dynamics, mastering values, leadership, and change (*Oxford: Blackwell Publishers, 1996*).*

Cossar, Faye. *Using Astrology to Create a Vocational Profile: Finding the Right Career Direction* (London: Flare Publications, 2012)

Diaz, Armand. *Integral Astrology: Understanding the Ancient Discipline in the Contemporary World* (New York: Integral Transformation, LLC, 2012).

Sheldrake, Rupert. *The Presence of the Past: Morphic Resonance and the Habits of Nature* (South Paris, Maine: Park Street Press, 2009).

Sheldrake, Rupert. *The Sense of Being Stared at* (New York: Crown Publishers, 2003).

Sheldrake, Rupert. *Seven Experiments That Could Change the World: A Do-It Yourself Guide to Revolutionary Science* (New York: Riverhead Books, 1995).

Wilber, Ken. *Boomeritis, A Novel That Will Set You Free* (Boston: Shambhala Publications, 2002).

Endnotes

1. http://www.khaldea.com/rudhyar/fromhtot_1.shtml Part 3. Bold is Rudhyar's emphasis, accessed January 2013.

2. http://www.khaldea.com/rudhyar/fromhtot_1.shtml Part 4, accessed January 2013.

3. http://www.beyondsunsigns.com/rudhyaraudioastrology.html#ta, accessed January 2013.

4. See Sheldrake's book "The Presence of the Past: Morphic Resonance and the Habits of Nature."

5. See http://www.astrozero.co.uk/articles/Uranus.htm, accessed January 2013.

6. Rupert Sheldrake, *"Seven Experiments That Could Change the World,"* 106-107.

7. I prefer holon, Arthur Koestler's term, to archetype here, as holons include all forms of matter and non-matter.

8. *"Towards a Responsible Astrology of the Future,"* AA Journal September/October 2009: 36-39.

9. Armand Diaz, *"Integral Astrology: Understanding the Ancient Discipline in the Contemporary World."*

10. Don Edward Beck and Christopher C. Cowan, *"Spiral Dynamics, mastering values, leadership, and change."*

11. Ken Wilber, *"Boomeritis, A Novel That Will Set You Free."*

12. Don Edward Beck and Christopher C. Cowan, *Spiral Dynamics, mastering values, leadership, and change.* Please note that these authors have gone their separate ways since this book was published. Cowan stays closer to the original SD model of Graves. Beck has joined forces with Ken Wilber, and they have created SDi, which includes Wilbur's integral thinking. For purposes here, I refer to the original SD, although both have the same basis.

13. http://themagicofbeing.squarespace.com/spiral-dynamics/, accessed January 2013.

14. Ken Wilber, "Boomeritis", 95-96.

15. http://www.barbaramarxhubbard.com, accessed January 2013.

16. Faye Cossar, "Using Astrology to Create a Vocational Profile: Finding the Right Career Direction."

17. Hillary Rodham Clinton, October 26, 1947, 8:02 am CST Chicago, IL, USA. Sun Opposition Ceres.

18. Aung San Suu Kyi, June 19, 1945, time unknown, Rangoon, Myanmar. Sun Trine Ceres.

8

The Death Chart

Maurice Fernandez

Horoscopic astrology has proven its fundamental value among practicing astrologers and their benefitting clientele. Regardless of the system one has adopted to interpret planetary cycles, the exact moment of birth is understood to capture essential information about the person. Character, weaknesses and strengths, along with his or her life direction, can be derived from the planetary configuration of the natal chart. It is a simple moment in time, but for the person born, no other moment precisely represents the deepest meanings of that life: past, present, and unfolding future.

Evolution is a time and space mechanism; however, as we progress through each fragment of time and space, we can capture more of what is beyond that, timeless—just like the full length of a movie composed of endless separated frames. The natal chart is founded on the moment (time) and place (space) of birth. When using astrology of the evolution of consciousness, a greater focus is put on the soul development when analyzing the particularities of a chart. Beyond identifying personality traits and general orientation, the premise is that the current life is the evolutionary continuation of previous incarnations; the frames that make the movie are not only about this life but include the whole sum of soul experiences through incarnations. Hence, the current natal chart also describes what themes the soul carries from previous lives and, accordingly, what the next steps are in the soul's evolutionary process. These past life signatures, commonly captured in unconscious memories, set the tone for present behavioral inclinations, instinctive attractions and aversions, and natural talents; a baby is not born blank, and the natal chart describes how consciousness is shaped by past life experiences and then how that spurs new cycles of becoming. There are multiple studies on the phenomenon of past life memories and the validity of reincarnation, but it is beyond the scope of this essay to delve into such research and debate the intricacies therein. For this purpose, I will attempt to keep these vast philosophical concepts simple but mention that the premise of this study is a fundamental understanding that life continues after death, but in another form.

From an evolutionary point of view, life is neither random nor completely fated; the evolutionary dynamics imply that the purpose of existing on this plane is to expand consciousness about the greater Truth of life, that which is beyond time and space fragments. The more conscious we become of the timeless Truth, the better we can navigate the waves of existence and experience an increasingly higher level of health and well-being within time and space—albeit such progress is not necessarily even and linear. Because the natal chart describes the next step, evolutionarily speaking, we can also detect early life conditions that will serve such purposes: family, culture, and general environmental conditions that serve as the platform for this life to unfold. Whether supportive or challenging, these early life factors are not random, but part of the evolutionary mechanism.

The Weight of Free Will

While the natal chart displays what our current evolutionary step is about, it does not predetermine how far we will go with it. We have capacities that provide us with a sense of purpose, and we have lessons to learn that pose a developmental challenge. However, some people will stumble over and over on the same issue, while others born with the same chart will master a lesson more rapidly and attain greater heights and depth under similar circumstances. The natal chart describes where we left off last time around, but regarding future development, it only describes orientation, probabilities, and potential. How much of that potential is realized is a function of free will.

We cannot change our charts because they are the fruits of our past life efforts, but we have the choice to make of them the best, worse, and everything in between. For example, using the natal chart of *Mohandas Gandhi* (see Figure 1), we identify intense planetary configurations that describe both past life themes and future orientation. Noticeably, he was born with Mars and Venus in Scorpio in the first house opposing Pluto and Jupiter in Taurus in the seventh house, all squaring a Leo Moon in the tenth house. We know his story, and we recognize that Gandhi used these energies to fight and transform (Mars in Scorpio in the first house) the abuse and excess of power, essentially associated with resource distribution (Pluto/Jupiter in Taurus) directed by the imperialism of the British Crown (Moon in Leo in the tenth house). Yet had we not known the individual, the chart describes different potential scenarios. For example, with Mars and Venus in Scorpio in the first house opposing Pluto in the seventh house, an individual is charged with anger that may easily be projected aggressively, perhaps towards members of the other sex. Maybe Gandhi even experienced some of these feelings in the course of his life, but what he choose to do with such a high charge made history and served as an inspiration for masses—he directed his personal frustration to stimulate change for the greater good. While his natal chart may have described a strong inclination for activism, it did not guarantee the full extent of his impact on liberating India and becoming the symbol of non-violent protest.

Free Will and Death

The extent of our free will is immediately associated with our level of consciousness. How deep we go or how little we learn along the way will determine the nature of our life circumstances; our actions engender results and realities that define the course of our lives. If someone is born with an angular Mars–Pluto opposition that suggests deep feelings of injustice and anger, the outcome from such an influence will depend on that person's free will to direct such intensity. When someone fails to channel such anger constructively and allows it to override common sense, a life of antagonism, ruptures, isolation and "emotional toxicity" is bound to manifest. Conversely, if he or she becomes conscious of it and introspects to understand the root of those emotions, such intensity can become potent energy that engenders transformative action, the very essence of activism. Instead of negative results, the same challenging configuration can bring about courage, risk, positive changes and growth. In conclusion, while a chart pattern describes a particular theme, that theme may be expressed in a variety of ways; consequently, there is no way to predict finite outcomes. Our free will provides us with the flexibility to generate completely different results from the same original themes.

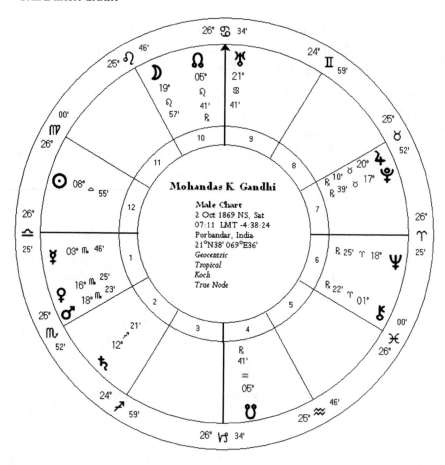

Figure 1 - Mohandas Gandhi's birth chart

Here is the vital question for our subject matter: If individuals born with the same chart patterns choose to express these influences differently, *will they die at the same time?* Without free will, the chart would describe a fated sequence of development, and thus death would be pre-determined and fixed for these people—but we know it is not the case. This assertion can be confirmed by statistics of twins born by caesarian at the same time, who, in most cases, will not die at the same exact time. People born with the same chart will confront the same themes in their lives, but they are bound to choose differently, and as a result, they affect the course of their evolutions and generate different circumstances. *As life takes a different turn, the moment of death will also change accordingly.*

114

We must then ask ourselves: if the natal chart captures planetary alignments that perfectly reflect our evolutionary development, is there a similar meaning to the moment of death and the planetary alignments of that chart? As it is with our birth, the death moment is not random but an important indicator in the sequence of our soul's evolution. *There is a reason why we die in one moment and not another, just as there is a reason why we are born in one moment and not another.*

The Death Chart

While more research is naturally invested in the meanings and influences of the natal chart, it is valuable to investigate death chart meanings and their role in reflecting evolutionary developments of the soul. From the perspective of the evolution of consciousness, death is not the absolute end of life but the end of a chapter in the sequence of the soul's evolution. Therefore, just as the natal chart describes past life dynamics setting the tone for current life purposes, the death chart reflects where the soul is at upon transitioning, and what its next step is in its evolutionary orientation.

Let us take a moment to understand death better. Death is arguably one of the most humbling experiences; it brings a complete and irreversible (in most cases) end to a whole life chapter. While we may have the power to postpone death, we do not have the power to avoid it. Death reminds us that we are not invincible, that we are not gods but mortals who are on an evolutionary journey. Evolution implies imperfection and bondage to time and space; time and space induce endings and beginnings; death is a reminder of our imperfect consciousness: that which needs to evolve.

As we evolve, we approach life more holistically and better navigate its currents. We realize new insights, make better choices, change forms and adapt, to live better. If we progressively manage life better, we also change the odds of our death. *If we live better, can we die later—or perhaps die better?* The death chart captures where we are when we die, and so the death chart reflects the efforts that we made to evolve in the course of this incarnation. Obviously, managing to live more consciously does not invariably imply that we live a longer life, for what matters is the timing of our death: the planetary alignments of that time and their meaning.

115

While we may learn to live better and sometimes cheat death (knowingly or unknowingly), eventually, it does have the last word. We reach the point when we cannot regenerate, and our energy is exhausted; we did the best we could to live well; and yet, we meet our ultimate limitation: we surrender to death. Our soul may continue on after death, but it remains that death is an ending that marks a fundamentally decisive moment in our evolution.

The death chart captures where the soul is at upon departing from the current incarnation. It shows what has been worked on, what gifts or complexes are being carried onward onto the next phase—in a way, *the death chart is a new birth chart*—yet one of its important values is that it can be referred to the natal chart so that conclusions may be drawn on the soul's development and/or continued direction the soul is taking.

Gandhi's Death Chart

We have discussed some of the prominent themes of Gandhi's natal chart (see Figure 1), notably his angular Mars–Venus conjunction in Scorpio opposing Pluto–Jupiter in Taurus and square the Moon in Leo (see Figure 2). This configuration naturally had numerous dimensions of influence in his life. On a personal level, it described his intimate emotional needs; on a collective level, it showed his public role as a freedom fighter who defied the status quo. With such a configuration, it can be derived that Gandhi's previous incarnation did not end peacefully but rather that he came from a place of confrontation, polarization, and great intensity. (Generally speaking, the first-to-seventh house opposition, particularly with Mars involved, suggests tension with the other sex, as well as confrontations with polarized adversaries.) With such a past life imprinted on his unconscious, we can expect that, as a young boy he would already tend to be emotionally reactive and naturally doubting of established rules. Knowing adversity, he would also need to measure his power with others and test his capacity constantly. For example, it is documented in biographical accounts that Gandhi confronted the legitimacy of child marriage customs when he was married at age thirteen by his parents. While he went along with the expectation, it raised many questions for him.

116

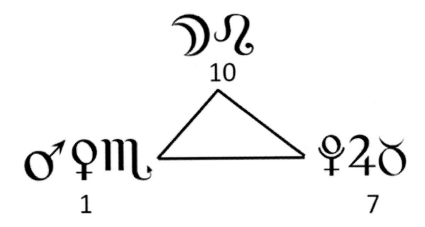

Figure 2 - Prominent configuration in Gandhi's natal chart

This T-square configuration suggests peaks of achievements (making a difference and being appreciated), contrasted by deeply humbling defeats; someone born with such a prominent Mars in Scorpio opposing Pluto is bound to experience the extremes of possessing power and then loss. Upon defeat, the Scorpionic theme intrinsic to this opposition would prompt him to reassess, regenerate, and reemerge with new strategies. We can assume that the legendary non-violent protest stance resulted from failing at first at other approaches.

In an adult, this configuration also reflects a powerful sexual drive. A person born with such a configuration may be consumed by his own instinctual drive, sometimes to a point where lust can lead him to betray his own values. An overpowering sexual drive can cloud one's judgment and engender poor choices. This prominent configuration (see Figure 2) reflects internal struggles with his own sexuality, from experiencing strong sexual powers to disappointment and crisis in sexual matters. The Scorpionic influence compelled him to transform and evolve his sexual approach (Mars and Venus in Scorpio) to ensure that sexuality does not lead him astray but, conversely, enhances his growth.

Author Jad Adams wrote a biography of Gandhi (*Gandhi: Naked Ambition[1]*) in which he described Gandhi's obsession with transcending his sexual desires and his goals of chastity. Below are selected quotes from an article written about the book.

It was no secret that Mohandas Gandhi had an unusual sex life. He spoke constantly of sex and gave detailed, often provocative, instructions to his followers as to how to they might best observe chastity. And his views were not always popular; "abnormal and unnatural" was how the first Prime Minister of independent India, Jawaharlal Nehru, described Gandhi's advice to newlyweds to stay celibate for the sake of their souls.

Two years later (after his marriage), as his father lay dying, Gandhi left his bedside to have sex with (his wife) Kasturba. Meanwhile, his father drew his last breath. The young man compounded his grief with guilt that he had not been present, and represented his subsequent revulsion towards "lustful love" as being related to his father's death.

Gandhi found it easy to embrace poverty. It was chastity that eluded him. So he worked out a series of complex rules which meant he could say he was chaste while still engaging in the most explicit sexual conversation, letters and behavior.

With the zeal of the convert, within a year of his vow, he told readers of his newspaper Indian Opinion: "It is the duty of every thoughtful Indian not to marry. In case he is helpless in regard to marriage, he should abstain from sexual intercourse with his wife."

Meanwhile, Gandhi was challenging that abstinence in his own way. He set up ashrams in which he began his first "experiments" with sex; boys and girls were to bathe and sleep together, chastely, but were punished for any sexual talk. Men and women were segregated, and Gandhi's advice was that husbands should not be alone with their wives, and, when they felt passion, should take a cold bath.

The rules did not, however, apply to him. Sushila Nayar, the attractive sister of Gandhi's secretary, also his personal physician, attended Gandhi from girlhood. She used to sleep and bathe with Gandhi. When challenged, he explained how he ensured decency was not offended. "While she is bathing I keep my eyes tightly shut," he said, "I do not know...whether she bathes naked or with her underwear on. I can tell from the sound that she uses soap." The provision of such personal services to Gandhi was a much sought-after sign of his favor and aroused jealousy among the ashram inmates[2].

The struggle with his sexuality is obvious, and his natal chart illustrates these biographical accounts. Since Gandhi was concerned about the right use of sexuality and consistently worked on evolving his approach (Scorpio Mars and Venus), we may expect that his life unfolded in a way that reflected his choices. Referring back to our subject matter, we can trace the development of these themes in Gandhi's life by analyzing his death chart (see Figure 3), and assess where he was, evolutionarily speaking, when his soul left his body.

Gandhi was assassinated on January 30, 1948, following four previous attempts. The time of the shooting is documented as 5:17 p.m. in Delhi, with a Leo rising chart (see Figure 3). The death chart becomes our reference to understand the orientation of his soul development from that moment, and to get an indication of how natal chart themes unfolded in the course of his life.

Gandhi's death chart portrays the circumstances of his life quite graphically. He passed while the sign of Leo was rising, reflecting the prominence he attained in his leadership position. The Sun in Aquarius in the seventh house, ruling the Ascendant sign, evidently describes his focus on freedom of rights and the liberation movement that he led. In the seventh house, the focus is on unifying adversities and bringing resolution between opposing parties; in his case, it had to do with the partition of India into Hindu and Muslim populations (later to be separated between India, Pakistan, and Bangladesh). The trine of his seventh house Sun in Aquarius to his Moon in Libra conjunct Neptune in the third house reemphasizes his effort to use dialogue rather than force in order to secure win-win solutions that would be fair to both sides. Mercury in Aquarius in the seventh house trining Uranus in Gemini in the eleventh house is another signature that reinforces the effort of dialogue, progressive thinking, and conflict resolution.

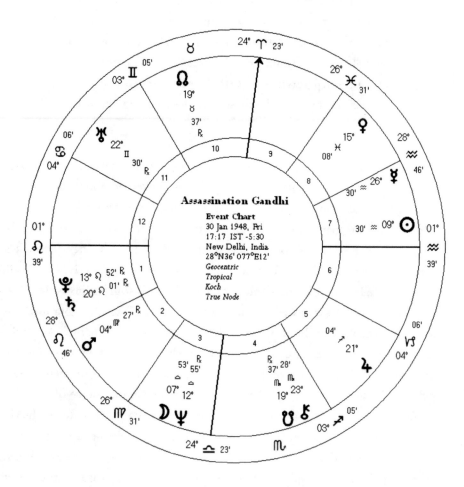

Figure 3 - Mohandas Gandhi's death chart

The Sun in Aquarius opposes Pluto and Saturn conjunct in Leo in the first house. This opposition underlines the fact that, despite the effort of dialogue and desire for fair play, political (Saturn) power (Pluto) struggles (first house) were still in effervescence. Pluto–Saturn in Leo in the first house describes an ardent need to change political systems and guarantee a breakthrough. On the one hand, this configuration shows the battle that Gandhi led against the imperial British crown, balancing force and determination (first house) with non-violence and progressive thinking (Sun in Aquarius in the seventh house); but it also shows the complexity of the new situation emerging: the partition of India and Pakistan was a bloody process charged with anger and resentment. The first house reflects the birth, the new era he created; and Pluto and Saturn in that house show a strenuous and convoluted labor process.

Pluto–Saturn in Leo in the first house square the nodal axis in Scorpio in the fourth house and Taurus in the tenth house—this configuration is another reinforcement of how fundamental and arduous the independence of India was, uprooting (Scorpio) many people from their homeland (fourth house), with the aim of establishing a more stable partition of land (tenth house Taurus). Yet Pluto–Saturn in square to the nodal axis shows that everything was still in process and not yet resolved. And indeed, to this day Pakistan and India are involved in land disputes over Kashmir.

On another level, we can look at the death chart to trace the development of the sexual theme we discussed earlier. The death chart has Mars in Virgo retrograde in the second house, widely opposing Venus in Pisces in the eighth house. Mars and Venus represent the sexual approach and needs (among other things). Venus and Mars are positioned in the sexual second and eighth houses; however, they are now in the (archetypically) chaste signs of Virgo and Pisces, in contrast to the highly sexual Scorpio placements in the natal chart. This configuration clearly describes Gandhi's effort and obsession about overcoming lustful desires and purifying his sexual nature. Mars in Virgo describes a strong need to control and purify the sexual impulse, while Venus in Pisces describes a need to transcend lust or, in other words, to put spirit over matter.

Venus in Pisces is also widely square a Uranus–Jupiter opposition in Gemini/Sagittarius, which shows how his efforts to be sexually abstinent were strongly governed by his mind (Uranus in Gemini) and his spiritual beliefs (Jupiter in Sagittarius)—he had a way to rationalize and argue his sexual approach (Jupiter opposing Uranus in a square to Venus). Venus and Mars are also the rulers of this Nodal Axis, emphasizing how important these themes were for him and will continue to be in his subsequent evolutionary processes.

Comparing the Natal Chart with the Death Chart

Much more can be derived from analyzing Gandhi's death chart, but its significance in describing and revealing evolutionary processes is already clear. Another valuable exercise consists in comparing the natal chart signatures with the death chart signatures to identify repeating patterns, placements, and degrees. I will only briefly address this comparison, mostly for the sake of stimulating readers to pursue their own research on the subject and demonstrate how rich this study can be.

Gandhi – Natal Chart	Gandhi – Death Chart
Seventh house Pluto–Jupiter square the Nodes in the fourth–tenth houses	First house Pluto–Saturn square The Nodes in the fourth–tenth houses
Mercury in the first house square the nodal axis	Mercury in the seventh house square the nodal axis
Sun in Libra in the twelfth house	Sun in the seventh house (Libra house) trine Neptune in Libra (natural twelfth house ruler)
Sun at 8 degrees Libra	Moon at 7 degrees Libra
Uranus in the ninth house	Uranus opposing Jupiter (natural ninth house ruler)
North Node 5 degrees Leo	Ascendant 1 degree Leo
Venus in Scorpio trine Uranus, opposite Jupiter, quincunx Neptune	Venus in the eighth house (Scorpio house) square Uranus, square Jupiter, and quincunx Neptune

Table 1 - Comparison of Gandhi's Natal and Death Charts

The recurring themes between the natal and death charts clearly reveal a direct correlation between the two fateful moments. As we can see with Gandhi's example, it is common to have the same theme repeat in the two charts in different forms: the same archetype can recur through house, sign, or by aspect configuration—as it is with Gandhi's natal Sun in Libra and then his death chart Sun in the seventh, natural Libra, house. So his Sun is connected to the Libra theme in both charts.

The Essential Value of Death Charts

While there is tremendous value in analyzing death charts, it is obvious that we will never have the privilege to analyze our own in this dimension. Many astrologers have tried to predict death, but from this study, we understand that the death moment depends on the free will factor, and therefore it is not a fixed matter—our choices and intervention alter our death circumstances. The only opportunity to explore our own death charts will be from the great beyond!

Similarly, we will never have the opportunity to discuss our clients' death charts with them, unless the astrologer is gifted with medium transcendental capacities to communicate with the deceased. The question, then, is: Why and when should we analyze death charts?

Evidently, whether or not we have the opportunity to share the insights with the deceased, the essential value of the death chart is that it works. The moment of death reveals a wealth of astrological information, and this provides us with a greater understanding of the phenomenon of death itself—if the death chart captures our evolutionary development, it does confirm that our actions during our life matter—nothing is wasted or unaccounted for. By further understanding and researching death charts of acquaintances or historical figures, we can better understand life on a general and personal level. Understanding death helps us live better.

It can also be valuable for the family of a deceased individual to gain greater insight into the evolutionary meanings seen in the departed one's life and death charts.

Damini's Death Chart

As we have described in the course of this essay, the death chart is intimately related to the natal chart. Notwithstanding, it can also be addressed as an entity of its own and reveal tremendous insight into soul processes. To illustrate this, let us use the example of a news case occurring on December 29, 2012. Damini was the victim of a gang rape in India (the name was given to her by the protestors she inspired). She did not survive her injuries and, following

13 days of battle for her life, she left her body at 4:45 a.m. in a hospital in Singapore. The following is from an article about the incident[3]:

> **(CNN)** -- A 23-year-old Indian woman, whose gang-rape aboard a bus in New Delhi spawned days of mass protests across India, has died, according to a doctor who was treating her at a Singapore hospital.
>
> "She had suffered from severe organ failure following serious injuries to her body and brain," Loh said. "She was courageous in fighting for her life for so long against the odds, but the trauma to her body was too severe for her to overcome."
>
> Students in New Delhi, India, on December 27, protest a recent brutal gang rape in the city. Authorities erected security barriers throughout New Delhi's key government district after two days of street battles following a woman's gang rape on a bus on December 16.

This horrific ordeal captured the collective mind and prompted protests to change laws in ways that would guarantee more adequate security for women in public places. Her real name had not yet been released as of this writing, so the nickname of Damini is used for her death chart (see Figure 4).

Damini passed as Jupiter in Gemini was setting on her Descendant, the apex of a yod configuration with Saturn in Scorpio in the twelfth house, and Pluto–Sun in Capricorn in the second house. Jupiter is also the ruler of the Ascendant sign. Yod configurations represent a clear intention to purify motives and realign actions. The apex of the Yod represents the cause as well as the direction of events, while the two legs represent the factors that need to be adjusted so that growth and a breakthrough may occur through the apex. The Yod often brings up deep crisis situations or circumstances in which we feel nothing is progressing in our lives and, no matter how hard we push, stagnation remains. One or the other, the sense of limitation continues until the matters represented by the legs are addressed and adjusted.

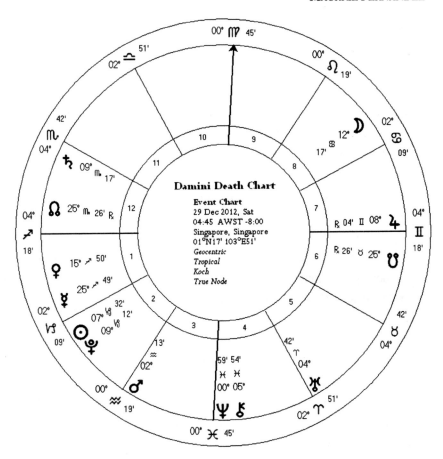

Figure 4 - Rape victim Damini's death chart.

The circumstances of Damini's ordeal have already caused uproar in India, and so her death generates a greater urgency about the cause of women's victimization in India and around the world. Her death chart thus captures a message that goes beyond her own personal reality and becomes a collective issue.

In a graphic manner, Jupiter in Gemini represents the bus ride where the gang rape occurred. Saturn in Scorpio in the twelfth house shows the overpowering use of sexual force and resulting victimization, with Pluto–Sun in Capricorn in the second house as an echo of the same misuse of sexuality (Saturn and Pluto are in mutual reception and therefore reinforce similar themes). Pluto in Capricorn and Saturn in Scorpio reflect the necessity to

125

change laws—they reflect corruption and the misuse of power (here sexual) so that the system (Saturn) may change and evolve (Scorpio).

Jupiter in Gemini as the apex points to the necessity for better education and media exposure of covered up, controversial, corrupt, and inadequate policies (Saturn in Scorpio in the twelfth house). "It needs to be talked about and brought to light" is Jupiter in Gemini's message.

Because Jupiter is in the seventh house of relationship, this position points to the overall gender imbalance that exists in India and the necessity for fairer policies supporting equality and opportunity for both genders.

Neptune positioned exactly in conjunction to an angle (IC) reflects the public nature of the circumstances of her death—she becomes a martyr and raises collective awareness in India and across the world. As it is, she is anonymously mentioned in an astrology essay as her story becomes the symbol for the cause and for so many other unheard cries—a phenomenon clearly described by a prominent Neptune placement. The collective message is also captured in her twelfth house North Node in Scorpio: she touches the collective unconscious (twelfth house) through her untimely death caused by criminal sexual behavior (Scorpio, Saturn in Scorpio).

She passes on a full Moon conjunct Pluto in the second and eighth houses, which are associated with sexuality, but also with safety (second house) and risk (eighth house); a full Moon death captures the powerful emotional event, and clearly her strong soul. The Capricorn-to-Cancer opposition captures the split existing between patriarchal and matriarchal essences strongly imprinted onto the culture—with a Cancer Moon in the eighth house opposing Pluto, the illustration of women kept hostage in the dungeon of the predatory lord of the underworld is obvious.

We know nothing at this point of Damini's personal life and who she was outside this tragedy, let alone her natal chart details. Notwithstanding, the death chart as a separate entity provides tremendous insight into her soul's developmental themes. The time her soul departed reflected the lessons to be learned. We see an evolutionary meaning to her death, and for those who have survived her; both those who know and those who do not know her personally, it provides more clarity on an otherwise senseless loss.

Conclusion

This essay is a brief introduction on a vast subject that invites a lot more study, both philosophically and with regard to astrological delineations. The important point is to realize how time and space factors, such as the events of our births and deaths, capture our evolutionary processes through the planetary clock cycles. As astrology essentially relies on our subjective earth perspective of the solar system and stars, it objectifies each person's existence and its processes: we realize that personal experiences capture a universal essence.

On the planetary plane of cyclic motion, each alignment is a part of the greater Truth. Some alignments will mark our births, our deaths, or other critical events of our lives, and accordingly, they will determine how we subjectively play out the greater essence of timeless Truth. In time and space, we spin the wheel until, perhaps, we find ourselves levitating in stillness at the epicenter of a spiral—then birth and death are but one.

Endnotes

1. Jad Adams - Gandhi: Naked Ambition; Quercus, 2011
2. http://www.independent.co.uk/arts-entertainment/books/features/thrill-of-the-chaste-the-truth-about-gandhis-sex-life-1937411.html
3. CNN:http://edition.cnn.com/2012/12/28/world/asia/india-rape-victim/index.html?hpt=hp_t1

9

Locational Astrology: A Transpersonal Perspective

Andrew Smith

Each one of us lives within a matrix of potential manifestation, woven together within a pathway of sacred geometry, held together by intention—a holographic projection onto which matter is outlined. Your life is embedded within this larger vibratory field of intelligence that is ever-changing and perpetually becoming conscious. As both our personal and collective consciousness more fully emerge, expanding inclusively, our awareness of our inner processing extends beyond the immediacy of our emotional–physical boundaries. Your life force is not simply contained *within* your physical bodies but extends across time and space as you draw into your Field people, ideas and circumstances that trigger a multitude of growth possibilities that ultimately serve to help you return to your Source.

Central to astrology is the awareness of change. As such, astrologers have become fascinated and absorbed by *time* as the agency of this process. From a historical context, time's centrality in astrology is an entirely understandable result of the calendric role of our predecessors. Even within modern astrology, the notion of cyclical or spiral time holds a tight grip around our practice despite the fact that our lives emerge not only *within* this abstraction but also within a *spatial* framework.

Prior to the publication of Albert Einstein's paper on special relativity in 1905, time was believed to be independent of motion, progressing at a fixed rate in all reference frames, despite evidence that space and time are actually an inseparable unit, a concept that can be found within Plato's third-century-BC writings[1]. There are even examples in nineteenth-century literature in which the idea of a unified space–time is discussed; e.g., in 1813, in his book titled *On the Fourfold Root of the Principle of Sufficient Reason*, Arthur Schopenhauer states that

...the representation of coexistence is impossible in Time alone; it depends, for its completion, upon the representation of Space; because, in mere Time, all things follow one another, and in mere Space all things are side by side; it is accordingly only by the **combination of Time and Space** that the representation of coexistence arises.

And again, Edgar Allan Poe, in his essay on cosmology titled *Eureka* in 1848, notes, "Space and duration are one." In 1895, in his novel *The Time Machine*, H.G. Wells writes, "There is no difference between time and any of the three dimensions of space except that our consciousness moves along it."

Yet despite this knowledge that space and time are inseparable, the spatial component of our internal psycho-spiritual process is infrequently written about and indeed not often practiced within astrology. If you really reflect on the *transpersonal* nature of consciousness it is clear that you do not simply exist in a specific location at a specific time, but you are deeply connected to all living (and non-living) things across *all* space and time. Not only do you draw people and circumstances into your life whose purpose is to support your spiritual growth during certain periods of time, but those messengers originate from, or reside in, a location in space.

Being born with the archetypal qualities of both time and space imbued within your soul means that no moment in time can ever reflect the same quality of experience and every individual soul therefore views reality through a unique lens. By extension, no two souls can ever attune to, or perceive, a region and its people in an identical manner, despite the existence of generalized cultural stereotypes within any given region.

To a geographer, something I was twenty years ago, a sense of place is made up of a mix of natural and cultural features in the landscape, which includes the people who occupy the place. A place may have a special energy due to its sheer beauty, geomorphology, or cultural significance (such as being found in literature, is historical, is portrayed in art or music, or holds specific religious focus) but it is humans who make places more special in their own minds. It is this power of common intention that creates a perception of the sacredness of space around a location. Therefore our sense of place is filtered by subjective experiences and we cannot objectively view reality outside of our own perceptual lens.

Broadly speaking, if you are an outdoorsy, mountain-hiking type, your resonance with city life is going to filter how you perceive an individual city. If you are not into architecture, the high level of imagination invested in architecture in Florence, Italy, will not really catch your eye in the way that it would for someone who really appreciates form and structure. Moreover, imagine you are on a romantic trip in Paris but whilst there you discover that your lover is cheating on you. The intense emotions that accompany such an experience would undoubtedly color your perception of Paris, and it would not be too surprising if you are unable to fully appreciate the architecture and other cultural nuances that make Paris, Paris.

You could argue the point that an issue manifests within a specific time frame as a result of the Soul's need to learn from this particular experience and that you could return to Paris some years later to appreciate what Paris holds. However, that may not be true. Your *unique* relationship with space means that you may continually attract particular psycho-spiritual themes in a particular area of the world, since that is what that location invokes within you as an individual to experience and integrate. You cannot therefore separate your own intrinsic psychic processes from your interpretation of space (or time), and therefore space is as essential a vehicle as time for psycho-spiritual growth.

The specific soul lessons necessary for your growth are held *within* a location are infused into the very fabric of both the people and culture as they literally embody the energetic vibratory potential that that locale holds for you. This embodiment is purely subjective, since the individual themselves may not have a strong resonance with what they embody for you. For example, if you have Mars Rising through the State of Kansas, your perception of the people and culture of Kansas will be filtered through the way that the Martian archetype is expressed within your chart. Irrespectively of whether any resident of Kansas has Mars accentuated in their chart, you will perceive them as being Martian, a fact also independent of the potential synastry you have with that person. In short, the experience of Kansas will provide for you an opportunity to understand/experience/unlock/ heal a particular aspect of the Mars pattern within you.

Since consciousness transcends space and time you do not have to travel to any given location to experience the potential that locale offers you. For example, this book contains contributions from authors who reside in differing parts of the world. I am writing to you from Dublin in the Republic of Ireland. You will have some sort of energetic resonance, constructive or otherwise, with both my style and way of approaching astrology. The traditional approach to understand that resonance is to check the synastry that you have with me (I was born on March 13, 1971, at 18:10 BST, in Derry, Northern Ireland). This will describe the energetic interaction that you will have with me and what I invoke within you (and vice versa). Indeed you might even check what transits you are experiencing as you read this book, which will highlight what is currently growing in your field of awareness. However, my writing is also produced within the space in which I reside. By exploring your astrological relationship with Ireland will inform you about what tends to get triggered when you encounter an Irish Soul!

Everything and everyone we encounter throughout our lives has a purpose, serving to assist us in healing the illusion of our separation consciousness and rediscover our whole being. By expanding our frame of reference to include the world as a canvas onto which our internal process is mapped, the potential for healing and spiritual growth is immense. Literally, your internal process is global!

The Locational Matrix of Your Birth Chart

Location holds at its core the potential to frame your internal process. The people, the culture, the geography and topography extant within each region can tell you much about the resonance of the planetary archetype within you as much as the element, mode, sect, decan, house position or planetary aspect. Therefore, by exploring the people and circumstances that arise from any given location, you can objectively explore the dynamics invoked within you by a certain place.

In addition to telling other astrologers that I have Pluto in my first house in Virgo, in opposition to my Mercury and square to my natal Mars (Figure 1), I can also inform them that I have Pluto in Umbria, Frankfurt-am-Main, in Perth, etc. (Figure 2). In itself, that means nothing other than that my relationship with those locations is filtered through a Plutonian archetypal lens. It says nothing about the way in which I engage or the level to which I operate within those locations.

My personal Pluto archetype rises through central continental Europe, extending on an arc from the polders north of Amsterdam in the Netherlands, through the Ruhr of Western Germany, through Baden Württemberg, into far eastern Switzerland and down along the spine of Italy. That Pluto rises means that these are locations where I literally *embody* the Plutonian archetype.

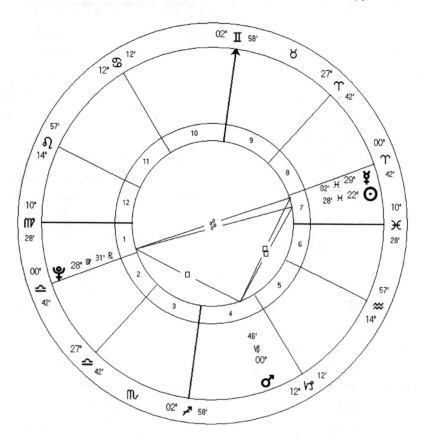

Figure 1 - Andrew's birth chart showing the Pluto patterning

When I was 19, whilst working in Long Island, New York (the longitude at which my seventh house Sun conjoins my Midheaven), I met a German lady. Our three-year long-distance relationship had a profound effect on me, as I experienced a number of events that, in hindsight, invoked my deepening and challenged me to awaken to who I truly am. Each time I visited my then-partner in Frankfurt, a differing layer of the Plutonian archetype was triggered - the suicide of my then-partner's ex; the marital separation of her parents due to infidelity; the death of her cat; connecting in with her friend-set who were Night Owls, extensively clubbing and experimenting (I have always been an early bird); let alone this relationship being my first serious sexual relationship. Not having the aid of astrology to illuminate why I kept 'having' those experiences, I began to fear travelling to see her, nervous anticipating what intense treat I would next experience!

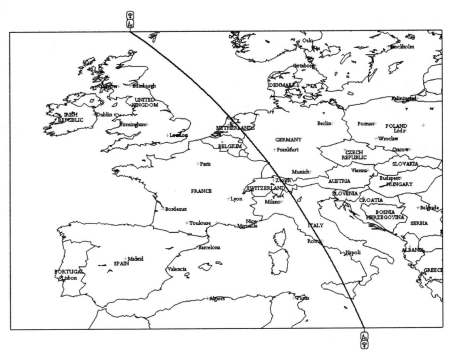

Figure 2 - Pluto rising through Europe for Andrew

Several years later, after discovering astrology, I sought to organize my honeymoon in Italy though the national airline company, Alitalia. I chose three locations and hotels from an extensive catalogue and put a deposit to reserve our package. Being conscious of my prior experiences in Germany and being aware that I was holidaying within my own Plutonian field, I decided to arrange a bank draft rather than writing a personal check for the outstanding balance on the off chance of a problem arising, since the bank was more likely to take care of their own check before a client's check. Two weeks prior to our summer solstice wedding, our tickets had still not arrived. I called to find out what had happened and was told that there was no record of my having paid for the package and therefore we had no honeymoon! After providing the company with the documentation from the bank, it transpired that the lady I had been dealing with had had a psychotic episode and had absconded with several clients' payments. The company was aware of this but had no records of who the clients were. Alitalia had our package on hold, hoping that I would contact them, and so we were able to resolve the issue swiftly.

When we arrived in Rome, we discovered that I had been intuitively drawn to the red light district of Rome. It was a beautiful hotel set in a very interesting environment! On our third day, we took the train to Florence, only to find that I had also managed to find a hotel located next door to a brothel! To add to the colorful surroundings, our retreat hotel in the Tuscany hills happened to be a Mafia family-run establishment; the family's head waiter took a shine to me, and so I had a card sitting on my desk with the name "Giuseppe" and instructions to call him if I ever needed assistance. Needless to say, it is still sitting unused on my desk!

More recently, a friend born with an exact Sun–Pluto opposition asked Karen (my wife) and myself to travel to Umbria, Italy, to help her with the development of a yoga retreat center in a Franciscan monastery that she had purchased. After several un-Plutonian days, I was asked to do a consultation for her gardener. It transpired he was a former KPP terrorist who was trying to start a new life in Europe, escaping the challenges of Kurdistan, where he had been nicknamed Jesus on the basis that he had saved more people than he had killed! His issue was that the Italian government would grant him a passport if he would spy on terrorist cells in Italy, something he did not want to do since he was seeking to transform his life and move away from his past.

The point of sharing with you some personal stories is to demonstrate that with increasing awareness of a planetary complex within you, what you experience becomes increasingly subtle. As you grow to understand what energetic potential a place holds for you, the fewer things happen to you, and the more conscious you become of what is emerging within your growth field. In short, events do not happen onto you, you happen onto events.

Planetary Symbolism within Locational Astrology

Our relationship with the planetary archetypes is rarely due purely to the dilution of the planetary meaning through its dialogue with other planetary archetypes at the birth moment. So I would strongly recommend that you do not apply simplistic cookbook interpretations, such as where Jupiter falls is where you will be happy; where Saturn falls is where you will be sad. Yes, you will experience the archetypal context of the planet invoked in a location, but you have to interpret it within the context of what that planet feels like within you.

As astrologers, we are in the business of interpreting symbols. Symbols are not theoretical abstractions that operate in a consistently objective and mechanical manner but are eternal, numinous, multi-leveled, metonymic and polysomic. They are ultimately transformative signs of alchemical process that exist independently of our egos, on other planes, where aspects of our being coexist elsewhere and are contextualized and filtered through cultural, personal and age-related lenses. For example, the meaning and experience of Uranus is quite different for a 29-year-old lady living in a culture with very strict social rules than it is for her equivalent living an open, liberal community!

Each astrological pattern contains within it multiple meanings, manifest across space and time, all of which are valid but some of which are only accessible once a certain level of awareness has been reached. If you are struggling with this concept of the simultaneous multivalent nature of astrological symbolism, please reflect on the popular cartoon series, the Simpson's, for a moment. The meaning derived from any episode is dependent upon the watcher's level of awareness. A child and adult can view the same show yet take a differing meaning from it. This stems from the fact that there exist differing levels of interpretation of dialogue that the characters make reference to. So a child does not "get" or appreciate some of Homer's satirical comments and really only sees the humor in his supposed stupidity, whilst simultaneously adults can appreciate the folly of human prejudices that are often depicted in the comfort that their children will not "see" what they "see." Both interpretations are apt; but although a child cannot really appreciate what the adult sees in Homer, the adult, having grown through childhood, can reflect on the innocence of the son's or daughter's laughter.

135

The practice of astrology is rarely separate from the prevailing consciousness in which the astrology operates. The dominant worldview in which we currently live not only seeks certainty and verifiable, reliable proof but is one that ultimately supports the notion that events happen onto people and not the other way around. This has slipped into astrological thinking, and it is common to read astrological literature that suggests that we are defined completely by our charts, forgetting that consciousness is really the key component within astrology.

Consequently, the way of thinking and the subsequent language used by astrologers reflects this mechanical reductionism—celestial determinism, prompting a sort of questioning that implies an abdication of self-responsibility, choice and self-determination, such as: is this relationship a good one? Will I be successful in this job? When will I be lucky? In terms of astro-locality: Will I enjoy this location? Will it be good for me?

Would it not be more constructive to ask clients to reflect on what they *need* to experience when traveling? Granted, given the constraints of the economic system we live within that yields the average employed person two weeks' vacation time a year, they will say, "Somewhere to relax, unwind and enjoy." However, our ongoing psycho-spiritual processes do not stop just because we take a holiday. We bring ourselves and our processes with us. Location has agency bringing into focus specific dimensions of our internalized processes in a more concentrated and overt manner. So you could reframe your question to your client, asking him whether he wants to travel to a place that will yield a deeper insight into a specific area of his life!

Another Plutonian Story

During a session, a client mentioned that she was about to take a dream vacation in Cuba. I noticed that this was an area where her Pluto squared her Ascendant. I felt I had two possible approaches to discuss this pattern with her: deterministic or awareness-orientated. I could inform her that this area should be avoided because hugely intense challenges could be invoked, culminating in the "death" of her relationship. Alternatively, I could discuss that inherent within this location is the ability to better understand the underlying psycho-spiritual components within her relationship.

The central crux to location from a transpersonal perspective is to refrain from making black or white judgment as to whether the latent potentiality of a location is either good or bad. Can we really say what is in a soul's best interest to experience in terms of ongoing psycho-spiritual development and evolution? All we can do is present the potential manifestation of the pattern and engage in a meaningful conversation so as to illuminate the growth opportunities.

I asked my client whether there was anything secretive between herself and her partner. She was not experiencing any transit or progression to her Ascendant or seventh-house ruler at the time, so she was surprised and a little disturbed by my comment, as she did not believe that there was anything hidden between them. Subsequently, we had an intimate conversation about the potential meaning of this aspect, exploring the various possible manifestations across a multitude of levels of interpretation.

Several weeks later, I got a call requesting an emergency appointment. She returned from vacation the day after she arrived at her destination, having discovered that her partner had been seeing his ex-wife for the past two years without her knowing! Actually the situation was less dramatic than it sounds. My client's partner had had a child from this previous relationship, which had ended under stressful circumstances. My client had found it strange that her partner had no contact with his son, given his gentle and loving personality, but had accepted his past and the situation. Her partner had been told by his ex that their son was to have no contact with his current lover and, if she discovered that he had acted against this request, he would never get to see his son again. For whatever reason, rather than confiding in his current partner about the difficulties he was facing, he chose not to disclose the request to my client and had spent time in his ex's home, trying to maintain this relationship with his son. The deception had been eating away at him for several months, and he confessed to my client on the first night in Cuba.

So which was the right approach? Tell the client not to travel because of the potential challenge? Or to travel with the awareness that hidden dimensions within the relationship may rise to the surface?

Over time, my client's relationship has become much stronger as a result of the experience. She was deeply disturbed by the lack of trust shown by her partner. She felt sad that her partner did not appear to trust her enough to share with her the deep strain he was experiencing between his unresolved past and his present. Also distressing was the fact that he made a judgment call concerning her potential reactions to his disclosure as opposed to openly discussing the situation with her, sharing with her the huge dilemma that he faced: the love for his child and need to maintain a relationship with him versus the love for his partner. They were, eventually, able to look past the incidentalness of the event and circumstances, to explore the deeper meaning in their process together and the reasons why this had arisen, in terms of healing patterns that both held around relationships, so they could grow together as a couple.

Transpersonally speaking, there is no such thing as 'good' or 'bad' in any event or experience. It is what it is. Everything that takes place in your life has a purpose. It occurs to teach you something, to heal something within you, to help you grow, to help you lift the illusory veil of the ego-mind and to move beyond the influence of the myriad conditional layers that life affords us: gender-related, cultural, age-related, karmic, familiar, experiential, parental, social, etc. It is not the job of an astrologer to help someone *control* their life by offer a judgment as to what is good or bad for another person. Can an astrologer really know what is truly appropriate for your growth? What would have happened if I had suggested to my client that Cuba was a "bad" place, given the so-called nature of a square from Pluto, and she had decided to holiday elsewhere? Would she have manifested that experience at that time in her life? I have no idea. However, as a result of spending time in Cuba, she had an intense experience that has subsequently helped her grow as an individual and her relationship to deepen as a couple.

As Within, So Without – your global psycho-spiritual process

It is our job to guide our clients to another way of looking at their choices. It is not that Egoic questions concerning wealth, health and happiness are redundant, but they do not serve growth in the same way that asking more conscious questions can, such as "Will this choice add to heighten my sense of self?" or in terms of location "Will this trip engage me in a clearer understanding of the roots of my fear?"

138

Since your psycho-spiritual process is inexorably bound to a sense of place the following are some ideas for reflection when considering how the *undiluted* planetary archetypes will resonate with you in terms of location:

The Sun - where my Light-Being is more acutely accentuated; where the true essence of my Light shines; where my individuation process is heightened.

What do the countries or regions through which my Sun lines traverse tell me about my sense of who I really am? Note what aspects of those cultures really do not 'work' for you in addition to what resonates, as it will show you what your light-being is truly like.

The Moon - where my Spirit listens to my Inner Being; where my Spirit seeks out a nourishing component within the cultural environment; where my inner process and dream-world is amplified; where my family complexes are emoted.

What cultural dimension of those geographic regions resonates, or feels disharmonious, with my soul? What do those reactions tell me about my comfort levels? Moreover, how does that culture seek to protect and nourish its people and how do I resonate with those emotional impulses.

Mercury - where my Spirit outwardly connects to receive messages; where I can learn about my way of thinking; where I bring information into my Mind.

How can my cognitive abilities be accentuated by literature and knowledge that stems from this region of the world?

Venus - where I can learn how I express myself with openness and love; where I learn about the value of love; where my individual Spirit resonates with beauty.

What cultural/topographical conditions and values do I find aesthetically appealing? What does this environment tell me about my value system?

Mars - where the Emotional Will of the Divine expresses itself through me; where I learn to manifest and to deal with my sense of being separate.

What do my experiences of the prevailing cultural attitudes teach me about my attitude towards assertion and competition/maintaining my independence/defining my boundaries/making things happen? How can I better direct my energy by drawing upon the passion of these cultures?

Jupiter - where I seek meaning; where I can receive healing on personal issues by expanding my consciousness through the belief system of those cultures.

How do the indigenous beliefs of this region reflect, or resonate with, my own belief system? What can I learn from the people and culture about my faith, healing or sense of adventure?

Saturn - where I can learn about the limitations of my ego; where I can ground myself; where I am 'encouraged' to be the parent/to stand on my own two feet/to become self-reliant and to develop wisdom

What cultural facets within these regions invoke a strong emotional reaction that informs me about the attachments within my ego? How would I be if I was truly left alone without support in this region?

Uranus - where I can step away from the norm and be free to express myself without limitation or emotional consideration; where I connect with my Divine Mind and develop my intuition; where I connect with insights and impulses to encourage my development to be truly free.

In what ways does this culture seek freedom and independence that reflects on my own desire to create space to be free?

Neptune - where my personal veil between various conscious realms is thinnest; where my sense of unity consciousness is most accentuated; where I can experience Divine Love; where I can feel confused, hazy and disconnected; where I seek to escape from the mundane.

In what ways does this culture seek to express the numinous and celebrate the Divine in a way that can support me?

Pluto - where I can experience the transmutation of my Being; where my deepest internal process is worked out so I can release and shed egoic attachments; where I can learn about power without ego, or experience the dark within my own soul through the misuse of power.

In what ways does that culture seek to empower or disempower its population in a manner that provokes a strong emotional reaction within me?

Some locational techniques

In short, location is individually meaningful. You do not have to travel to a location to invoke an experience and to activate your emerging potentiality.

The world is your oyster and can literally come to you! You are surrounded by people and ideas within the books on your shelves. Each author became a conduit for their inspiration somewhere on the Earth, and whilst those locations maybe meaningful for their own soul growth, their work has touched you and shaped your awareness in some meaningful way. If you look at the planetary pattern that is accentuated within the location where the author wrote his/her book you will gain insight into what is being invoked within you by their words and creativity. If an author is writing from an area of the world where your Sun is angular, then his/her words will trigger the Solar complex in your life; if your Saturn is emphasized then the house, house ruler, the aspect patterns made to your natal Saturn will be highlighted, irrespectively of the content of the book.

When working with a client I use very detailed maps, including all the minor aspects, parans, and local space, to explore what a location holds for them, generating modified astrocartographic maps to highlight the specific theme pertinent to the client needs. For example, if the issue of vocation is under discussion, I produce a geographic map plotting where the rulers of the second, sixth and tenth houses rise, set, culminate and anti-culminate in the region of the world in question so we can explore where people, circumstances, books and wisdom fall to assist the potential of the client's vocational life (Figure 3). Aside from house rulers there may be other significators specific to the client's chart that I will include. For romance, I look at the rulers of the fifth and seventh houses; for spiritual direction, the fourth, eighth and twelfth house rulers; for property, the fourth house ruler, along with the Moon and the Nodes; for writing, the third and ninth house rulers in addition to Mercury.

Additionally I use the eighth harmonic aspects to examine where the potential being discussed will *manifest*, and twelfth harmonic aspects, as well as the quintile series to look at where there is potential flow and release of tension and strains. The latter can be used to highlight locations of opportunity wherein the struggle to manifest is less resistant.

I also focus on the least aspected planet within a chart since it operates as a vital link between the more consciously developed energies, highlighted by the more active planetary archetypes (the most aspected planets) and the more unconscious or mysterious archetypes of the Self as indicated by the under-aspected planets. This un-integrated planet appears to form a bridge between

141

the normal mode of functioning and the vital springs of the dormant, potential personality, which lie untapped and yet remain fecund, possessing enormous psychic potential. Robert Couteau's inspiring work on *The Role of the Least-Aspected Planet in Astrocartography*[2] was seminal in this line of investigation. He has discovered that many people produced the life's work, or at very least are remembered for what they did, in the region of the world that accentuated their least aspected planet.

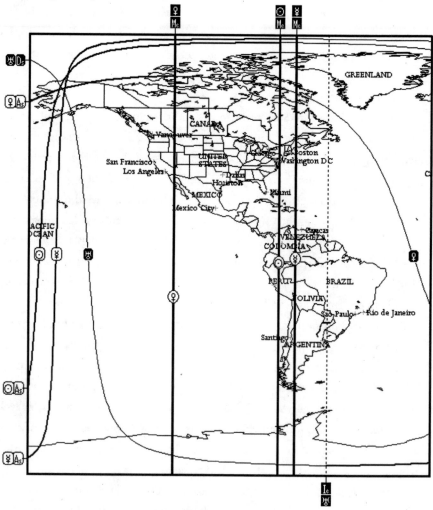

Figure 3 - ACG Maps for Andrew Highlighting the Vocational Planets

I also explore where the potentiality of the client's *emergence process*, as symbolized by the transits and progressions, takes place. For example, if a client is going through an eighth harmonic transit from Saturn to Venus, it amazes me how frequently that client would intuitively feel drawn to spend time in the area of the world where their Venus falls. What we discuss is the relevancy of either spending time directly in that locale or, at very least, invoking the energy of that location using a variety of apotropaic rituals so that the energy of that location literally comes to the client. I ask him/her to become aware of people and circumstances in the coming weeks that "arise" in his/her life—people or circumstances associated with those locations—as a concrete manifestation of that internal developmental process, since those people/circumstances are literally carrying the energy potential of this transiting signature.

There are additional techniques that you can also use to add to an understanding of your growth process. For example, local space astrology is a technique akin to Feng Shui, using the azimuth and altitude of the planets to create a chart showing you the directions that the planetary archetypes are projected out from you. This chart can be used to map onto specific locations. For example, from a local space perspective, my Venus line goes through the very street in Dublin where my wife resided at the time that we met in 1994. Does that mean that where Venus falls for anyone is where that person will find love? No. My Venus resides in the fifth house, in trine to my Moon in Libra, so my relationship with Venus is very relationship-orientated. However, let's say it was my Mars through this same location. That does not mean I will not be romantically drawn into the relationship. What it does mean, however, is that the archetypal potential of my fourth house Capricorn Mars, ruling my eighth house, would be invoked as a central function of this relationship, and the relationship itself would become a vehicle to play out ways that I would need to learn to assert myself more clearly, etc.

Summary

To draw this chapter to a conclusion there is no outside and inside at a higher level of awareness. Nothing is separate and everything is part of the One. Therefore, our souls exist across space and time, and we operate in differing realities simultaneously. Whilst I have not discussed the implications that history, deep memories, timing, astral projection and the like have on astro-locality, what we are seeing with locality is a more complete process of our return back to the light and the truth of our complete interconnection with people and circumstances from all over the globe, throughout time and space. We are afforded a much deeper view of the workings of our consciousness at play. By changing our questioning and languaging, we empower people to really understand the resonance that space holds for them in their individuation processes, rather than allowing them to be limited by the impositions of what we believe is happening in any given location. It is my belief that, as astrologers, we are supposed to be empowering people to live more consciously, to shed the layering of their own ego development, and to help them take the steps back towards their internal home, the sense of who they really are.

Endnotes

1. Plato wrote about a vast Field in which humanity is embedded, called the World Soul or *Anima Mundi*, wherein your individual soul is ultimately interconnected to all other souls that in turn are part of an immense One Soul.
2. http://www.dominantstar.com/astro02.htm

10

The Vertex: Fate, Serendipity and Attraction

Julene Packer-Louis

Have you ever thought of someone and that person phoned, emailed, or happened to be at a function or a store at the same time as you? Have you ever been mulling over something and an answer came through a song on the radio? Have you ever put an item on your wish list and, without telling anyone, just happened to get that as a gift? Have you ever had a chance encounter via being in the right place at the right time that provided something significant in your life? Have you ever wondered why freak accidents happen—you just happened to be in the wrong place at the wrong time? Chances are some of those things have happened to you. This is the Vertex in action.

These chance encounters can be seen through the Vertex. The Vertex is the intersection of two great circles; it has no physicality what-so-ever. Yet transiting, progressed and solar arc directed planets trigger our natal, solar arc and progressed Vertex in various ways. Also the progressed, solar arc and transiting Vertex triggers our natal, solar arc and progressed planets. It is this interaction between our natal, progressed and solar arc planets and Vertex that times the chance events or encounters in our lives that are riddled with synchronicity and seemed fated or destined to come to pass.

The Vertex is associated with fate or karmic destiny and is the least conscious point in our chart. Of course, our entire birth chart can be viewed as karma, destiny, a natal promise or propensity toward certain experiences, and we are relatively conscious of working with these energies as we strive toward becoming who we want to be. We feel the pull toward the things we are trying to achieve or attain and the push away from that which we no longer want. We are conscious of our life dreams and goals and choose to do something to take part in manifesting them. We see all this reflected by the Nodes, the planets, and the four angles of our charts. The Vertex operates differently. The serendipitous chance encounters of the things that just happen to us out of the blue, things we did not make conscious choices about, are the Vertex.

The Vertex is often referred to as the third angle. It is formed by two great circles whose intersection provides local space coordinates for a specific geographical location at a specific date and time. The Ascendant and Midheaven are the two more commonly used angles that provide local space coordinates for a specific date, time and location. All three of these angles are part of an axis whose counter-point is the opposing intersection of the great circles at the exact opposite degree of the zodiac. Therefore, all three require an accurate birth time. The intersection of the Ecliptic and Horizon in the east form the Ascendant, and the Descendant is formed by their western intersection. The Medium Coeli, or Midheaven, is formed by the southern intersection of the Ecliptic and the Meridian, and the Imum Coeli is formed by their northern intersection. The Vertex is formed by the western intersection of the Prime Vertical and the Ecliptic. The Anti-Vertex is formed by the eastern intersection of the same.

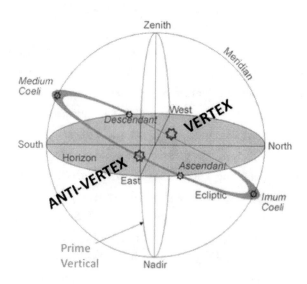

Figure 1 - The Vertex

The fact that the Vertex is found in the western half of the chart is important to its meaning because the western hemisphere deals with *others*. Therefore the Vertex represents the people, places, events and situations that come to us seemingly via external forces, rather than what we self-initiate in the

146

eastern hemisphere, which is likely to be a more self-oriented directive. The word vertex comes from the Latin root *vertere*, which means to change, turn or spin. These Vertex events often seem to indicate change, where we encounter a turn of fate or happenstance that spins us in a different direction. Therefore, the Vertex is often referred to as the least conscious personal sensitive point.

Lorne Edward Johndro (1882-1951), an engineer and sidereal astrologer, is often credited as being the first to research this axis. Johndro considered the Ascendant Axis to be magnetic and the Vertex Axis to be electric. In fact, he called the Anti-Vertex the Electric Ascendant. Some sources state that Charles Jayne (1911-1985), a Uranian astrologer, independently began researching this point at the same time. Much of Jayne's work revolves around the GEM theory (gravity, electrical, magnetism) whereby the Midheaven correlates to gravity, the Vertex to electricity, and the Ascendant to magnetism. Regardless of whether Johndro was first or if this concept was a simultaneous arising for both men independent of each other, they did collaborate about the Vertex via the exchange of letters. They tested the Vertex with solar arcs and agreed that the Vertex was the most fated and least conscious or involuntary angle, whereas the Ascendant was the least fated and most conscious or voluntary angle.

When the Vertex is the angle activated by transits, progressions or solar arcs in our major life events, it indicates the manifesting or altering of destiny beyond our conscious effort—a turning point in life or milestone at a fork in the road of life's journey that we did not anticipate, or that which happened through a series of synchronicities whereas activation of the Ascendant and Midheaven by transits, progressions or solar arcs indicates the consciously chosen events that we strive towards with dedication and determination to achieve or succeed as planned.

Since 2002, I have been teaching timing of events to western astrology students at the International Academy of Astrology. Through the numerous events studied by myself and my students, the Vertex has proven to me to be just as personally sensitive as the Ascendant and Midheaven in the timing of monumental events in life. However, the Vertex has a very different quality. The Vertex seems to have a more fated or karmic quality to it than the Ascendant and Midheaven. My experience with the Vertex has also proven it to be the least conscious, and often unconscious, personal sensitive point where

147

karma, destiny and fate become manifest as if by happenstance, serendipity, or synchronicity of being in the right place at the right time, or sometimes even at the wrong time.

Fate, Destiny, Karma and the Law of Attraction

Fate and destiny are loaded words that mean different things to different people. Webster defines fate several ways, including inevitable, often adverse and final outcomes. I prefer the first definition Webster gives for fate: "the will or principal or determining cause by which things in general are believed to come to be as they are or events to happen as they do: DESTINY."[1] My favorite Webster definition of destiny is "a predetermined course of events often held to be an irresistible power or agency."[2]

I believe we choose our fate by our actions and thoughts, both conscious and unconscious. Our actions create karma. Karma is the universal law of cause and effect that guarantees we reap what we sow at some point or another. Our thoughts and actions predetermine the results of our actions. When our karmas unfold and manifest as people or events, it is the reaping of what our actions have sewn. According to Eastern philosophy, karma is not the absence of free will. It is not things preordained by the universe over which we have no control. It is what we preordain through the free will of our own actions. Some karmas are fixed, such as how tall we will be, our eye and hair color, our biological parents, and our propensity towards encountering certain lessons in this life. How we choose to deal with our inevitable lessons through our thoughts and actions is our free will, and that has a big role in our karma as well. "But in the present moment, the attitude adopted by the individual towards all that he faces is not predeterminded."[3] Many great Yogis say, in some form or another, that it is not destiny that makes us who we are, but what we make of what happens that determines our destiny.

The law of attraction is closely related to what we think about, we bring about. *The Dharmapada* states, "Mind is the forerunner of all actions. All deeds are led by the mind, created by mind."[4] Whether these are things we are consciously trying to attract or things we are unconsciously attracting without intending to, and whether we give these things a good or bad value judgment, our thoughts play a role in the law of attraction as well. So we are constantly attracting the fruits of our intentions and actions both through universal laws and via our thoughts and actions.

For instance, we sometimes think about someone and that person calls or emails or we encounter them somewhere. That's an example of the law of attraction that comes about by thought alone. However, it is much harder to attract a job, for example, by just sitting around and thinking about it. That occasionally happens, but the odds are very low because we are only using one universal law. If someone thinks about a job and actually gets off their duff and takes action to land a job, their odds increase exponentially. We can see this difference in the astrology of the angles. If you are thinking that you really need a job or would like a different career, and then in a chance encounter you are offered a job or even told about one that would be perfect for you, that is the Vertex. Then when you put yourself out there and take action to apply for the job, it becomes the conscious use of the Ascendant, Midheaven and associated planets. The difference between these three angular axes is that we are more conscious of the actions we take with the Ascendant Axis and Midheaven Axis, whereas we are least conscious of the actions we take to land in chance encounters with the Vertex.

While we can attract things through all planets and points in our natal chart, the Vertex indicates the things that we are least conscious of attracting to ourselves. You can look back at both positive and negative events in your life that you did not consciously bring upon yourself or strive toward and see that the Vertex was activated by transit, progression or solar arc. These can be big things, such as an accident or meeting a person who was very significant in your life. They can even be small things, such as - seeing an outfit in a store window and then receiving it as a gift. It is synchronicities of all shapes and sizes that can be seen through the Vertex.

Earth's Electromagnetic Field and Schuman Resonance

However, the problem with unconsciously attracting these things is that they seem to be beyond our control—they just happen to us. It gets chalked up to fate, karma, or synchronicity because we all know there is no such thing as coincidence. My question for anything that is unconscious is, how do I go about making it conscious? If the Vertex is a point where fate, destiny and serendipity manifest without our conscious effort, can we use it consciously to activate the law of attraction, and if so, how? To answer these questions, we have to understand a bit about electromagnetic fields and the Schuman Resonance.

The earth has an electromagnetic field. Our bodies have electromagnetic fields. Stars, including our Sun, have electromagnetic fields. So do planets. We say "seeing is believing." Yet visible light is only a tiny portion near the middle of this spectrum of wave lengths and frequencies—a spectrum that tells of a vast array of electromagnetic interactions in the universe. There is also electrostatic energy in the building blocks of matter. The electrostatic force between an electron and a proton in an atom is stronger than the gravitational force between them. Therefore, we might postulate that the electrostatic force of the universe is stronger than the gravitational force. Our personal interactions with these electromagnetic and electrostatic forces of the universe can be explained through the Vertex and Anti-Vertex. They can help us tap into the Law of Attraction when we learn to decipher our Vertex story and use that axis consciously. How so? Because of the Schuman Resonance.

The Schumann Resonance is the global electromagnetic resonance between Earth's surface and ionosphere that is excited by lightening. (Between the surface and ionosphere are the layers of our atmosphere: troposphere, stratosphere, and mesosphere.) The frequency Earth emits as the Schuman Resonance is 7.83 hertz (Hz). Earth does have a hum. Perhaps this hum is the "om" heard by the ancient Rishis: the sound vibration of all creation where in the beginning there was a word. This frequency, 7.83 Hz, is an ELF (extremely low frequency). It is lower than radio waves and not depicted on the usual diagrams of the electromagnetic spectrum. However, it is within the range of frequency that our brain waves operate.

Our brain waves dip to their lowest frequency during our deep restorative sleep. This is the delta wavelength, between 0.5 - 3 Hz. We dream at theta, which has a frequency of 4 - 7 Hz. Subliminal messages are picked up on the theta frequency. Also, deep meditation occurs in theta. Alpha is our daydreaming and meditating state and has a frequency of 8 - 13 Hz. Beta is our awakened state of 14 Hz. The Schuman Resonance of 7.83 Hz corresponds to the alpha-theta border of our brain waves. The alpha-theta border can be reached in meditation and deep daydreaming, in which you become unaware of your surroundings, yet are not quite asleep.

As children, when we were more open and absorbed information like sponges - our brains operated from a dominantly theta state. Many sources say that around age six, the beta frequency starts to dominate in our brains, as we get filled with unconscious paradigms and automatic ways of behaving and reacting as a result of our conditioning. However, I think it might more likely to be around age seven when we have our first Saturn square.

If we can learn to access the alpha-theta border, we can consciously work the Law of Attraction. When our brains are operating at 7.83 Hz, our thoughts and visualizations can ride out into the universe with the Schuman Resonance, where they then get reorganized in what Deepak Chopra calls the quantum soup and come back as manifest events. This is why I think the Law of Attraction does not always work. We have to be in the right state of mind, literally operating at the right frequency. What we put out with the right frequency at the Anti-Vertex, Johndro's Electric Ascendant, rides out with the Schuman Resonance and comes back at the Vertex as manifested events. The problem is, we are usually not conscious at that frequency. However, we can become conscious of that frequency and use our Vertex axis to help us with the Law of Attraction, and combining this consciousness with consciously directed action helps as well.

Your Vertex Story

The Vertex axis helps us to see what is manifesting unconsciously in our lives. The sign polarity of the Vertex and Anti-Vertex shows us the preconditioned types of thinking and automatic ways of behaving that are behind our unconscious attractions. The house polarity shows the areas of life where we most readily experience this and the people and things we have an attraction or affinity toward.

The house of the Vertex shows the area of life where things tend to converge or manifest as if by chance encounter or synchronicity. The sign of the Vertex shows the manner in which it does so. The planet that disposits the Vertex (the planet that rules the sign the Vertex is in) tells about the people and events that manifest through our Vertex. The house and sign of the dispositor of the Vertex give the more complete story as to what is driving the Vertex into action (the planet), as well as how it is doing so (the sign) and where (house in which the Vertex resides and the houses it rules). This information gives you two or three additional areas of life to work the law of attraction via the energy of that dispositing planet.

The house of the Anti-Vertex shows the area of life where our unconscious thoughts co-create what manifests at the Vertex, and also indicates what we have a natural attraction to or affinity toward. The sign of the Anti-Vertex shows the manner in which we put out unconscious signals. The house and sign of the dispositor of the Anti-Vertex gives the more complete story as to what is driving the unconscious thoughts (planet), as well as where (house in which it resides and the houses it rules) and how (sign of the dispositor).

Aspects to the Vertex add even more information about the things you unconsciously attract. Planets aspecting the Vertex add people and things related to that planet. The sign describes those people or things. That planet also adds two or three more areas of life: the house the aspecting planet is in and the house or houses the aspecting planet rules. By the time you are done, you have quite the Vertex story to unravel to understand why and how you attract the things that you do.

One of my Vertex stories involves an accident I was in when I was nine years old. Surely I did not consciously set out to be hit by a car while crossing the road and to break the femur bone in my thigh. I have a Mars–Uranus conjunction that tells of my natal propensity for accidents. Jupiter, the ruler of the thigh and dispositor of my Vertex, is also conjunct Mars and Uranus. Mercury, the dispositor of my Anti Vertex, rules cars and disposits my Mars. So we see that part of my Vertex story is going to involve an accident that seems to just happen to be by chance - being in the wrong place at precisely the wrong time. Of course, transiting Mars was activating my chart that day. It was in a partile (same degree) square to my natal Sun. Although Mars makes either a waxing or waning square to a planet every year, this time it was significant because transiting Uranus was trine my natal Ascendant, bringing my body into play. The fated or synchronistic encounter part of the tale, however, can be told through the Vertex.

My sister and I were called home for dinner from across the street. There were cars parked along the roadside, and we couldn't see to cross. Without consciously thinking about the ramifications, I walked out between parked cars into the road to see if it was safe for my sister to cross. The Moon is quite evident here, as I was putting out thoughts of protection. My natal Moon is semi-sextile my natal Anti-Vertex and quincunx my Vertex with a one-degree orb. What happens next is a result of taking that step at the precisely the wrong time, as shown by the transiting Vertex of that moment. Two cars were coming, one from each direction. It mattered not if I ran across or ran back—either way, I was getting hit. The transiting Vertex, which has an average speed of roughly one degree every four minutes—as do the transiting Ascendant and Midheaven—was in partile conjunction to my Moon and in partile square to my Mars, which sits between Jupiter and Uranus. So while the accident is of course seen through the planets, the timing of the precise moment in which the accident occurred is told through the transiting Vertex. The transiting planets set up the event for that day and the transiting Vertex provided the moment of that day.

There is something important to note regarding aspects to the Vertex Axis. Remember this is the least conscious, most fated axis in your horoscope. So keep your orbs tight, around two degrees, allowing three for a conjunction. Don't try to pull in every aspect or celestial body imaginable. Keep it simple. Nature operates on simplicity, and the Vertex is associated with the divine synchronicity and the organizing principal of the universe beyond our normal level of consciousness.

A conjunction to the Vertex is an opposition to the Anti-Vertex and vice versa. In your natal chart, planets conjunct the Vertex indicate that you attract things related to that planet. Planets conjunct the Anti-Vertex indicate you have unconscious output relevant to that planet.

Planets squaring the Vertex Axis indicate the challenges you attract. This tells where you need to take action to stop attracting negative things unconsciously, or, to start attracting things consciously. The eighth harmonic semi-squares and sesquiquadrates work the same way as the squares. Don't underestimate those eighth harmonic planetary aspects to the Vertex. They are just as powerful and prevalent in manifesting events as conjunctions, oppositions and squares.

Planets in trine to the Vertex Axis represent what is flowing easily into and from your unconscious. This, therefore, indicates your conditioning and

153

programming. In fact, a trine to the Anti-Vertex can be troublesome because it indicates an unconscious thought pattern that flows effortlessly without obstruction. So pay attention to the theme of that planet in trine - its sign, house, and house(s) it rules—to see what programs are on auto pilot regarding what you attract. Planets sextile the Vertex are the opportunities of which you are least conscious. They are not usually too much use until you learn how to work with the Vertex consciously. A trine to the Vertex is a sextile to the Anti-Vertex and vice versa. By looking at your natal trines and sextiles to the Vertex Axis, you can ascertain what opportunities are brought your way via your automatic response system of unconscious, free flowing, pre-conditioned, thought processes.

Quincunxes to the Anti-Vertex indicate you have to make an adjustment in your level of consciousness to work with that planet. Quincunxes to the Vertex indicate the things you attract where you feel darned if you do, darned if you don't—as with my accident—I was darned whether I ran forward or back. These are life's conundrums that you attract. Of course, a quincunx to the Vertex is a semi-sextile to the Anti-Vertex and vice versa, but the affect is much more obvious when focused on from the quincunx.

Once you have determined 1) the sign polarity of your Vertex axis, 2) the house polarity of your Vertex axis, 3) the dispositor of the Vertex, its sign, its house and houses it rules, 4) the dispositor of the Anti-Vertex, its sign, its house and houses it rules, and 5) aspects to the Vertex axis including the signs, houses, and houses ruled by the aspecting planets, you'll discover that unconsciousness affects several areas of life. Use that information to determine what you put out unconsciously through the Anti-Vertex. Recognize how it came back to you as manifested people, places and events through the Vertex.

It is actually easiest to work this backwards. Rather than thinking, *"What does this mean? What am I putting out or attracting unconsciously?"*, think of things you have attracted in the past and of chance encounters with someone or something that led to a significant event or relationship. Then see how that is reflected in the astrological notes you just took on your Vertex. Watching this unfold in your own life is a really good way to see the Vertex in action. Seeing through hindsight how you attracted things unconsciously in the past can help you understand how to use that energy consciously to attract what you want in the present, as well as predicting when it will manifest in the future.

154

The Vertex Axis holds the key to utilizing the law of attraction consciously because it is the electric axis with correlations to the Schuman Resonance. Once we see our Vertex themes through the lens of astrology, we take strides to make the unconscious conscious. We can tap into the Law of Attraction consciously by first seeing through astrological analysis of past events and people we've attracted. We can see through hindsight how negative thinking and acting brought on negative events, while positive thinking and acting brought on positive events, through the Vertex portion of the astrology of those events. In my story, the accident was evident in several astrological factors, but the Vertex showed the role of my unconscious action without thinking. When we understand our personal Vertex stories in hindsight, we can apply that knowledge with conscious foresight to find auspicious times to set the intentions and actions in motion to manifest our desires. Those auspicious times will be told through transits to your natal, progressed and directed Vertex and also through your progressed and directed Vertex making aspects to your natal and progressed planets.

The Vertex and Relationships

Understanding the Vertex also works with attracting people into our lives. Sure, the Nodes, the Descendant and other astrological factors show others' comings and goings as well. But again, Vertex axis encounters are the people that come into our lives by chance or serendipity when we weren't looking for them to appear. Take a look at the Vertex contacts between your chart and the charts of others in your life. All sorts of people come and go in our lives. Sometimes it is difficult when they go if you didn't consciously choose the separation. Often when relationships have ended, their karma is finished. Sometimes we leave prematurely because we don't want to face the karma, and so we attract that same relationship dynamic again and again until we eventually do face it. Other times we stay too long because we fear change and attract all sorts of things that back up our fear of change, keeping us locked where we can no longer grow and evolve. Understanding the role that person had in helping you with your karma, and vice versa, can help make sense of the reason others come and go throughout our life time. This can be any person including but not limited to a boss, business partner, neighbor, teacher, friend, family member or romantic partner.

Of course, the astrological synastry between you and another person will tell the whole story, but the Vertex connections with others can help you understand the less conscious relationship dynamics you are working on together. Knowing about your progressed and directed Vertex dynamics can shed light on the issues arising together in the present, as can looking at your composite Vertex. Then it's up to you to check in with yourself. Are playing out the less conscious patterns behind your mutual attraction in a negative unhealthy way? Or are you working together to raise your consciousness in that area, to grow and evolve together in manifesting those dynamics in a more positive, healthy way?

None of us exists in a vacuum. We exist in relation to others. We create our relationship dynamics through our thought patterns. Whatever we think someone is doing to us, we will perceive it in his or her actions whether that was the intent or not. Working with the Vertex in relationship astrology helps to see what is real and what is illusion, identifying how past conditioning runs the less conscious and often automatic thought process. It can be a monumentally enlightening step toward consciously creating healthier relationships with others and your Self, the Atman—your divinity behind your ego.

Another personal example (as I am not at liberty to share other people's stories) is a story regarding relationships. I met my husband at my old job while my astrology career was in the early stages—a job on the side. I have Venus in the sixth house, and it is conjunct his Sun. We were friends for about two years before becoming romantically involved. We worked in a factory, and occasionally there would be too many people for the jobs, and some of us would get sent home on a fairly rotated basis. Usually it was just one person. But on this day, it was both my friend (who later became my husband) and I was sent home simultaneously—less than ten minutes into the shift. We decided to go to breakfast and wound up spending the whole day together. This was the beginning of our relationship evolving into something more. That year, transiting Pluto made three conjunctions to our Venus–Sun synastric conjunction, so it could have happened any time during that year. Of course, as soon as I got home, I had to pull up the astrology because I was dying to answer the burning question, *why now? Why today?*

Transiting Saturn had moved into the degree of his natal Vertex that also happened be the degree of my progressed Vertex but in different signs. Transiting Venus was sextile our Sun-Venus conjunction, partile my Venus in a two degree orb to his Sun, providing a three day window of opportunity to reinforce the Venusian relationship theme, while transiting Saturn was activating our Vertexes in the midst of transiting Pluto triggering our Sun-Venus synastric conjunction. But it gets even better—the transiting Vertex opposed our Sun-Venus conjunction, and I was sent home as the Vertex was opposing my Venus!

Vertex Example of Fate and Synchronistic Timing of Coming into Destiny

Since the Dalai Lama was most likely fated to become the Dalai Lama, we should see this written in his Vertex story. We should also seeing the Vertex activated when he was officially installed as the spiritual leader of Tibet as a small child. We could see many other fated events of his life as well, if space permitted.

The Dalai Lama has his Vertex in Scorpio in the fifth house and Anti-Vertex in Taurus in the eleventh house. The Anti-Vertex is disposited by Venus in Leo. He unconsciously or automatically, without thought, puts out genuine love and wishes for comfort and well-being for his country and for humanity as a whole. Pluto is the modern dispositor of his Vertex. Pluto is trine his Vertex and sextile his Anti-Vertex. This is an unconscious opportunity to assume power and, with Pluto conjunct the South Node, we can see that it is part of his life path. As a leader, he encountered power issues with the Chinese government. The traditional dispositor of his Vertex is Mars in the fourth house, in quincunx the Midheaven. Remember, quincunxes to the Vertex are conundrums. Part of his Vertex story is facing a conundrum involving his leadership or position of status that involves his home or country. His Vertex is quincunx to Mercury in the twelfth house. Mercury is the ruler of his fourth and twelfth houses. He had to face the conundrum of leading his country into exile.

157

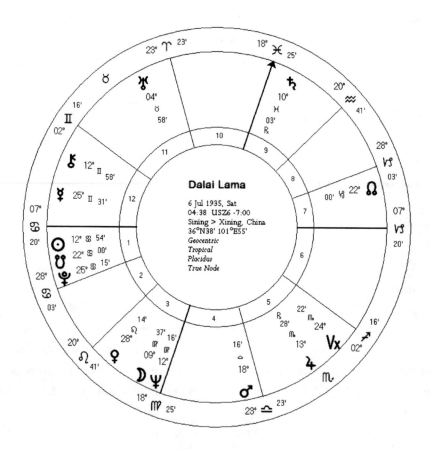

Figure 2 - Dalai Lama

While we could find many other astrological factors that indicate he is a spiritual leader, it is through the Vertex that we can see the less conscious aspects of his story and the things that just happened to him. He probably did not set out in life thinking, "I'm going to be the next Dalai Lama." They found him as a small boy in a rural village, and he correctly identified objects belonging to the prior Dalai Lama, without prior conscious knowledge of these items. This brings us back around to the Anti-Vertex dispositor being Venus in Leo.

Let's now examine the date he was officially installed as the spiritual leader of Tibet. Below is a tri-wheel. The inner wheel is the Dalai Lama's birth chart. The middle wheel is his secondary progressions for the date of the ceremony that officially installed him as spiritual leader of Tibet: February 22, 1940.

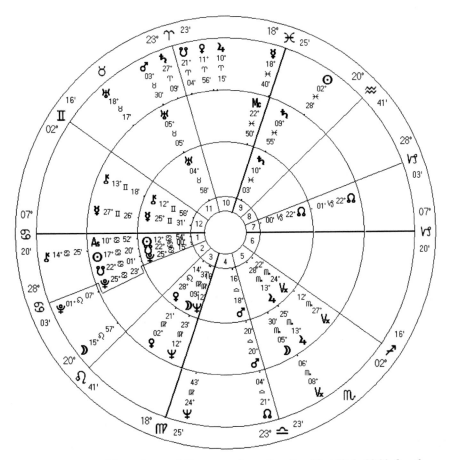

Figure 3 - Transits and Progressions for the 22ⁿᵈ Feb 1940 for the Dalai Lama

The outer wheel is the transits for Feb 22, 1940, in Lhasa, China, where the ceremony took place. I could not find the time, so I cast for noon.

Transiting Neptune at 24 degrees Virgo in the outer wheel is sextile to his natal Vertex at 24 degrees Scorpio and trine his Anti-Vertex at 24 degrees Taurus on this date. Neptune is also the modern ruler of his Midheaven and was in sextile to Pluto when he came into spiritual power. That delineation pretty much writes itself!

There is a Yod with the progressed Vertex at 27 degrees Scorpio in quincunx to progressed Mercury at 27 degrees Gemini and transit Saturn at 27 degrees Aries. The Vertex and Mercury are in quincunx natally as well, so the fact that the aspect still holds by progression at this young age is no big deal. The big deal is that transiting Saturn moved into position to create a Yod—and surely the boy's life circumstances changed at this time. He went to live in the Potala Palace and was educated in scriptures along with other monks pursuing doctorates in Buddhist studies.

Transiting Jupiter, the traditional ruler of his Pisces Midheaven, is in a sesquiquadrate to his Vertex and semi-square to his Anti-Vertex. There are two other major configurations that play off the Vertex. Dane Rudhyar called an eighth harmonic Yod a Finger of Fate. This is one planet in sesquiquadrate to two planets that are square each other. In Finger of Fate number one, we have the natal Vertex in sesquiquadrate to transiting Jupiter and also to the progressed Ascendant. This represents a fated ascension to a public position. In Finger of Fate number two, we have the progressed Vertex in sesquiquadrate to the natal Sun and transiting Venus. Venus is the Anti-Vertex's dispositor. The Sun is natal Venus's dispositor.

So the timing seen through the Vertex confirms that this was a fated event. He was only two years old when he was discovered to be the Fourteenth Dalai Lama. And incidentally, he set off on a three-month journey to the Potala Palace in Lhasa in the summer of 1939, accompanied by family members and the search party who had discovered that he was the Dalai Lama.[5] It was June of 1939 when Saturn first hit 27 degrees and made that Yod partile (progressed Vertex, progressed Mercury and transiting Saturn, all at 27 degrees). His ceremony the following February was at Saturn's last pass over 27 Aries. This is the final milestones of the life-changing story that unfolded through the Yod with the Vertex.

Summary

Take a look at the Vertex Axis story in your chart. Think of a few events in your life that occurred that you did not consciously seek out. Don't look for things represented by other angles, such as a marriage, purchase of a home, career milestone, etc. Look for something you weren't planning, and find that event in your natal Vertex story. Then look to see how it was timed by transits, solar arcs, progressions, or whatever you normally use. Injuries and accidents often show up with both the Ascendant and Vertex involved because they are chance events that impacts your body. If it was a person rather than an event you encountered, the meeting could show up in synastry as well as transit, solar arc or progression.

I'll leave you with one last example, a definite Law of Attraction Vertex story. I was looking for a Pampered Chef ice cream scoop - one of those scoops that heats up from the warmth of your hand and goes through the ice cream with the ease of a knife in soft butter. Once you have that, you don't want any old ice cream scoop—an object attachment ensues—so the ice cream scoop is a Venus object for several reasons. I could not find one for sale anywhere. My Anti-Vertex is in the eleventh house in Gemini. I was at an astrology conference when I overheard a woman saying she sold Pampered Chef. So I found what I was looking for by being in exactly the right place at exactly the right time to overhear that precise sentence of that particular conversation. After we became friends and exchanged birth data, I learned her Venus is partile conjunct my Vertex. I was in an eleventh house situation, over hearing a conversation (Gemini). I had been putting out that I wanted a Venus object, and lo and behold, the person whom I overheard had Venus conjunct my Vertex.

There are no coincidences, only synchronicities. These synchronicities can be viewed astrologically through the Vertex Axis. I hope this chapter has inspired you to explore your Vertex and see how it unfolds the stories of your chance encounters and seemingly fated events orchestrated by the synchronicity of the organizing principal of the cosmos.

Endnotes

1. Merriam Webster, *Collegiate Dictionary Eleventh Edition*, (Merriam Webster Inc., 2003), 456.
2. ibid, 339.
3. Brian Hodgkinson, *The Essence of Vedanta* (Arcturus Publishing Limited, 2006), 197.
4. Ananda Maitreya, translation of *The Dharmapada*,(Metta Foundation, 1995), 1.
5. Dalai Lama Website http://www.dalailama.com/biography/chronology-of-events, accessed February 1, 2013.

11

Transcendence:

The Archetype of Masculine Transformation through the Mars Cycle

Adam Gainsburg

"We humans serve the... Self – and in this service we may discover our essential humanness, our history and our value beyond the personal limits of our own experience." [1]

– Gregory Max Vogt, *Return to Father*

Introduction

Perhaps the last planet to come to an astrologer's mind when asked for the transpersonal dimension in consciousness is Mars. The ancient link of the god Ares with self-directed action, personal will, and concrete achievement is as alive today as it has ever been. Indeed, there does not seem to be much mainstream credence given to the ephemeral or non-local dimension of experience or the higher qualities we each possess. Collectively, we seem to be in love with a reductionist view of the individual that conveniently fuels our idolization of our ego in mainstream media. Yet if it is true that humanity is imbued with a transpersonal dimension of beingness, then each planet in astrology signifies not only a material dimension but a facet of that larger, transpersonal Self we all share.

Masculinity

As this exposé addresses this higher dimension of Mars, it is necessary to outline the masculine principle itself. What follows is not a description of the male gender. Male-ness and masculinity are quite different. As the masculine and feminine principles exist well beyond our ability to conceive of them in totality, this picture of masculinity must remain a working draft. It attempts only to evoke the quality or tone of authentic masculinity:

> The Masculine principle in creation is the urge to move away from its own source, to penetrate into indefinable spaces, and forever seek.[2] It is chaotic in its absence of pattern. It will disrupt and shatter structure, organization and stagnancy. The Masculine evolves in humanity from additive subjective consciousness into reductive objective consciousness. Masculinity houses the archetype of the individuation impulse, the urge to develop a singular, defining identity. Its experience exists within a context of singleness, and has a natural antipathy toward being consumed, overwhelmed, or homogenized. It is the Masculine that seeds creation to occur through its instigating, fertilizing, energetic nature. The Masculine part of humanity can be individualistic, inconsistent, eruptive, solipsistic, competitive, hierarchical, and alienating, but also progressively idealistic, non-violent, entrepreneurial, visionary, emotionally powerful, detached, and deeply committed through a service-oriented vision.

Masculine Symbols in Astrology

While astrology categorizes every planet as masculine or feminine (often changing the designation if placed in morning or evening sky), a transpersonal view suggests that there are two main symbols for the primary Masculine or yang force: Mars and the Sun. Jupiter is most at home in adventurous Sagittarius and hidden or renunciatory Pisces (according to traditional astrology), and its significations are in fact a blend of masculine and feminine core drives; it connotes exaggeration and an increasing involvement in one's expanding ability to integrate information. Thus, it is less succinctly a masculine image. And though Saturn is infamous for its association with our patriarchal value set as a culture, the essential significations of the planet are the keeping of order and assuring continuity, a blend of masculine exertion and feminine

163

inclusiveness. Thus let's focus on the Sun, the other central masculine symbol in astrology.

The astrological Sun represents the unfocused qualities of ever-present activity and aliveness in that activity. Astrology continues to promote the Sun alternately as an individual's basic identity, the main symbol for one's masculine nature, the co-symbol with Saturn for the Father archetype, and the Moon's partner as the primary masculine symbol. Though accepted and widely in use, these assignments do not address the actual dynamic of the Sun itself.

The astrological Sun infuses everything with its vital current of outward-moving energy (*prana* or *chi*). *It is indiscriminate aliveness.* For the human being, the Sun is the quality of his/her raw current of life force. It should not be seen as that which gives rise to an individual's quintessential and base nature, but as that which provides the energy for it. We express *as* or *through* our Sun sign in a visible, lighted and recognizable way. In this way, the Sun can be seen as the *universal additive* for the collective or as a *personal battery* for an individual. The Sun is masculine for two reasons: it provides us with the energy to be alive, to be seen, and thus to be an individual; and its energy is outward-moving. As we'll see, it is the Sun–Mars relationship which is the more accurate signifier for *logos* and spiritual insight.

Mars

Astrology's most direct symbol for the masculine drive is Mars. The planet's physical progression through the solar system symbolizes the *archetypal development* of masculinity from lower to higher forms, both individually and collectively. As an archetype, Mars represents the pre-conscious will to live, how we enact our desire, and how we individualize ourselves, ultimately and paradoxically, to our liberation. Mars is also our sexual drive, experience of our power, and proclivity for competitiveness, impatience, anger, or violence. Its archetypal energy is characterized by inconsistency, aggressiveness, intense focus on a goal, outward-movingness, curiosity, competitiveness, directness and inconsistency.

164

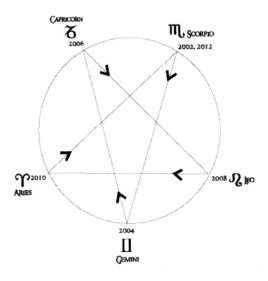

Venus Archetypal Journeys 2002-2012

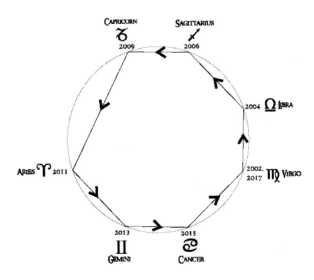

Mars Archetypal Journeys 2002-2017

Figure 1 - Venus' consistent eight-year pentacle (above) in contrast to Mars' irregular shape (below). Listed years and signs indicate the start of a new cycle.

The *geocentric* path of Mars—how Mars appears to us Earth dwellers—mirrors these *egocentric* expressions of masculinity. Mars tracks an inconsistent and at times extremely variable path through the solar system. *"Mars' succession of phenomena and rhythms of movement are most difficult to comprehend. Its motions, whether considered spatially or temporally, show irregularities and variations to a degree not found for any other planet."*[3] This trait is in direct contrast to Venus' ongoing consistent orbit. We can compare the signs of Venus and Mars at the start of their respective cycles. In Figure 1, each labeled sign and year indicates the start of a new geocentric cycle (Venus–Sun cycle and Mars–Sun cycle). The pentacle shape formed by Venus every eight years remains for us a consistent metric for tracking the Earth–Venus–Sun and Earth–Venus–Moon relationships accurately over long periods. In contrast, Mars cycles never form consistent relationships from one cycle to the next (see Figures 1, 4).

Mars' apparent antipathy toward regularity reflects in each of us the ever-present choice to leave the familiar, ingrained, or condoned reality frame. This instinct can be refined through the course of a life, but the source drive responsible for it remains. Natal Mars remains natal Mars. The "terrible twos" period of childhood shows this. The twenty-sixth month of life is in fact the first astrological (minor) Mars return, when the child is for the first time exhibiting behavior and speech that emanate from his or her growing *masculine* individuating urges—to separate from parents, the familiar "safe" ground, and the known past.

Though only a minor return, the two-year return is the most significant of all the Mars minors because it is the *first* outward exploration of uniqueness (see Note 12). Thus, it is the most obvious departure from familiar behavior and temperament. Until the second birthday, the child lives in a largely undifferentiated state, requiring everything from the parents. When Mars returns to the child's birth placement at approximately 26 months of age, the spark of Mars' fire becomes unavoidable.

The Three Stages of Transformation

From many years of seeing clients in a healing and transpersonal setting, I have formalized for myself a three-stage model of the transformational process (Figure 2). While each stage is associated with one of the two principles, these labels describe the quality of the stage itself, rather than the content of any specific process.

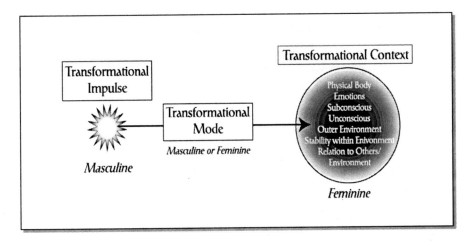

Figure 2 - The three stages of the archetype of transformation

The Transformational Impulse is like a spark, an outward-moving energy likened to a synaptic explosion that causes a disruption to stasis. Its intention is to shed the old and reach for something new, greater and unknown. Its spark is unpredictable and eruptive, seeking to interrupt or penetrate extant form.

The Transformational Mode is a type of reaction or a chain of events. It describes *how* the impulse is meant to be realized. The mode's primary action can occur through an intense, forced *expansion* beyond one's known and comfortable definitions, or through an equally forced *descent* via profound surrender and release of the familiar.

The Transformational Context is the container in which the transformation occurs and is experienced. The context can be the body, the psyche, one's relationship with one's environment, one's relationship with Other, or any other identifiable "environment." The *context* also describes the matter of the transformative dynamic—which issues, resistances, and possible outcomes, as well as what and how support might come.

The three stages are not consecutive in the traditional sense. They are closer to being simultaneous or non-linear.[4] The *impulse* sparks to life a process that instantaneously begins the *mode's* operation, which in turn produces the *context* to be actualized. Whether the desired outcome is realized in forty seconds or forty years is determined by the individual's sense of safety.

The Archetype of Masculine Transformation

There is much available literature on the many manifestations of transformation—psychologically, culturally, and even financially. Yet there is a significant absence of literature distinguishing the masculine from the feminine transformational modes.

If we examine how transformation has been described, we find "a dark night of the soul," "an underworld experience," "ego death," "hitting bottom," "a loss of self," and "a breakdown." They each imply a kind of catastrophic *loss* of something vital and needed, a movement *downward or inward,* and the experience of *being overwhelmed or subsumed.* From this view, severe changes are thought to occur only in *dark* places, *under* our surface persona, which *threaten* our survival, stability and happiness, and *into* which no normal person would choose to go. While they are accurate descriptions of our emotional and psychological experience, they do not describe the archetypal movement of consciousness manifesting as the individual's experience. Without the latter, there is no context in which to see the transformative intent, and thus no broader perspective to provide guidance. Therapy can devolve to superficial treatment at best and misdiagnosis at worst. The italicized words above in fact describe the uniquely feminine mode of transformation, which I call *transmutation.* This term signifies the processes of death of the animated self, cyclicity and the potential for regeneration.

This poses an intriguing question: Why has the archetype of transformation become culturally defined through the feminine mode? Three facts help to shed light on this. First, any experience of authentic change will trigger emotional, psychological and even physical *experiences* of pain, isolation or discontinuity. Our immediate experience within the body is a domain of the feminine principle, just as the body itself is. Second, our patriarchal perspective purports misogynist values stemming from a radical reaction to its matriarchal predecessor. Cultural patriarchy and its injurious misunderstandings about what our intra- and intersubjective norms should be are pandemic. Third, our culture's projected fear of death and the resulting refusal to address death as an integral, powerful and sacred threshold of life originate in the threat implied from *any* unknown thing. In one view, death is king/queen of the unknown. Because death is out of one's control, so the projection goes, it is natural to make every attempt to cheat, beat, avoid and fear it.[5] In other words, our culturally unconscious assignment of all transformational experiences to the realm of the feminine lacks *objectivity*. Thus objectivity – a decidedly masculine archetype – becomes a kind of "medicine" for our cultural soul.[6]

All the while, our innate femininity is without question returning to her rightful place as our intrinsic relationship with all life. The feminine principle is that which returns us to our source (whereas the masculine principle pulls us away from our interior source). In the mythic sojourn of the Heavenly Queen Inanna into the underworld, we are shown exactly why the feminine transformational mode is so essential for life on earth and in body: Inanna "goes down" in order to regain/re-contact/re-associate with the singular source of feminine power: "the abyss that is both source and end of all being."[9] It is a monotonic abyss, lacking any familiar artifacts for ego. It is an interior, featureless ocean holding life itself in its balance. This feminine dyad of Heavenly Abode and Underworld Abyss imaged in the Inanna story cellularly reifies the primal laws of nature that subject all life to live and die in cycles of changing patterns. The path of descent–death–rebirth–ascent is the experience she must have to re-contact the feminine source, to play her part in the ongoing re-empowerment of authentic femininity.

In a counseling environment, observing the distinctions between masculine and feminine energies can greatly assist the stabilizing of a transpersonal context. Our clients then gain the added advantage of knowing the context within which their change is occurring, which can significantly ease egoic contraction and hasten a new, sustainable self-image. Briefly described:

- Transformation occurring through the masculine mode, or *transcendence*, is a final departure away from something lesser/more stable/more known and towards something greater/broader/beyond/unknown.
- Transformation occurring through the feminine mode, or *transmutation*, is a downward- or inward-facing surrender or profound loss of relation causing a change in fundamental self-structure.

169

While authentic transformations in general broaden our vision, refine our context, and enlighten our awareness of our essential selves, the masculine modes occur through *outwardly directed movement of energy* and necessitate an *expansion* within the psyche. Naturally this is the inverse movement of the feminine mode; both are equally valid and beneficial. Within masculine-specific transformations, there is an upward or outward departure from the known self for something bigger, broader, and beyond it. Going beyond one's known reality is indicative of the masculine pattern of transcendence. The effect of such experiences is an expansion of personal context. Masculine transformations produce a greater capacity to be *objective,* to perceive *outside* of one's context. Naturally, the outer-moving modes of masculine transformation intend a masculine result: *detachment, objectivity, vision and a broader wisdom.*

Unconditional love

The Mars Cycle

The astrological Mars cycle signifies the process of collective masculine consciousness in specific and unique ways. It is composed of the relationship of Mars and the Sun in space and time. The combined symbology of Mars and the Sun is a powerful, multivalent image, and one that offers a unique and renewed map of transpersonal development through robust, healthy forms of masculinity.

Astrologically, the sign that Mars occupies within this cycle indicates that moment's (or native's) pertinent masculine expression within the overall intent of the cycle. And the spatial distance or *elongation* between Mars and the Sun indicates the phase of Mars within his cycle.[7] The phases of Mars thus signify how an individual is imprinted to contribute substantially to an improved society, nation, world or cosmos, a type of personal *masculine dharma.*

The first appearance of Mars rising before the Sun in the morning (Mars' heliacal rise) occurs when Mars is approximately 15° in front of the Sun. It is this first appearance of Mars in our eastern sky, known as his Emergence Phase, which visibly signals we are in a new cycle (see Figure 3). The astrological sign of Mars here at the emergence phase determines the developmental intent or signature of the entire cycle, just as an individual's birth chart determines his/her developmental intent throughout life.

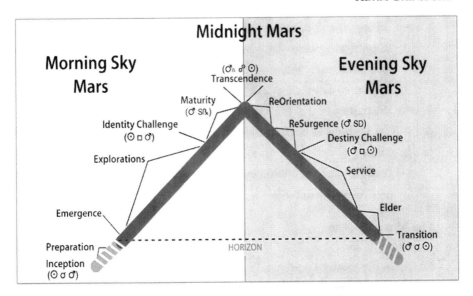

Figure 3 - **General structure and phases of the Mars cycle. This sky path describes the elongational relationship between Mars and the Sun as seen from Earth each day of the cycle's 26-month duration**

The Mars cycle actually begins with the Mars–Sun conjunction prior to his heliacal rise. Mars here is invisible to us and symbolizes a type of conception event. In the Mars cycle, his conjunction with the Sun is known as the inception phase to echo the inchoate conception of physical life. As described earlier, Mars and the Sun are the main astrological symbols for the masculine impulse within consciousness. Where Mars is the masculine drive itself, the Sun is the animating and non-specific life force infusing all manifestation. In context of the Mars cycle, the Sun symbolizes the vivifying force for each cycle's intent. "The creative Mars energy emanates from the symbolic Sun—source of perpetual vitality…"[8]

As stated, the celestial sky path that Mars follows is highly variable, reflecting the nature of masculinity:

- The synodic period between two successive inception phases (Sun–Mars conjunctions) can vacillate by as much as 1½ months (between 24 and 26½ months).[9]

171

- From the beginning of the cycle—Mars–Sun conjunction or inception phase—to its midpoint—Mars–Sun opposition or transcendence phase—Mars may cover as little as 113° of the zodiac to as much as 211°.[10]
- Mars may begin its cycle superior or inferior to the ecliptic.[11]
- Its visibility is best at successively later times every two years (minor return).[12]
- Mars' major returns repeat in a staggered pattern of alternating 15- and 17-year intervals.[13]

The Mars Phases

Similar to the modern conception of the moon's eight phases determined by the Moon–Sun elongation, the Mars cycle has thirteen phases or sub-periods, each possessing unique developmental characteristics within the cycle's intent (see Figure 3 and Table 1). With knowledge of Mars' cycle, we know not only *what* is being worked on (the sign of Mars at any point), but also *how* it's happening (the phase of Mars). In other words, we are able to tap directly into masculine consciousness at any point along the cycle and know what's developing. For example, if we observe morning-sky Mars 17° from the Sun, we know that Mars is just about to complete his emergence phase; we are sealing our collective intention for the new cycle and ensuring we are clear in our "marching orders," as it were.

As another example, if Mars is in Libra during the explorations phase of the Taurus cycle, collectively we are forging our inter-subjective position with others so that we can stabilize and support a more reliable, pleasurable way of life. Again, these interpretations apply to the level of the collective psyche. Natal delineations become deeply personal for clients by contextualizing all the "content" of their personal experience (natal chart) into a collective, intelligent process (natal Mars cycle and phase).

Midway through the cycle, the transcendence phase occurs. The transcendence phase divides the full cycle into two halves of about one year each. Each half has its own astronomical indicators and is quite different in archetypal quality.

172

Mars Journeys 1968-1983

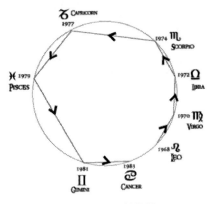

Mars Journeys 1985-2000

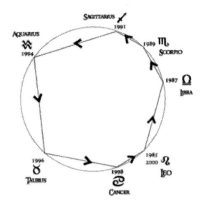

Mars Journeys 2002-2017

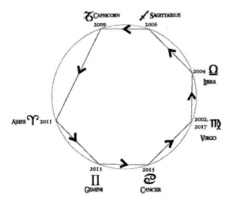

Figure 4 - "Patterns" of the Mars cycle for three synodic periods show no consistency. Each intersection of an arrowed line with a circle's circumference indicates a new Mars

Morning Sky Phases	Mars -Sun Elongation (°)	Evening Sky Phases	Mars–Sun Elongation (°)
1. Inception Phase	0–3	7. Transcendence Phase	178am–178pm
2. Preparation Phase	3–15	8. Reorientation Phase	178–130*
3. Emergence Phase	15–18	9. Resurgence Phase	130*–94
		10. Destiny Challenge Phase	94–86
4. Explorations Phase	18–86	11. Service Phase	86–38
5. Identity Challenge Phase	86–94	12. Elder Phase	38–15
6. Maturity Phase	94–178	13. Transition Phase	15-0

* Denotes approximation at stationary direct.

Table 1 - Mars cycle phases with Mars–Sun elongation in degrees (°)

Morning-sky Mars ascends out from the glare of the rising Sun in the east and brings a focus on the development of self-identity. This year-long period (Phases 1–6) represents the development of *subjective masculinity* through stabilizing the sense of self (inception, preparation, emergence, and explorations phases); breaking down and releasing what is no longer relevant about the self (identity challenge phase); and finally, refining a self-image as a direct result of the new information gained (maturity phase) (see Figure 2). Through this first half of the cycle, Mars discovers his uniqueness not only through experiences of success and connection but also through those that block his illusions and over-dependence on old behaviors. Mars is required to release his myopic, impulsive, confrontational and resistant patterns. This long period of time is needed to root him in a new self-definition and prepare him for the evolutionary goals of the transcendence phase. Mars' morning-sky development is homologous with the astrological progression from Aries to Virgo.

The evening-sky Mars period (Phases 8–13) comprises the latter half of the cycle and focuses on developing *objective* consciousness through the trial-and-error application of the subjective identity for a social purpose. During this period, Mars is seen to descend gradually towards the western horizon, which symbolizes his increasing refinement, broader vision and devoted service. His diminishing brightness through this period symbolizes the decrease of individuated, noticeable identity. In its place arises an increasing commitment and ability to blend personal desires with the social need. The night-sky progression correlates to the Libra-to-Pisces progression.

Full masculine maturation requires the successful development of *both* the morning-star archetype of breaking a wild stallion (first half of the cycle) and the evening-star archetype of the naïve outsider or resistant loner coming to accept his destiny to lead (second half of the cycle). This is the simplest and most basic way to frame an understanding of the developmental structure of the cycle. To appreciate the cycle on its many levels of meaning and thus to incorporate it into chart interpretation, each phase needs to be studied—both archetypally and through case examples.

The Transcendence Phase

Each of Mars' thirteen phases possesses essential challenges and gifts in the form of potentialities to be actualized by us. At a collective level, the function of the transcendence phase (Phase 7) is to provide a fundamental transformation to our collective consciousness. Mars' astrological signature at transcendence signifies *how* and *around what issues* the entire cycle will transform. This phase is signaled astronomically by retrograde Mars' exact opposition with the Sun. Depending on application, this phase can represent:

- the *completed development* of subjective consciousness (Figure 5A),
- a threshold process marking the *shift* from subjective to objective development (Figure 5B), or
- the *inception* of objective development (Figure 5C).

The transcendence phase produces a challenging and deeply transformative metamorphosis of the masculine function within us. It may then be surprising to learn that the transcendence phase is the shortest phase of the entire cycle.

175

The entire phase lasts all of three days, with a pinnacle or peak experience of only 35 hours. This runs contrary to astrological folk wisdom, which purports that longer transits lead to deeper changes. Why then should it command so much attention? [14] As we'll see, the masculine mode of transcendence is the material inverse of the feminine mode of transmutation.

The transcendence phase sees Mars reach a unique confluence of astronomical alignments that do not occur individually at any other time, yet together they are responsible for the unique archetype of masculine transformation itself. The factors are:

1. Mars is *closest* to Earth (perigee) and *brightest* in the night sky.
2. Mars is in *fastest retrograde motion* (appearing to move backward in the sky).
3. Mars is *in opposition to the Sun* (furthest from the Sun).

Mars Closest and Brightest

Recall that transcendence is the archetypal expression of profound transformation through the masculine mode. Yet in the transcendence phase, we do not find Mars hidden away, deep in a "below place" as we do with Venus in her transmutation phase (superior conjunction). He is not surrendering vital aspects of his nature and is not preparing to die in the traditional sense. In fact, Mars is nowhere near the Sun. Rather, he is highest in the night sky and sustains his longest visibility while also being closest to Earth (perigee), where his reflected light is shining most impressively. Even with naked-eye observation, we can often note his red color. "At a bright opposition [transcendence phase] Mars outshines all the fixed stars.... To be sure, Mars only lights up for a relatively brief time to such an impressive radiance."[15]

Here at the culmination of his morning-sky subjective development period (see Figure 5A), with Mars brightest and closest, he is symbolically full of his accomplishments, boasts his true colors, and secretly looks to what to do next. His overt visibility in the night sky is the first qualitative distinction of masculine transformation and challenges the general assumption that all transformations occur in and through dark places.

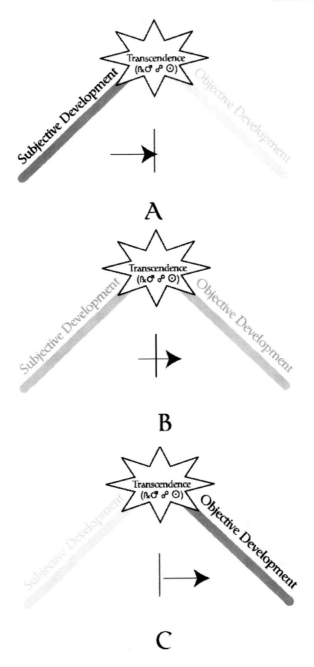

Figure 5 - Mars' transcendence phase framed as (A) a completion of
the subjective development period, (B) transition from subjective to
objective, or (C) inception of objective development

Mars Retrograde

Retrograde is the phenomenon of the visible planets appearing to move backward relative to their forward direction. When Mars is retrograde, his otherwise active, uncontrolled, doing-oriented, outward-moving nature becomes blocked or retarded by an unprecedented invisible wall of limitation. Astrologer Maurice Fernandez describes Mars retrograde: "What is put into question is one's mode of actions, assertion of power, and defense mechanisms."[16] Vedic astrologer James Kelleher describes Mars retrograde as "energy becoming excessive, spilling over and imploding."[17] Astrologer Jeffrey Wolf Green notes that within the Mars retrograde dynamic, "the instinctual energy to take action on the desires emanating from the soul becomes inverted."[18] The intensifying limitation or blockage to one's further freedom of movement arises not necessarily due to personal contraction but because consciousness here is attempting to leap *upwards*, rather than forwards. In this sense, transcendence represents a quantum shift to another octave of development; it is not just a next lesson within the same octave. It certainly ushers us into a very different kind of challenge in that there is literally nothing we can *do* except to allow, upwards and outwards.

Not only is Mars retrograde here, but he is also at his *fastest* retrograde velocity. Mars is journeying across the greatest amount of interior space in the shortest amount of time. This is highly unusual for Mars. What began five weeks earlier as an unsettling feeling at his retrograde station during the maturity phase has now intensified into a shattering of the structure of self-identity. The maximum retrograde velocity portends a sort of identity-death-march for Mars.

The retrograde effect also produces a build-up of energy which otherwise finds externalization when Mars is direct. The energy accumulates, creating a need to release it in some manner. Release or appeasement comes either through a sustained introversion and regular withdrawal from others, providing a "safe space" in which to discharge that energy, or through periodic outbursts. Astrologer Martin Schulman has written that Mars retrograde creates "an inability to regulate [the otherwise natural] flow of energy."[19] As we will see, retrogradation effectively blocks Mars' tendency to remain in the familiar and known, thus helping to catalyze the transcendent experience.

178

Mars opposition Sun

Mars' exact opposition (180°) with the Sun lasts for 35 hours in the very heart of the transcendence phase. It is the phenomenal trigger for the noumenal presence of transcendence, once the other celestial factors are in place.

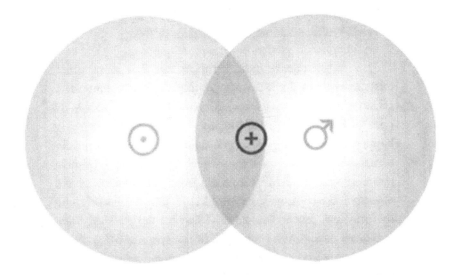

Figure 6 - The moment of transcendence as seen from the north ecliptic pole. Earth occupies the shared space, or vesica, of Mars and the Sun at their opposition

The Mars–Sun opposition can symbolize the furthest psychic distance, the maximum separation, or the strongest tension between masculine *self-identity* (Mars) and *self-essence* (Sun).[20] The developmental goal of the entire first half of the cycle (morning-sky Mars) is to deliver Mars to this point.

Once the exact opposition is reached, there is nowhere left for Mars to go, no further differentiation to be realized through his own efforts. This is the evolutionary wall described above. But the masculine impulse cannot go away just because there is no more material distance from the Sun to achieve. It pushes the identity past its need for rational, dependable self-image. This allows the raw masculine nature or *experiential impulse itself* to be released into a state of boundlessness. We might think of this as an expanding away from its relative identity back into its source state. Homologous with femininity's primordial

179

return to source through decay and death, the masculine finds its return through a symbolic evanescence into an original, self-less state.

Loss of the Self

The 20th century mathematician, gold miner, philosopher, and mystic, Franklin Merrell-Wolfe, describes his experience of this:

> "... [I]t suddenly dawned upon me that a common mistake made in the higher meditation...is the seeking for a subtle object of...something that could be experienced. At once, I dropped expectation of having anything happen....Then, with eyes open and no senses stopped in functioning—hence no trance—I abstracted the subjective moment—the "I AM" element—from the totality of the objective consciousness manifold.... I found myself above the universe, not in the sense of leaving the physical body and being taken out in space, but in the sense of being above space, time and causality. ... I felt intangibly, yet wonderfully, free. **I sustained this universe and was not bound by it.**"[21] (emphasis added)

Founder of the interspiritual movement and renowned scholar and Christian mystic Brother Wayne Teasdale (1945–2004) talked about his experience in a different way:

> "I was sitting in my room and the room began to dissolve. Everything dissolved. I was no longer in the world and I found myself in this infinite expanse of light, with no structure, no form, no colors, no shape.... **I was not aware of myself at all**. I was only aware of what I call the primordial act of identity of the Godhead. How God is God. The simplicity of an act of self-relation...."[22] (emphasis added)

The combined effect of Mars' three unique sky factors pulls the masculine dimension of our being out of our structured identity and releases it into an unfettered, pure awareness.[23] The goal of the first half of the Mars cycle is here undermined and exponentially realized courtesy of our transcendent potential.

The purpose of the transcendence phase is to radically dissociate the true Self from its identity shell, freeing it into vast boundlessness and reifying our eternal nature. In this experience, we transcend our relative reality of "self experiencing the world" and return to primordial awareness itself, unlimited and free.

The Collective Lost and Retained

Without some type of structure to sustain a stable self-image, the masculine loses its ability to be expressed in form and returns to pure and indefinable principle. This forces a conflict in the psyche. Where once we could depend on physical Mars to be the symbol we needed it to be—the masculine within and without us—now it can no longer house and reflect that projection. Before our collective eyes, Mars becomes an entirely different image reflecting masculinity in an entirely new way. This conflict exists at the very center of masculine transformation. If Mars has lost self-identity and yet is still Mars, what does the *Transcendence Phase Mars* signify for us? Is something retained?

There does seem to be retention of...something. From outside the transcendent experience looking in, there is what I refer to as an *echo signature* of the masculine. This signature does not carry the recognizable qualities we've come to associate with Mars up to this point in the cycle. Recall that the transcendence phase is the experience of transcending the limitation of subjective development (self-identity) signified by Mars' sojourn through our morning sky. With Mars beyond structure, the only quantity left is the original, vivifying, indiscriminate energy for the cycle itself: the Sun (exact opposition). Transcendent Phase Mars becomes completely infused by the illuminating solvent or universal additive quality of the Sun as its echo signature: still masculine, yet no longer direct, "driven" or focused.

From inside the transcendent experience, there is no coherent or identifiable masculine signature. The transcendent is a non-local, non-direct and non-specific expansiveness. When Mars returns to this boundlessness at each retrograde opposition with the Sun, he becomes transparent. This is such an extreme departure from his otherwise driven and demonstrable nature that

181

conceptualizing "transparent Mars" may be a stretch. But this is the precise purpose of the masculine annihilation experience – *to obliterate and then re-source the identity*. I have come to see Mars' transcendent phase as a *returning*. I envision it as a re-expansion back into original vastness, a kind of reconnection with essential nature through a subsummation of the local self. Such nature has been described by many wisdom traditions alternately as non-abiding, non-dual mind; absolute subject; diamond body; undifferentiated awareness; and Big Heart Big Mind.[24] This state has also been termed "the mind of Lord Shiva," or the obliterating, omnidirectional dispersion of consciousness into and away from everywhere and everything.

Transcendence Phase Traits in Natives

Transcendence phase individuals are attempting to harness, actualize and then balance or integrate *spiritual vitality*. As natal Mars signifies both the way in which we move in the world and the way we enact our deeper desire or purpose, the essential challenge is how to retain or substantiate oneself as pure awareness within the somatic and psycho-emotional context of the local self.

Transcendence phase individuals possess an intensified awareness of and strong sensitivity to the power in higher states of consciousness. This can produce a buildup of psychoid pressure if the individual has not created a personally relevant means of releasing it. Such pressure is produced whenever the individual rejects—consciously or otherwise—the inherent safety of the larger self, or becomes overwhelmed by constriction of material life. We can see this symbolized in Mars' retrograde station, which results in the exact Sun opposition. This dynamic portrays a pattern of repeated build-ups and releases. Such releases can be conscious, instinctual or subconscious. They can produce bursts of creativity or insight, energized performances, or long periods of focus and endurance. They can also occur as long periods of isolation, overwhelming frustration, or intense self-criticism, even leading to self-inflicted injury or suicidal attempts. It should be noted that such behavior does not result from one's natal Sun–Mars opposition alone. The larger chart picture must be taken into account. Over time, individuals learn how to embody—rather than dissociate from—their own vitality and drive sooner, before explosions of release become necessary. As they embody their uniquely higher octave and higher octane energy, the former overwhelming of the subconscious diminishes and transforms into the energy of possibility, conscious alignment and right motivation.

In counseling situations, I have observed that these individuals have a "porous" energy field, making them more sensitive to and inspired by other levels of reality, yet greatly challenged in integrating this trait in functional ways. They will be energetically sensitive, highly talented, seemingly divinely inspired, not always grounded or often in their body, repressing their anger, and trusting only in the non-physical realms. Impatience can become conflated with their drive to serve, improve or change things. Such drives often mask the hidden fear that they'll never accomplish what they most wish to. Their interests may move them toward the esoteric, yet their emotional illiteracy may impede integrating those interests into mundane life. These individuals tend to be more susceptible to unwanted energies from others or their surroundings. Yet they can be quite unaware of how sensitive they are. Sometimes an unexpected angry outburst is the only evidence. This susceptibility/sensitivity can trigger self-doubt, self-cruelty or external reactions typically indicative of Mars retrograde individuals.

In general, they can be strongly motivated to live out their life's desire and be quite clear they are tapped into their higher consciousness. Their capacity to manifest it provides a consistent litmus test of their ability to do so. There also seems to be a theme of assumptive beliefs about how reality should be, which had previously led to beliefs that the problems in the world (or with themselves) are broader than they can overcome. The isolation response is very strong here because the implicit drive for individuation (Mars) has reached its pinnacle (opposition) with no safe next step available.

These natives were born with the Mars and the Sun maximally distant from one another, creating the most elongated electromagnetic relationship in the entire Mars cycle (see above, The Transcendence Phase). Thus they find it more difficult to become aware (Sun) of the source of their inspiration or desire (Mars).

In significant relationships, their inconsistency can alternately create:

- *codependence* – an over-reliance on others for safety, acceptance or consistency indicating a refusal to embrace oneself,
- *isolation* – a perceived need to distance themselves from perceived threats, or
- *immaturity* – an irresponsibility with their intimates' feelings.

The sign, house and aspects of natal Mars reveal which pattern(s) is most active. Earth and water signs and houses tend toward codependence, air and fire tend toward isolation and immaturity. Intense aspects involving Mars would further restrict Mars' freedom, while more easeful aspects would indicate an unwillingness to change.

This codependence, isolation or insensitivity will create experiences involving being "taken for a ride," abandoned, or attacked—emotionally, ideologically, spiritually or otherwise. Those individuals I have observed do in fact eventually recognize that something in the way they are managing their unique gifts is not aligned with others, and this misalignment or ignorance is responsible for their feeling alienated.

These individuals are imbued with a personal potential and collective *dharma* to live and exemplify that there is a greater reality beyond one's personal reality, there is more to existence than the self, and their authentic masculinity is just the right vessel for their unique gifts to find expression.

Known Transcendence Phase Natives

Artist Frida Kahlo – July 6, 1907; 8:30 am; Coyoacan, MX; Source: birth record (AA)

Judy Garland – June 10, 1922; 6:00 am; Grand Rapids, MI; Source: birth registry (AA)

TV Prophet David Icke – April 29, 1952; 7:15 pm; Leicester, England; Source: mother's memory (A)

Surrealist painter Paul Rebeyrolle – November 3, 1926; 4 pm; Eymouteirs, FR; Source: biography (B)

"Spree" killer John Allen Muhammad – December 31, 1960; 6:12 am; New Orleans, LA; Source: birth record (AA)

184

Conclusion

The transcendence phase of the Mars cycle strips our adherence to subjective ground. It plants seeds for the planet's subsequent evening sky phases in which we learn to devote more of ourselves to others and to societal needs. What this requires is a self-definition which includes the capacity to be altruistic. The transcendence phase creates for Mars the alignment for this potential to become actualized by freeing the masculine essence from its fundamental self-associations, allowing it to re-contact its source—boundless, non-self-centered awareness. Identity is disbanded, re-merged into the vastness of the eternal.

As the transcendence phase ends, Mars begins returning to "normal" reality in the subsequent re-orientation phase with an entirely new basis for self-construction that must be integrated. Over time, our expanded awareness of societal needs, a growing desire to serve those needs, and the actual capacity to do so all increase. Personally, we experience the empowered blessings from devoting our fuller Self to a more accurately conceived worldview. The masculine thus re-discovers a new domain into which it can actively assert itself, participate, explore, learn, improve, and be with others. The lofty intent of all Mars cycles is the evolved expansion of consciousness through its expressions. This is redefined each 26 months as a new Mars cycle begins and is catalyzed about a year later in its transcendence phase.

Transcendence Phase Dates: 1899–2020

Dates indicate exact the transcendence event, or exact Mars–Sun opposition. The transcendence phase has a period of three days, or one and a half days on either side of the event. The sign of entire cycle is that of Mars at his emergence phase or heliacal rise.

Date	Sign of Entire Cycle	Position of Mars at Transcendence
January 18 1899	Capricorn	28° Cancer 43' Rx
February 22 1901	Pisces	2° Virgo 57' Rx
March 29 1903	Taurus	7° Libra 26' Rx
May 8, 1905	Cancer	17° Scorpio 32' Rx
July 6, 1907	Leo	13° Capricorn 23' Rx
September 24, 1909	Virgo	0° Aries 42' Rx
November 24, 1911	Scorpio	1° Gemini 48' Rx
January 5, 1914	Sagittarius	14° Cancer 36' Rx
February 9, 1916	Aquarius	20° Leo 02' Rx
March 15, 1918	Taurus	23° Virgo 52' Rx
April 21, 1920	Gemini	0° Scorpio 56' Rx
June 10, 1922	Leo	18° Sagittarius 53'Rx
August 23, 1924	Virgo	0° Pisces 14' Rx
November 4, 1926	Libra	11° Taurus 12' Rx
December 21, 1928	Scorpio	29° Gemini 28' Rx
January 27, 1931	Capricorn	6° Leo 53' Rx
March 1, 1933	Aries	10° Virgo 49' Rx
April 6, 1935	Gemini	15° Libra 59' Rx
May 19, 1937	Cancer	28° Scorpio 20' Rx
July 23, 1939	Virgo	29° Capricorn 34' Rx
October 10, 1941	Libra	16° Aries 48' Rx
December 5, 1943	Scorpio	12° Gemini 45' Rx
January 13, 1946	Sagittarius	23° Cancer 15' Rx
February 17, 1948	Pisces	27° Leo 55' Rx
March 23, 1950	Taurus	2° Libra 01' Rx
April 29, 1952	Cancer	11° Scorpio 10' Rx
June 22, 1954	Leo	3° Capricorn 07' Rx
September 9, 1956	Virgo	18° Pisces 35' Rx
November 14, 1958	Libra	24° Taurus 16' Rx
December 28, 1960	Sagittarius	9° Cancer 18' Rx
February 2, 1963	Aquarius	15° Leo 30' Rx
March 7, 1965	Aries	19° Virgo 17' Rx
April 13, 1967	Gemini	25° Libra 21' Rx
May 29, 1969	Leo	10° Sagittarius 31'Rx
August 8, 1971	Virgo	17° Aquarius 26' Rx
October 23, 1973	Libra	2° Taurus 04' Rx

December 13, 1975	Scorpio	23° Gemini 31' Rx
January 20, 1978	Capricorn	2° Leo 10' Rx
February 23, 1980	Pisces	6° Virgo 20' Rx
March 29, 1982	Gemini	10° Libra 55' Rx
May 9, 1984	Cancer	21° Scorpio 22' Rx
July 8, 1986	Leo	18° Capricorn 08' Rx
September 26, 1988	Libra	5° Aries 41' Rx
November 26, 1990	Scorpio	5° Gemini 53' Rx
January 6, 1993	Sagittarius	18° Cancer 13' Rx
February 11, 1995	Aquarius	22° Leo 54' Rx
March 17, 1997	Taurus	26° Virgo 46' Rx
April 24, 1999	Cancer	4° Scorpio 05' Rx
June 13, 2001	Leo	22° Sagittarius 45'Rx
August 28, 2003	Virgo	5° Pisces 01' Rx
November 7, 2005	Libra	15° Taurus 00' Rx
December 24, 2007	Sagittarius	2° Cancer 36' Rx
January 29, 2010	Capricorn	9° Leo 47' Rx
March 3, 2012	Aries	13° Virgo 39' Rx
April 8, 2014	Gemini	18° Libra 56' Rx
May 22, 2016	Cancer	1° Sagittarius 47' Rx
July 27, 2018	Virgo	4° Aquarius 08' Rx
October 13, 2020	Libra	21° Aries 04' Rx

Data generated by Sky Engine Software™ www.SkyEngine.us.

Endnotes

1. Gregory Max Vogt, *Return to Father,* Spring Publishing, 1998.
2. As such, a woman's *masculine nature* may be just as important for her development as her *feminine nature.* Astrology is a highly accurate tool for determining the unique qualities of both men and women's feminine *and* masculine aspects.
3. Joachim Schultz, *Movement & Rhythm of the Stars*, Anthroposophic Press, 1987, p. 169.
4. The Christian mystic, author and teacher Brother Wayne Teasdale describes the act of identity-creation or identification as "an act proceeding from itself, into itself and integrating itself, without really moving. I call this an unmoving movement. And this goes on for eternity." From a conversation between Brother Wayne Teasdale and Ken Wilbur, www.integrallife.com.

5. The closed mind with which we as a culture face death equally shuts out greater capacities to live more fully. Only in death do we come to know life. *"And so long as you haven't experienced / this: to die and so to grow, / you are only a troubled guest / on the dark earth."* ("The Holy Longing" by Goethe, as translated by Robert Bly in *The Rag and Bone Shop of the Heart*, 1992.)

6. The term "Medicine" originates from Native American wisdom. In my astrological and counseling work with the asteroid Chiron, an individual's Sacred Medicine is the developmental result of a successful receiving and embracing of one's Sacred Wound. For more, visit www.soulsign.com/chiron-book.

7. The spatial relationship between any planet and the Sun can likewise indicate that planet's cycle or transformational quality and framework within consciousness.

8. From "Mars – A Tool for Survival of the Spirit" by Linda Reid, *The Traditional Astrologer Magazine*, 1998.

9. Calculated from the average of 129 Mars cycles self-conception phases, transcendence phases and transition phases between the years 1910 and 2172.

10. From inception phase to transcendence phase for 102 Mars cycles from 1900 through 2172.

11. 129 Mars cycles between the years 1910 and 2172 reveal that Mars begins a cycle inferior (south celestial latitude) 38% of the time and superior (north celestial latitude) 62%.

12. We see two distinct types of Mars returns: "minor" and "major." Minor returns re-occur each 23½ to 26 months when Mars reaches the zodiacal degree of birth.

13. Major returns are also called synodic returns and occur only at ages 15, 32, 47, 64, 79, 96 and 111.

14. The same question might be asked of the solstices and equinoxes, times of great import but very short duration. I conclude from this that it is not the *quantity* of time but the *quality* of the specific energetic alignments occurring *within* that time window that dictate a timing's import, relevance and power.

15. Schultz, p. 174.

16. From private email correspondence.

17. From private email correspondence.

18. Jeffrey Wolf Green, *Pluto, Volume II: The Soul's Evolution Through Relationships*, Llewellyn, 1997.

19. Martin Schulman, *Karmic Astrology Volume II: Retrogrades and Reincarnation*, Samuel Weiser Inc., 1977.

20. I teach an astrological opposition as a "pulling-away conjunction" and as the alchemical *separatio* (Edward Edinger) which possess the archetypal intent to *reveal* what is held tightly within or in between two forces.

21. See *Pathways Through to Space*, Franklin Merrell-Wolfe, 1983.

22. Quoted in a conversation between Teasdale and Ken Wilbur recorded for www.integralnaked.org, February 2005. The quotation continues with: "…And what I saw is the Divine is a community of consciousness. And that it's utterly, utterly simple. It's so simple you can't get a hold of that. Realizing that this isn't adequate to the reality of the Divine, the act of identity is an act proceeding from itself, into itself and integrating itself, without really moving. I call it an unmoving movement. And this went on for eternity."

23. This conceptual framework—"essence-into-container" or "held-into-holder"—describing how the One (essence) becomes known (through containment) replicates how the masculine (held) and feminine (holder) perpetually reunite.

24. These conceptualizations are from Zen Buddhism, Tibetan Buddhism, Hinduism, and Christian mysticism as interpreted by Ken Wilbur, Andrew Cohen and others. Particularly influential has been Genpo Roshi.

12

Changing Relationships:

A Transpersonal Approach

Margaret Gray

> Love is not only about the relationship between two people,
> it is an affair of the soul that embraces everything of importance
> to the soul, some of which may have nothing directly to do with
> the relationship
>
> - Thomas Moore

The focus of this chapter is on exploring some of the changes we are invited to integrate and co-create with the current transits in the arena of relationships, from an archetypal, psychological[1] and astrological perspective. As we increasingly remember who we truly are and what our soul journey is about, our relationships are also required to undergo a process of depth transformation. Although this is taking place in all of our relationships, this chapter is primarily concerned with intimate partnerships.

An Overview

Although change is an innate feature of our evolutionary journey on this planet and beyond, the threshold we are currently crossing as a collective is of unusual proportions. This is both in its nature and the extent to which it is affecting all aspects of our existence. Living at this core time therefore offers each of us a powerful invitation to pioneer the co-creation of a new paradigm within ourselves and in our relationships. This paradigm is based on the authentic conscious alignment of our personality with our soul self.[2] A soul self which in its essence consists of pure unconditional love, most easily experienced and expressed through the conduit of our heart.

This is not a new paradigm of course, but more a way of being and relating which we have largely repressed, suppressed and disassociated from over the centuries. Initially doing so for the purpose of aiding our survival as a species, over time we allowed our defenses to solidify into a way of existing that is survival based, rather than heart centered. This widened the disconnection between our personality and our soul self. In consciously restoring this connection, via a deepening and expansive opening of our heart with the help of the current transpersonal planetary transits, we are more likely to be able to co-create authentic, soul-aligned relationships based on unconditional love.

This model of relationships primarily involves a shift from a place of 'what do I need' to a place of 'what can I offer/share'. In so doing we remove our core motivation from the strictures of a predominant self-surviving ego/mind, to an ego that is heart centered and therefore soul connected.

So what is the difference? At its simplest, when not aligned with our soul self, our ego takes rather than gives, fears rather than loves, restricts rather than expands. In opening our heart to unconditional love, we fully align ourselves with our soul-self creating the possibility for authentic reconnection with ourself and others.[3]

The Buildup to the Current Changes - Recognizing the 'I' to Create the 'We'

In line with the innate perfection of the Universe, our current transformation couldn't have taken place without the previous evolutionary stages that equipped us for this major threshold crossing. This included the assistance of many Promethean teachers along the way. Following in the footsteps of the Uranian god who risked the wrath of Zeus to bring the gift of fire to humanity, these teachers sought to light the fires of enlightenment on a collective basis in preparation for the current changes.

Freud and Jung, who both had North Node in Aries, played a major part in awakening us to more comprehensive theories of personality than had been previously conceived. Their valuable contributions included the concept of the unconscious as an active part of the personality as well as the importance of developing a central sense of Self. Jung in particular was instrumental in highlighting the process of individuation, the reconnection with our sense of 'I' which astrologically is the foundation for the ignition and expansion of the solar light in our chart.

The absence of at least a partially formed sense of self in an intimate relationship can be challenging in several ways including that: the motivation to be in a relationship is more likely to arise from a feeling of emptiness and a fear of aloneness, rather than love. On this basis relationships are likely to eventually disintegrate.

Additionally: deep loving intimacy reconnects us with the memory of our original oneness, requiring a temporary transcendence of our illusory sense of separate self. As we blend our individual solar light with that of our significant other a more expansive and enriching solar light is created which is illustrated by the composite Sun. However, we cannot transcend our individual solar light and blend with that of another if it's largely unformed and barely lighting.

This is particularly relevant with the transit of Neptune in Pisces as this Dionysian god is inviting us to remember who we truly are as we re-connect with our oneness with all.[4] With Neptune's primary energy being one of dissolution, we are more likely to fear the potential of Neptunian disintegration within relationships if our sense of self feels unformed. Hence our inner defenses may be unconsciously activated, resulting in intimacy being kept at bay or sabotaged.

Ultimately the integration of the self with the 'self and other' in relationships, is best described as the balance of the Aries/Libra and 1st/7th house axis.[5] This is an integral theme in all our birth charts but is particularly highlighted as a core soul theme for anyone with planets or nodes in these signs and houses.

In addition to bringing our focus to the need to develop our sense of self, Jung in particular also paved the way for the increase in popular awareness in the '60s of so called 'new age' teachings. Crossing borders from East to West, alternative healing modalities formed a Mercurial bridge, between mind and body, 6th/12th house matters. Tools such as yoga, acupuncture, Reiki, TM meditation, chakra healing bodywork and many more, flourished at this time. Not surprisingly Pluto was in Hermes ruled Virgo at the time.

With Neptune traveling through Scorpio, we were also reminded of the potential sacredness of sex through the increasing popularity in the West of the arts of Tantra and Kundalini. This counteracted the predominant traditional Western religious view of sex being solely for the purpose of procreation or as something to be transcended. Together with the many forms of yoga that increased in popularity, these approaches paved the way for a greater understanding of the integration of spirit, mind, body and emotions. There was also a growing awareness that the 'divine' does not reside in an external paternal all powerful and sometimes fearful punitive god, as prescribed for centuries by some of the more traditional religions. However in these early stages of retaking power back from religious organizations, many initially handed it over to Eastern gurus and teachers, rather than fully integrating it within. Nevertheless, the stage had been set for the personal empowerment required by the current transits and the new relationship paradigm.

Meanwhile, collective structures to do with relationships, such as the institution of marriage, were also being challenged as to their real function and purpose. With divorce rates rapidly increasing[6] we were challenged to consider whether the institution of marriage is fundamentally based on self-empowerment, unconditional love and expansion or on expectations, disempowerment and co-dependency?

These challenges were also reinforced by the second wave of the Women's Movement' in the 60's 70's and 80's. With perfect timing it invited us as a collective to further recognize, re-own and reintegrate the feminine archetype within both genders in a new way. This helped to counterbalance the over active and often distorted masculine archetype that had particularly dominated western culture. In his book 'The Passion of the Western Mind', Rick Tarnas aptly describes that "the crisis of modern man is an essentially masculine crisis, and …its resolution is already now occurring in the tremendous emergence of the feminine in our culture"[7]

Astrologically this accurately describes collective attempts to reconnect with the lunar realm of reflection and feeling, to aid in rebalancing the dominance of the masculine realm of thinking and action, which prevailed since Patriarchy. In taking an evolutionary view of our development, it can be argued that the original purpose of the dominance of the masculine energy had successfully served its cause of "evolving the autonomous human will and intellect: the transcendent self, the independent individual ego, the self-determining human being in its uniqueness, separateness and freedom."[8] However, to do this, "the masculine mind had repressed the feminine" eventually requiring a rebalancing of these two archetypes, which had been successfully highlighted by the Women's Movement.

This re-igniting and re-owning of the feminine[9] principles within us occurred at the same time as mass media exposure of sexual misconduct by both gurus and religious organizations alike, reaching a heightened visibility when Uranus moved into Sagittarius. The time had come for us to take our power back from the guru/priest, on whom we had so easily projected the Father archetype. In so doing we were a step closer to re-integrating the feminine and masculine archetypes within.

At a deeper level we were preparing to integrate more fully as a collective that we didn't need any intermediary to access the divine/spirit part of us. This freed us to move towards a more consciousness based model of relationship anchored in authentic self-empowerment. Astrologically on a macro level we could describe it as the integration and balance of the four elements: fire (Intuition/spirit), earth (body), air (mind) and water (feelings). On an individual micro level it involves the conscious development and expansion of our solar center with the assistance of the other planets. Psychologically this is based on a conscious awareness of self, which is dependent on the integration of all aspects of our personality. From this place of wholeness we can effectively move from more limited approaches in relationship based on: "what can I do to change someone to suit my needs?" to a more expansive inclusive "how can I fully accept the other and love them as they are?" This takes us closer to relationships based on unconditional love with no judgments or expectations.

Co-creating a New Paradigm

In co-creating something new, the first inevitable step involves releasing and transforming the old. Since Pluto's move into Capricorn in 2008 the backbone[10] structures of our collective, including education, politics, finances, religion and healthcare, have been undergoing monumental transformation. With so much attention and panic by the media on the financial and political

194

structures, it has been easy to ignore the changes that have been occurring within relationships.

By its nature, Pluto invites powerful and empowering transmutation and transformation, ultimately leading to the rising of the Phoenix from the ashes. Like the volcanic activity of Madam Pele, the initial stages of this process require a bringing to the surface of all that has been repressed over the ages and a cleansing of what is no longer required. As the molten lava surfaced and flowed whilst Pluto traveled through the first decanate of Capricorn, we have been individually and collectively faced with exploring relationship structures that were not authentically in sync with our soul self.

The challenge so far has been threefold:

1. Releasing destructive patterns within our relationship with our self that are not based on authentic self-value and self-love.

2. Clearing unhelpful relationship patterns and paradigms from this lifetime with current and past partners and parents, as well as from our ancestral line and past lives.

3. Strengthening and/or re-constructing, an authentic integrated personality with a strong yet flexible ego. This can more easily facilitate the challenge of transformation, whilst also supporting the integration of the personality with the soul self.

All three are of course interrelated.

Since Uranus in Aries started squaring Pluto, the transformation process has speeded up and put additional pressure to focus on our individual inner changes. This doesn't mean that we can't be in a relationship during this transformative process, but the structure and nature of the relationship has to allow each person to empower and transform themselves fully. This would not be possible within co-dependent or addictive relationships which are intrinsically based on fear, control and the illusory belief of power residing outside the self. With the core of self-empowerment residing in self-love and self-value, paying heed to the placement of and transits to Venus in our birth chart can greatly assist us at this time.

195

One of the requirements of the new relationship paradigm is for both individuals to do their individual soul and personality work at a similar pace. Differing levels of consciousness and individuation, can throw relationships out of balance, potentially hindering growth for all involved. This may result in a temporary respite from the relationship for one or both individuals to invest in personal development.

In releasing the old relationship paradigm, there's also a greater urgency to transform and heal inner parental archetypes as well as ancestral and past life relationship complexes. Like Inanna's journey to the underworld, our purpose is to let go of old complexes and stories through owning and integrating transpersonal planets in the natal 4th and 10th houses as well as aspects to the Sun and Moon. This may involve returning for periods of time to significant geographic locations including our place of birth, to complete the clearing.

The above tasks are very much a work in progress.[11] As deeper and deeper lava like material has been surfacing from our personal and collective unconscious, Saturn which is in Scorpio until 2015 in mutual reception to Pluto in Capricorn, has also been assisting us in the process of cleansing and transmuting.

Spiritual Partnerships

The Integration and Synthesis of Dualities

Despite both archetypes belonging to the realm of the feminine, to date, mythology, psychology and astrology have mostly differentiated between the lunar and Venusian principles. Attributing unconditional love to the lunar 'maternal' realm, Aphrodite's ability to love is associated with desire rather than compassion. Liz Green describes them as: 'psychological opposites' yet 'two complementary faces of the feminine. The Moon needs to belong to someone, preferably a family or group.... but Venus is her own self ...she does nothing in order to be loved, because she is the essence of the beloved'[12]

The gift of our lunar essence, best described by the sign and placement of the Moon in our chart, is our ability to offer love. This includes and starts with self-love, with its associated gifts of compassion, empathy and nurturing, regardless of any conditions. The gift of Venus is to remind us that without

196

self-value, we are unable to recognize the true value of the other. Our previous relationship paradigm included a split between these two archetypes in the arena of intimate relationships, mostly relegating maternal nurturing to our blood family and tribe, including our close friends, as our adopted tribe. Although the lunar archetype was included in the arena of intimate relationships, the expectation was that the Venusian archetype would dominate this sphere. Hence we seem to have struggled with the possibility of integrating desire and pleasure with unconditional love. Yet in moving towards rebalancing the predominance of the patriarchal masculine with the feminine, we are ideally seeking to integrate the archetypes of both Venus and the Moon into our intimate relationships.

The other important polarity we are seeking to integrate in relationships, is between the earthbound Saturn and the expansive celestial Jupiter. Particularly visible in the institution of marriage, the more restrictive Saturnian archetypes of duty and obligation, seemed to predominate until relatively recently. From the 60's onwards the pendulum swung more towards Jupiterian freedom, leaving an ongoing struggle to integrate these two apparently opposing principles represented by Zeus and Kronos. With these two deities coming together, the possibility of expansive, joyful, conscious relationships, within the containment of love, based on individual freedom rather than restrictive duty, becomes a reality. This I believe was one of the key learning points of the Jupiter Apex opposite Venus Yod on December 21st 2012 which had already previously highlighted in the May 18th 1989 Yod and was repeated on March 17th 2013.

One potential way to integrate the above dualities in this new relationship paradigm is by our soul-self becoming the observer alchemist who blends polar energies into a new unified form. A useful symbolic description of this process, is the image of the dot within the circle of infinity. Imagining the polarity initially as an opposition between the two planetary energies, with the surrounding circle representing the soul self; the resulting energy of the blending of the two energies is the dot in the center. This is beautifully described by June Singer in the following quote: "the newer paradigm that is now emerging begins with awareness of a total unified scheme of reality. It entails a sense of participating in an overarching oneness, not as a separate being but as a particular manifestation of the whole".[13] This ancient symbol of the dot within the circle, has been used throughout the ages to represent cyclic perfection as well as the creative spark of divine consciousness, depicted in many cultures as the Sun or Ra.

Hence, rather than eliminating the duality of both of these valuable archetypes, one of the keys is to engage with each side, releasing what is no longer needed and integrating what is of value. This process is best described by Thomas Moore as 'the need to deepen each side, to imagine each alternative further ...eventually...a third possibility comes into view".[14]

From Conditional to Unconditional love

The current shift in relationships from conditional to unconditional love based on authentic inner soul work, is beautifully described in the myth of Psyche and Eros.

Envious of the beauty of Psyche[15], Aphrodite sent her son Eros[16] to destroy her. However, when Eros saw Psyche, he was so struck by her beauty that he accidentally stabbed himself with one of the arrows he used to make mortals fall in love. Instantly struck by love, Eros rescued Psyche from the rock she had been condemned to by her father and took her to a beautiful palace where he told her that he was her destined husband. Upon Eros' request Psyche promised never to look at him. The couple married with Eros continuing to only visit his bride in the dark of night.

All went well until Psyche's envious sisters suggested that she should try to look at her husband as he was probably an ugly monster. Paying heed to their words, Psyche shone a light on Eros when he was asleep. Totally stunned and jubilant at how handsome he was, she tripped and pricked herself with one of his arrows thereby instantly falling in love with him. However, awoken by a drop of oil that Psyche accidentally dropped on him Eros realized that his bride had broken the promise made to him and he left her. At that instant the castle disappeared and

Psyche found herself back on the rock, heartbroken at the loss of the husband she had now fallen in love with.

Searching for her beloved, Psyche successfully completed numerous challenges set for her by Aphrodite. Still in love with his spouse and in despair of ever being reunited, Eros begged Zeus for help. The god of the heavens agreed to grant Psyche immortality and the couple was reunited. Aphrodite forgave Psyche and there was a second joyful wedding amongst the gods on Mount Olympus.

This myth describes the necessary internal journey we are required to undertake if we wish to create an authentic external 'marriage' with another. In the context of the current transits it describes the challenges that relationships are currently facing in releasing old relationship paradigms and embracing a new way of being that is heart and therefore soul centered. An authentic soul based love comes from challenging our deepest fears and complexes rather than insisting on preserving our naivety as in the case of Psyche or maintaining control as in the case of Eros. In coming together for their second marriage as empowered individuals we are reminded of the power of combining soul with passion, rooted in unconditional love and compassion[17] rather than expectations. This is the true meaning of spiritual partnerships and particularly of twin soul relationships.

Twin soul Relationships - Transformation and Transmutation

In moving to a new relationship paradigm our desire to reconnect with our twin souls feels more urgent. These are souls whom we have had a depth loving connection and agreements with over many lifetimes and whom we instantly recognize when we look into each other's eyes. Our main agreement is a commitment to ongoing mutual soul growth. Although it is one of several possible spiritual partnerships, it is in all likelihood the most intense and passionate one. In reconnecting as twin souls, the individual energies ignite and expand, creating a powerful healing and transformative force.

One of the keys to sustaining a twin soul relationship is for the two individuals to consciously maintain a sacred triad between each other and the greater soul of the relationship, whom they are in service to. Consciously retaining individual and joint awareness of the greater spiritual purpose, maintains an easier flow of energy, similar to the trine configuration in a chart. This helps to dissipate potential oppositional confrontations between the two individuals that can easily occur in the alchemical transformational and transmutational nature which is at the heart of twin soul relationships. Unconditional love and an ongoing commitment to the relationship and to individual self-growth form an alchemical container for powerful transformation to occur. If this is not present, projection of unresolved issues, such as a lack of individuation from family of origin, is likely to make the relationship unsustainable in the long term, as it will hinder rather than enhance the soul growth of both individuals.

With twin soul relationships reoccurring in many lifetimes, it is only a depth awareness of their individual complexes that can also assist the couple to differentiate which relationship dynamics belong to this lifetime rather than previous ones.

As with any relationship our involvement in a twin soul relationship is always subject to free will and choice. However often it is not an easy decision as the consequences can feel heavy on our heart. This is aptly described by past life regression therapist Dr. Brian Weiss "destiny dictates the meeting of soulmates. We will meet them. But what we decide to do after that meeting falls in the province of choice or free will. A wrong choice or a missed chance can lead to incredible loneliness and suffering. A right choice, an opportunity realized can bring us to profound bliss and happiness". [18]

Creating Something Bigger

If the myth of Eros and Psyche were to continue after their second marriage, the outcome of their deep love would most likely result in an expansion of their joint energy fields into the universe for the benefit of all. This could take place through a creative project, a contribution to the collective and/or through the birth of children.

Unlike previous relationship paradigms which have been predominantly based on the willingness of both partners to meet each other's personality and practical needs, spiritual partnerships are based on supporting and enhancing each other's soul growth as equal partners on life's journey. Like Psyche and Eros, both individuals need to engage with their shadow self as well as having the capacity to forgive each other's human imperfections. This can only fully take place in the context and container of unconditional love, which in turn is dependent on the ability of both individuals to recognize themselves in the other. The now commonly used greeting 'Namaste,' meaning the soul in me recognizes the soul in you, is a reminder of our sameness, notwithstanding our uniqueness.

With several years of Chiron[19] traveling alongside Neptune first in Aquarius and then in Pisces, we have been offered a truly unique opportunity to dissolve and release the human wounding of separateness. Similarly to homeopathic remedies which often heal through offering us an initial experience of the symptom we are seeking to clear, the initial feeling of this transit for many was one of loneliness and confusion as the suppressed feelings came to the surface. This is most likely to have been felt by those with strong aspects between Neptune and the personal planets in the birth chart as well as Pisces and/or Neptune on the angles. Also for the generation with Chiron in Pisces, who experienced Neptune conjunct natal Chiron at their Chiron return and those who went through the midlife transit of Neptune square Neptune between 2012 and 2013.

With the veil lifting and the distancing in the sky between Chiron and Neptune, we are now healing the above illusory sense of aloneness and increasingly engaging with the Neptunian awareness of our innate interconnection with all.

What can assist us in our Intimate Relationships?

1. Continuing to engage with Saturn in Scorpio to authentically face our greatest fears and engage with the dissolution and release of the energies that have been tied around our complexes. This work includes pulling back our projections from our loved ones and taking full self-empowered responsibility for our choices. Saturn in Scorpio can also assist us to reconnect with our deepest passions within ourselves which we can then choose to express in our relationships. Honesty and authenticity are required at all times with

this configuration, particularly in the Plutonian arenas of sexual intimacy and shared resources. The natal house which Saturn is currently transiting as well as the house and sign position of natal Saturn will give an indication of which fears and complexes are ready to be released.[20]

2. Embracing the energy of the Uranus/Pluto square to release, transform and transmute any parts of ourselves which are not authentic and in alignment with our soul self. This is an ideal time to create a new sense of self that is strongly grounded and aligned with our soul. Depending on the overall elemental balance in our chart we can choose from a variety of therapeutic tools that are easily available. Predominantly earthy individuals may for example find bodywork, exercising in nature and sculpture helpful and within their comfort zone. However it can also be useful to move outside our elemental comfort zone. Hence for anyone with a lack of air, tools that include breathwork can be of great assistance.

The energies of the square can also assist us in releasing and transforming the structures within our relationships that are not aligned with our soul self, knowing that the releasing process also contains the seeds of an innovative new birth. For some couples this may involve building some time apart into the relationship whereas for others it may involve structuring in more creative time together. Mapping the current Uranus/Pluto transit on the composite chart of the relationship in conjunction with where it lands on the individual charts can assist in assessing which relationship structures might benefit from being transformed.

3. Engaging with the energy of Neptune in Pisces to remember who we truly are as equal yet unique creative parts of the whole, on a spiritual journey in human form on this planet. Through loving ourselves and each other unconditionally with compassion and total acceptance and allowing our heart to take the lead over our mind, we can truly create heaven on earth. This nonverbal energy is particularly accessible through the creative arts including music, poetry, art, photography and dance as well as through spiritual tools

202

such as meditation, yoga, color, sound and crystal healing, energy work and guided visualizations.

All of this is a work in progress. In the meantime I leave you with a final quote from the wise musings of Thomas Moore:

> The point in a relationship is …to lead us into a profound alchemy of soul that reveals to us many of the pathways and openings that are the geography of our own destiny and potentiality.

Endnotes

1. Based on the original Greek meaning of the term Psychology as the study of the *psūchê* meaning soul/spirit

2. The term Soul Self is used in this context to describe the part of each of us that is aligned with our soul, which in turn is a part of the divine and which Jung said "might equally be called the God within us". Ideally the ego revolves around it "very much as the earth revolves around the sun". (C.G. Jung Two Essays CW 7)

3. For more information on working with the ego from a new paradigm you may wish to refer to Eric Meyers book *The Astrology of Awakening Volume 1: Eclipse of the Ego*

4. The potential for this is particularly highlighted for anyone going through their Neptune square Neptune transit. This is discussed later in the chapter.

5. Not surprisingly both Freud and Jung had their natal sun in the 7th house

6. From 1960 to 1980, the divorce rate more than doubled. *National Affairs*, Issue 1, Fall 2009.

7. Richard Tarnas, *The Passion of the Western Mind*, pp. 442- 443.

8. Ibid.

9. In using the terms "feminine" and "masculine," I am referring to the archetypal qualities within each of us, rather than to gender differentiation.

10. Capricorn rules our skeletal structure.

11. These are not new tasks for many of us. The difference at the moment is that the current transits offer us the possibility of resolving ancestral and past life issues in a way that was not likely to have been consciously available to us before now.

12. Liz Greene and Howard Sasportas, *The Inner Planets,* p. 73

13. June Singer, *The Power of Love to Transform our Lives and Our World,* p.142

14. Thomas Moore, *Soulmates,* p. 149

15. Meaning: soul/spirit

16. Meaning: romantic/erotic love

17. Described by Buddhism as one of the four elements of true love. The other three are: Maitri meaning loving-kindness, Mudita meaning joy and Upeksha meaning freedom Thich Nhat Hanh, *True Love,* pp. 1 -4

18. Brian Weiss, M.D. *Only Love is Real* Grand Central Publishing. New York. Boston. 2000. Preface

19. The Centaur Chiron is known as: the wounded healer. His position by sign and aspect reminds us of our wounding as humans, which when faced with compassion and understanding can turn into an ability to offer healing to others. For further information, you may wish to consult Melanie Reinhart, *Chiron and the Healing Journey* and Zane Stein *Essence and Application: A View From Chiron.*

20. For further information on Saturn in the natal chart and by transit, you may wish to consult Greene, Liz. *Saturn: A New Look at an Old Devil* and Sullivan, Erin. *Saturn in Transit.*

13

Killer in the Home

Sherene Vismaya Schostak

> The deadly arrows do not strike the hero from without; it
> is himself who hunts, fights, and tortures himself. In him,
> instinct wars with instinct; therefore the poet says, "Thyself
> pierced through" which means he is wounded with his own
> arrow.
>
> – Carl Jung[1]

With so much getting stirred up in our collective unconscious regarding our relationship to violence—the most recent topic being gun laws—this subject matter seems more critical than ever. If we are to become the change we wish to see in the world, we have got to look at how we handle the loaded guns in our own souls. How can the horoscope reveal how we deal with our own defenses, anger, violence and psychic weaponry? This chapter will take a Jungian astrological approach to delve into the inner "killer" as saboteur versus mass murderer approached from a Jungian astrological approach. I will break down the relevant archetypes and decipher how they might be reflected in individual natal horoscopes. Where is this inner killer lurking in our own psyches? How is this destructive energy constellated? It sounds so foreboding at the onset.

Of course, most of us would like to believe we are quite sweet and civilized and the killers are those evil gun-toting hillbillies or psychos "out there." In fact, the killer is closer than we would like to think. In Jungian terms, the killer is often a negative aspect of the animus or unconscious masculine archetype of reason and spirit in women. The counterpart in male psychology is the anima or soul archetype for men—and she certainly has her own mysterious ways of "killing softly." in a different way. Although we will be focusing on how the animus becomes constellated for women, this chapter should useful to men in understanding deeper unconscious aspects of the feminine within and without.

> The animus is the deposit, as it were, of all woman's ancestral experiences of man - and not only that, he is also a creative and procreative being, not in the sense of masculine creativity, but in the sense that he brings forth something we might call... the spermatic word.
>
> - Carl Jung[2]

The animus is the unconscious masculine constellation found in the female psyche. Also known as spirit or the spiritual force in a woman's psyche, the animus serves as a bridge between the ego and the unconscious as a woman becomes more conscious and individuated from her personal, familial and ancestral complexes. The animus is also considered a composite of all of the male influences and imagery in a woman's life—and potentially past lives—that have left an imprint upon her psyche. The father complex is one of the greatest influences in forming the animus.

The absence of the father during crucial developmental years can constellate either a negative or positive father complex, or some combination thereof. The positive version is the search for an idealized older father figure or external sources of validation and self-esteem, with a hyper-emphasis on worldly achievement. A negative version creates great fear and distrust of men and, authority, and great difficulty finding success in the world.

From a psychological perspective, one would definitely want to inquire deeper into the residual influence from the relationships with the father and grandfathers, both maternal and paternal, in understanding the makeup of the animus. The killer animus is born from a negative father complex. It is a deeply distorted version of what went awry in the relationship with the father, as we will see Sylvia Plath's case demonstrates. Later in this chapter, we will examine the loss of losing her father at the young age of eight and how powerfully that loss imprinted her psyche and affected the development of her killer animus.

For a more direct experience of what the animus is like, you can catch a glimpse of his influence through your self-talk. According to Jung, watch for any absolute statements or harshly negative blanket statements that you make about yourself, your creative work, or especially the men in your life. There is something very limiting about the voice of the animus, and he would have you always err on the side of the negative or the worst-case scenario. You'll hear him say things such as, "It's just the way things are," or, "Whatever, I don't want it anyway." It has the ring of the overly cynical Saturnian attitude of, "It is what it is." There is something very cynical and life-draining about the energy of the negative animus. Anytime you feel, "What's the point?" or "Why bother?" with that certain and arrogant defense, you can bet you're in animus possession.

According to Jung, the best defense against the animus is to think of putting his negative opinions, assumptions, and predictions in a test tube and sealing it up and moving forward with conviction and commitment. If you give the animus free rein, he will surely throw black paint all over everything and have you continually doubting or second-guessing—looking for the holes in everything. Marion Woodman's analyst used to tell her to take the animus out for a good drink.

The negative animus often appears to women in dreams in the form of a killer, as a means of revealing self-destructive aspects lurking in the unconscious. The transformational potential of working with the animus is the bridge to the spiritual and creative potential of the soul. Of course, the work must be followed up with years of intensive self-analysis, inner work, and journaling practice to see real results.

Astrology is an excellent tool for mapping out or zeroing in on this deep and challenging process. I would like to propose a theory of how to uncover the animus potential in the horoscope, specifically the killer energy inherent in the more negative unconscious aspect. Most simply, we would look to Saturn, the Descendant, and any powerful aspects to either of these. I have found this to be quite a consistent and reliable method in my sixteen years of private practice as a Jungian therapist and astrologer.

In her book *The Ravaged Bridegroom*[3], Jungian analyst Marion Woodman has said the loaded gun is either aimed within or pointed out. Either way, the energy is deadly. It may consist of repressed rage, fear, self-loathing, or some other amalgam of destructive instincts buried in our shadow—aspects of ourselves that we started rejecting around the age of seven, during the first Saturn square, when the shadow and seventh house of the horoscope first began to crystallize. Any and every aspect we have decided is "them," and not "us," or that lives outside of us becomes part of the shadow. Any forbidden, rejected, shamed, unloved, intolerable, ridiculed, or simply ignored aspects of the self often gets constellated in the shadow. By studying the archetypal forces surrounding the Descendant/seventh house cusp of the horoscope and any aspects to the planetary lord governing this house, one can gain insight into the shadow energy. Although the first instinct when thinking about the inner killer may be to check out where Mars or Pluto are lurking in the horoscope, I recommend first working with the seventh house aspects for clues and then integrating Saturn, and then of course looking at Mars, Pluto, and the nodes for a deeper understanding of the composite of potentially destructive energy within. The less conscious water houses—fourth, eighth, and twelfth—can also reveal deeper aspects of unconscious underpinnings of the shadow constellation. However, that level of detail is beyond the scope of this chapter. For the purpose of honing in on the inner killer in the space allotted, I will focus mostly on the Descendant and Saturn.

Let's take a quick tour through the shadow aspect of the animus by sign. You can apply the descriptions below to themes around Descendant and Saturn configurations in the horoscope.

The Aries Shadow

When embracing the Aries shadow, one immediately thinks of primal scream energy. It is helpful to consider where anger, selfishness, aggression or competition was denied to the child or rejected in the child's instinctual responses. You often see anger internalized or expressed more passive–aggressively when this shadow energy is struggling for expression. Migraines or general fatigue often arise when the individual has no way of directly expressing frustration or other competitive instincts.

Shadow symbols: the bossy boss, bitch, competitor, warrior, man or woman with a gun, weapons, boxers, competition, war, battle scenes, fights, accidents, injuries, ambulances, rams.

The Taurus Shadow

A fear of loss of control or possession over the love object can often arise. Here we would look to see what Venus is trying to express in the horoscope. Is there a wound around beauty, the voice or the body? Food and money often play an important role in helping this individual come to consciousness. A fear of losing control or losing what one values most and holds most dear could be deeply buried at the core of this shadow complex.

Shadow symbols: dogs, clingy or dependent characters, robbers, lost wallets, food (especially sweets), jewelry, money, bulls, roses, fabric, grass, earth, gardens.

The Gemini Shadow

Lies, lies, lies, yeah. This is the "one foot out the door" shadow. Duplicity and evasiveness play an important part in uncovering the shadow energy of the Trickster. One often finds a puer or puella (the eternal youth archetype) terrified of growing up. Commitment issues often plague the life of this shadow figure. There is a quick, mercurial "I don't wanna grow up" rebellion to this shadow that prefers causing mischief and quickly slipping in and out of situations to avoid getting "caught" or "trapped." Inner splits and Jekyll-and-Hyde kinds of dramas ensue.

Shadow symbols: words, messages, doubles, twins, doppelgangers, magicians, salesmen, homosexuals or bisexuals, bad boys, teenagers, innocent boy or girl turned killer, monkey, gossip/tabloid, lies, books, school, neighbors, lovers, other languages.

The Cancer Shadow

The Cancer shadow may reveal an overwhelming need to be babied and taken care of. However, any needs for nurturing may be so repressed and deeply buried that the individual covers them up by being ridiculously self-sufficient. Longing for the past, withholding affection or just a generalized sense of apathy may feel pervasive. The shadow will convince this individual that her needs will never be met—so why get emotionally close or too involved with anyone? Yet at the bottom of this shadow is a strong need for emotional contact, support and connection.

Shadow Symbols: bottles, photos from the past, mother figures, food, babies, nostalgic places, bathtubs, kitchens, vessels, pearls, breasts, nursing, childhood, photo albums.

The Leo Shadow

This is the "attention whore" shadow needing (if not demanding) proper respect, appreciation, and recognition. The need to be treated as special or part of the elite dominates the unconscious responses of the Leo shadow. There is a bit of a super star or rock star complex that wants to be spoiled, pampered and fawned over. At the core of this shadow is the need to feel cherished and deeply loved, but this is often masked by a need to collect admirers and more superficial attention to prove how "wanted" the individual is.

Shadow symbols: celebrities, luxurious settings, red carpet, velvet, diamonds, queens, cats, fame, the stage, rock stars, gold.

The Virgo Shadow

This is the selfless helper shadow who wants to take no credit for any work or service. The problem with this shadow is that so much work and attention are spent taking care of others that often a huge well of worry and self-neglect can kick in. The shadow may make itself known in a hypochondriacal fashion with a slew of mysterious symptoms or overall malaise. Physical complaints, excessive worry or just a nervous edge to the personality may dominate when the individual has lost connection to her own inner life and magic. There can also be a bit of the Madonna/Whore complex; the individual is split between purity/celibacy and a dark subservience to the sexual needs of others.

Shadow symbols: hermits, simple folk, workers, ascetics, monks, healers, nuns, secretaries, nurses, janitors, aids, witches, madonnas, blue collar workers, prostitutes.

The Libra Shadow

This is the *too good is no good* shadow. The need for harmony, connection and partnership may be terrifying to the individual afraid to lose independence. Underlying a lot of bravado and seeming aggressive energy may be a soul simply scared of rejection, not being liked, or not being good enough. There is a strong need to feel one is sweet and likable—and, most importantly, beautiful.

210

Shadow symbols: weddings, beauty queens, models, the scales, court, couples, relationships, doves, peace, makeup, symmetrical images, roses, rose quartz, trials.

The Scorpio Shadow

Many deep and dark secrets are buried in this shadow. This is the jealous femme fatale shadow, often cloaked in a persona of wanting to be loving, loyal and supportive. If you dig deeper, you'll discover a ruthless need to be number one and possess the object of one's desire. You may also discover a terror of death and loss of control similar to the Taurus shadow. A person may have to work hard to recover the depths of her sexuality with this shadow.

Shadow symbols: death, graves, funerals, crows, skulls, sunsets, killers, poison, insects, subways, snakes, debt, taxes, underworld scenes, black imagery.

Sagittarius Shadow

Here you may discover a bit of a dogmatic shadow lurking behind an extremely intelligent and seemingly versatile facade. As mentally flexible, tolerant and neutral as this person may like to believe she is, when you scratch beneath the surface you'll often uncover some very rigid beliefs that are not up for debate. Although this individual would never want to consider herself a preacher, often you'll find her shadow working a serious soapbox or two.

Shadow symbols: religious figures, gurus, teachers, debates, Santa Claus-type figures, horses, open fields, airplanes, sky, foreign people, foreign lands, scriptures, rainbows.

Capricorn Shadow

This shadow is likely to give all of her power and authority over to another while repressing her own need for structure, discipline and boundaries. It may be easier to remain in the role of the child and force others into the role of the strict or overly controlling parental figure she is afraid of owning in her own psyche. Here is where people often fall into sadomasochistic patterns. If one

211

does not own and integrate some aspect of shame or self-doubt, one may constantly feel criticized, rejected or judged by the partner or others.

Shadow symbols: wise elders, mountains, rocks, traditional scenes or images, antiquity, time, clocks, aging, father figures, bosses, authority figures, black imagery, stones, dryness, winter.

Aquarius Shadow

All of the kinkier and eccentric aspects of the self often become concealed in this shadow. There is a hidden need to shock others in a way to test or perhaps push them away. There is often a fear of losing one's individuality or quirky and unique aspects by getting too close to others. Often there is a dreaded refusal to get lost in a crowd or just become one of the masses.

Shadow symbols: electricity, friends, communities, crowds, groups, electronics, anything kinky or bizarre, rebels, humanitarians, stars, the universe, altruism, people with a detached or objective demeanor, lightning, breakthroughs.

Pisces Shadow

Meet the savior complex and victim/perpetrator constellation. As with Pisces in general, there are multitudes of possibility with this shadow. The strongest themes seem to revolve around feeling victimized or helpless to change one's circumstances, addictions, or any other arena where there has been a merger, submersion or fusion with someone or something idealized. If this someone or something is not truly of the realm of the divine, there is trouble as disillusionment and disappointment prevail.

Shadow symbols: ocean, swamps, swimming pools, fish, spiritual places, ashrams, hotels, mystics, unicorns, other worlds, fog, steam, deception, dancers, musicians, poets, illusions, mirages, addicts, wells.

> What we women have to overcome in our relation to the
> animus is not pride but lack of self-confidence and the
> resistance of inertia. For us, it is not as though we had to

212

demean ourselves, but as if we had to lift ourselves" - Emma Jung[4]

One of the most obvious ways the killer energy operates is through self-sabotage. In trying to write this chapter, I have had to contend with the killer/saboteur aspect of my animus (Gemini) attempting to cut me off from finishing with the cleverest of ploys, just as the animus is wont to do. The "cutting off" aspect is very common for the animus. I can attest to the truth of the above quote, by Jung's wife, about the animus: the inertia aspect. Each time I sat down to write this chapter, I was instantly overcome with extreme exhaustion no matter what time of day it was or how much sleep I had gotten the night before. Some nights I would actually go to bed by 6:00 PM just to avoid writing. And then of course come the clever forms of distraction and procrastination. Everything and anything one can possibly imagine would come up as an interruption at the precise time I had set aside to work on the chapter.

Barbara Hannah has said that the animus cannot stand to be written about because he does not want to be revealed or "found out." If you saw the film *Sylvia*, you might recall the famous scene in which she is struggling to write poetry and instead ends up baking a huge collection of pies every day while the page remains empty. That is a classical description of how the animus likes to block, stifle, sabotage and create inertia. It also sounds very much like unconscious Saturn influence. Thus making this energy conscious is incredibly valuable in "unlocking" our creative potential and becoming conscious of the roots of our individual styles of inertia and procrastination.

But what about the more foreboding aspect of the animus killer? There is a version that feels far more akin to a bad nightmare or a horror film than a state of inertia. I will share a personal account of my own animus experience. This will illustrate how close to "home" this killer can be, while also lending a useful portrayal of some rather classic Jungian themes around the killer energy of the animus.

I was recently divorced and was also recovering from two important deaths, all within one six-month period, marking a huge turning point in my life. I had formed a pretty close friendship with a man who was coming to visit me the following day. That night I had this dream:

I am in my office when I hear a knock on the door. I open the door to discover a sweet and innocent little boy with a dog. The boy wants to come in. As soon as I invite him in, a menacing figure comes out of the shadows and forces entry into my office. The little innocent boy and dog were the dacoit. I realize I am in deep trouble. This killer intends to rip me to my death—limb by limb. In my horror, I realize I have no protector. No father figure. Not even my (ex)husband.

As dreams often are, this dream was far ahead of my consciousness and my life and would take about a year or so to reveal many of its secrets and insights to my conscious mind as it "played out" in my next relationship. I certainly got to meet my animus and the killer inherent within. The next several months brought me face to face with the depths of my unconscious killer: fear, hatred, self-loathing, anguish, criticism, death, rage and every other destructive instinct we would all like to believe only exist in the worlds of killers and psychotics. They are we. If you've ever fallen "madly in love," you may very well have had the opportunity to meet this killer. Sometimes this aspect of the animus is known as the "Demon Lover" because of that possessed state we often feel and the accompanying horror when things go awry in the love affair. If you've ever felt your life force being sucked out of you, or as if you're constantly walking on eggshells, or "in the presence of a real God"...you know you're in animus country.

Often this energy will meet you in the form of an addiction. Any state of possession where the mind finds itself continuously and relentlessly obsessed is part and parcel of this archetype. Any form of self-sabotage will reveal the inner killer, even if he or she is killing us softly. My natal Saturn in Taurus (the dog symbol) is in a tight opposition to my stellium of Scorpio planets (Sun, Venus, Jupiter) in the twelfth house (which might also explain my fascination with such a dark subject matter). You could almost call my twelfth house "killer in the home," with Pluto/Mars lording over it and the conglomeration of the death archetype residing within. My Gemini Descendant might explain the "innocent" little boy who lured me into allowing the actual killer to emerge from the shadows. The killer in my dream was old and Saturnian—gaunt, dry and severe. Since Mercury is the ruler of my seventh house, it might also explain why I feel the need to write and teach about the animus. My Mercury is in Scorpio in the twelfth house and squares my Aquarius–Leo nodal access in the third and ninth, which doubles this theme of teaching/writing about death/killer/animus issues (when the animus lets me).

Sadly, we see how far the animus can go in the suicides of so many creatives. As noted earlier in this chapter, Sylvia Plath comes to mind, as her story is a sad but classic case of the animus tragedy. The final stanzas of her poem "Daddy" reverberates with archetypal imagery so representative of Saturn and also her inner animus constellation:

If I've killed one man, I've killed two—
The vampire who said he was you
And drank my blood for a year,
Seven years, if you want to know.
Daddy, you can lie back now.

There's a stake in your fat black heart
And the villagers never liked you.
They are dancing and stamping on you.
They always knew it was you.
Daddy, daddy, you bastard, I'm through.[5]

Plath clearly projected much of her animus onto her husband (poet Ted Hughes), which is why the relationship was so fraught with passion and crippling pain. What made it even more dangerous is that he embodied the very form of written expression with which her own animus had to compete. She lost her father at such a young age (and during the critical time of the first Saturn square), which obviously set the stage for a very powerful father complex. That level of loss and abandonment for such a sensitive soul led to her first suicide attempt at her second Saturn square at age 21. She had a very powerful Saturn in the late degrees of Capricorn, making it extremely dominant in the chart.

You can hear in this poem how the relationship with the father constellated an inner fascist/killer/dictator, with deadly and debilitating consequences for her psyche. You can feel the resounding Saturnian archetypes in almost every image of this poem, from the title to the barbed wire fence to the black boot to the bones to the black heart—and all of the fascist imagery. The vampire image is often linked with the animus killer as it drinks the life force—drinking her blood for seven years (Saturn cycles). Since Capricorn is often linked to the Devil archetype in the Major Arcana of the Tarot, it is the Demon Lover.

To make matters even more intense, Plath's Saturn was in a cardinal T-square with Pluto and Uranus. The missing leg of the square is Libra, which is the sign of her Moon—an archetype/image found in many of her poems:

If the Moon smiled she would resemble you.
You both leave the same impression
Of something beautiful, but annihilating.
Both of you are great light borrowers. (from *The Rival*)[5]

Plath's chart had a Leo Descendant, and the ruler of her Scorpio Sun (Pluto) sat in her fifth house of love affairs and creativity. Although they do not form a grand cross by degree, the Saturn–Pluto–Uranus–Moon influence can be seen in her relationship to her animus killer. Stealing the light (similar to Lucifer) is another frequent image of the animus or Demon Lover.

On the positive side, her inner animus was a genius and clearly one of the most powerful poets in history—but he was also a deadly killer. At the time of her Saturn return at age thirty, Sylvia Plath committed suicide.

How to heal, transform and integrate this inner killer? I recommend working with your own dream imagery, or the dream imagery of your clients, in relationship to Saturn/seventh house themes to better elucidate what the animus/shadow is trying to make conscious. The horoscope is a wonderful tool to help you hone in on specific archetypal themes. By exploring these themes in a sacred temenos (space) with your client, you bring awareness to the personal evolution in her process of self-understanding, or as Jungians would say, individuation or wholeness. For eons, we have heard astrologers say "do your Saturn, do your Saturn," and you can make him an ally instead of the god that devours your creativity and innocence. Working with the animus is similar.

When Sylvia Plath separated from her husband, Ted Hughes, she revoked the projection of her animus that had been deeply entrenched in her

216

relationship with him from the get-go (as expressed in her very Venus–Neptune-themed poem "The Hanging Man": "By the roots of my hair some god got hold of me. / I sizzled in his blue volts like a desert prophet....").[5] It was after the separation that she stopped baking pies and started writing some of her best work. Sadly, she relapsed, feeling betrayed by him, and her own deteriorating psychological state led to animus possession, and ultimately the death archetype became tragically concretized in suicide.

So it may be with individuals possessing a strong Pluto/Saturn nature unless they can channel it into something powerfully creative and die a little each day to the old outworn garments of Self in a conscious manner. When we can embrace and love our inner killers, that destructive energy becomes powerfully creative, and we can triumph over inertia. This is a daily battle and constant struggle for women. We must literally fight the inner killer to keep our creativity alive and thriving.

> Dying is an art, like everything else. I do it exceptionally well. I do it so it feels like hell. I do it so it feels real. I guess you could say I've a call.
>
> - Sylvia Plath

Endnotes

1. Jung, Carl. *Symbols of Transformation, Collected Works 5*, p. 291. (Princeton University Press, 1957).

2. Jung, Carl. Anima and Animus, in *Two Essays on Analytical Psychology, Collected Works 7*, p. 208. (Princeton University Press, 1966)

3. Woodman, Marion. *The Ravaged Bridegroom: Masculinity in Women.* (Inner City Book, 1990).

4. Jung, Emma. *Animus and Anima.* (Spring Publications, 1957).

5. Plath, Sylvia. *Collected Poems.* (Harper Perennial Modern Classics, 2008).

14

No Such Thing as Source?

Toward an Understanding of Sacred Duality in Evolutionary Astrology

Adam Elenbaas

Let me start by saying that I am admittedly someone who likes to push the buttons of those who hold common New Age beliefs and dogmas, and this feature of my personality is probably as pathological as anything I ever take the time to call out or criticize. Nonetheless, if I had to describe my spiritual practice in this lifetime, I would say it has been the mental and intellectual exploration of the opposites. I read everything I can of world religions and philosophy, astrology and metaphysics, and I take time to see both the similarities and the differences in various metaphysical systems of thought. I also try to see these similarities and differences in myself and in my everyday life.

For the past few years, I've resisted the common urge to reduce all world religions to oneness; I am instead interested in understanding the very real differences between metaphysical dispositions. I have found that, by doing this, I am resisting the urge to get trapped by my fiery Christian Protestant upbringing; instead, I am opening myself to truly consider many different ideas about God, the Universe, evolution, the soul, etc. After all, it's just so easy to make everything about oneness, package it like a sticker with all the religious icons spread out in a circle like a 1970s smiley face, slap a few posts about unity and wholeness on my Facebook wall, and get nice and comfortable in yet another version of the same old evangelical tunnel vision. In the New Age, I've noticed, Jesus is just called "oneness," sin is now called "separation consciousness," and salvation is called "awakening to the source."

I've recently come to something like a working hypothesis about the Sun and the Moon in astrology that has helped me to understand the two major spiritual/metaphysical types of dispositions that I've come across, both in my reading of other popular astrologers and thinkers in the metaphysical fields, and in terms of the major ways in which spiritual people end up polarized within their own spiritual practices.

The Solar Spiritual Philosophy

From the solar point of view, spiritual life is about linear evolution. We originate from a non-dual source energy or singularity point, and we are returning to that source. Some people go so far as to say that the source energy point is God (and God doesn't have to be an old man in the sky; God can be a more evolved singularity or source point). This view closely relies on (and popularly explicates) the Big Bang and expansion theory of the universe, in which the universe begins with a kind of non-dual singularity point (which defies or cannot be explained by the laws of physics) and explodes outwards. As the universe appears, duality appears. Duality, as source theorists explain to us, is the manifestation of seemingly separate systems, bodies, and time and space itself, all of which have their essence in the creation/explosion of an original, perhaps non-dual, "source."

From this point of view, duality has its origin in non-duality. This is of course logically problematic. How can we say that non-duality is the source when the very concept of *source* implies the notion of something extending from the source or holding space for the source? Non-dual enthusiasts will tell you that you have to let go of the logical mind and embrace paradox in order to grasp their thinking about source. Similarly, scientists will tell you that the original singularity point cannot yet be explained by the laws of physics.

Should we really put our faith in a non-dual source that we can't quite talk about in a logically cohesive way? And why do we keep trying to do so?

A case in point is the violently solipsistic New Age tome, *A Course in Miracles*. Insisting that God or the true, non-dualistic self is the only truth, the book—which claims to be the channeled voice of Jesus—struggles on for hundreds of pages, like Plato on a bad acid and cocaine rant, trying to say that there is only one truth, one reality, one higher self, and that we should do away

219

with all dualistic ideas of selfhood. The course does this, of course, while always simultaneously doubling back to say that these non-truth dualism delusions are also the truth. By the time I had finished the book, which I read in earnest (and even performed all 365 exercises), my largest question for the transmitted text was, "So how does it feel to have the world's largest case of linear thinking denial?"

Joseph Campbell aptly summarizes the masculine or patriarchal solar philosophy in his *Masks of God* series:

> The Patriarchal point of view is distinguished from the earlier [lunar] archaic view by its setting apart of all pairs-of-opposites—male and female, life and death, true and false, good and evil—as though they were absolutes in themselves and not merely aspects of the larger entity of life. This we may liken to a solar, as opposed to lunar, mythic view, since darkness flees from the sun as its opposite, but in the moon dark and light interact in one sphere.[1]

Similarly, in many evolutionary astrological communities, the highest levels of consciousness are imaged as those closer to the Sun, which is likened to the non-dual source. The element of the Sun in astrology is similarly likened to fire, another masculine or *yang* element. Of course, these non-dual points of view mostly come from men, and they are, as *A Course in Miracles* is, solipsistic and unavoidably dualistic in their logic. The word "highest" or "higher" is a word of dualism. The very words *non-dual* and *source* are both, at their worst, frustrated manifestations of the very same religiously fueled illogical impulses that led the male church fathers to condemn sin, condemn the body, and condemn women. They are the very same impulses that will always insist upon the linear evolution toward something non-dual, which is also claimed to be the only reality anyway. This extreme solar thinking, in all its illogical fumbling, makes a case for both the superiority and total dominance of an energy (the singular solar energy) that is always, no matter how illogically or paradoxically it tries to fight or establish itself as the sole reality, entangled with something "other," and someone "else."

220

At its best, the solar philosophy gives us real linear growth experiences and a linear evolution paradigm (which we can probably all agree is a valuable spiritual reality). The solar philosophy also reminds us that forms have essence. At its worst, the solar paradigm forgets its dependency upon, and rages against, the lunar paradigm, insisting its comparatively relative schema isn't real, or worse, is demonic or evil or less evolved.

The Lunar Philosophy

In contrast to the solar point of view, Joseph Campbell writes of the lunar point of view: "The wonderful ability of the serpent to slough its skin and so renew its youth has earned for it throughout the world the character of the master of the mystery of rebirth—of which the moon, waxing and waning, sloughing its shadow and again waxing, is the celestial sign."[2]

From the lunar point of view, there is no such thing as source energy without the simultaneous existence of life forms through which the life force can be incarnated, reflected, and circulated. To the lunar, the source does not come first or beget duality because, to the lunar, there was never a beginning or original begetting; and there will never be an end, either, to the dance of the opposites.

From the lunar point of view, there is no oneness without duality. There is no essence without form. No good without evil, and no consciousness without unconsciousness. The lunar viewpoint is therefore, generally speaking, more readily in touch with the presence of the Sun, or source, as its equal opposite than the Sun is of the Moon as an equal opposite. The solar point of view tends to see itself as absolute, as all that there is, as the point from which everything generates and returns; and yet it cannot divorce itself from its equal opposite relationship to the manifestational and reincarnational lunar.

In terms of a spiritual philosophy, the lunar point of view is thus quieter about any transcendent mission. The lunar philosophy is about imminence: This is it. There is no evolution toward something. There is no awakening. There is no grand design toward which we are heading. There is no source/God. There is no problem of evil or free will. There is perhaps no continuous or higher organizing "self" either. There is only the infinity of time and space and the flowing dance of the opposites. Progress and growth and

221

evolution toward anything, including the non-dual, are to the lunar as transient as the breath in and the breath out.

To understand the lunar philosophy in terms of a new popular theoretical physics standpoint, we might invoke the recent cyclic universe theory of Paul Steinhardt and Neil Turok. Imagine two infinite membranes and imagine space between them. They have been and always will be colliding with each other. Each time they collide the membranes create big bangs, or universes. The universes expand and then contract, and then the membranes collide again and the process repeats. There is infinite time and space. There is infinite time and space, infinite duality (i.e., the presence of the opposites – truly opposite yet interconnected – infinite and without origin). Singularity, from this point of view, is just an illusion of a never-ending, always existing cyclical process. The source is not an ultimate origin point, and therefore it's not a final return point either; it's just one aspect of an endless dualistic fluctuating.

Of course, this view is no less spiritual and no less capable of imagining or experiencing what we might call divinity or even linear evolutionary growth focus; it's just that we don't need to imagine *source* as beyond or behind or above the dualistic "illusion" that we're trying to "evolve through" right now. We don't have to fight endlessly against our common sense, trying to imagine oneness without using contradictory dualistic logic. From this point of view, all of the source conceptualizing of the universe that we do is merely like one half of the brain (the half that works with linear understandings) gently and occasionally colliding with the other half of the brain (the one that understands the flow of the opposites) to create another new process that doesn't have beginnings or endings.

Utopian Thinking and the New Age

Many New Age thinkers want to transcend the ego. But from the lunar point of view, the ego is also just the presence of divine imminence. There is no need to transcend it. In a similarly illogical move, non-dual proponents will tell people that the ego thinks it's the center of the world, absolutely separate and distinct, in no way involved with the world "out there" – and it will do everything it can to maintain its illusion of sovereignty and avoid the oneness of all things. The irony of this point of view is that the ego is cast as a separate

222

part of the psyche or selfhood, and it is done so from a position that doesn't believe in such distinctions to begin with. This is like saying that the ego is a real illusion. It's nonsensical. Non-dual thinkers will also tell you that we each have an internal observer, and that that observer is what's real. This, again, is just another way of valuing the objective, dissociative faculty of the mind over and above the subjective sense of "I." Both are real and dependent upon each other. We can identify a certain paradoxical "sameness" of the two different qualities (objectivity/subjectivity), and yet there is no need for a value judgment about which is better—their sameness or their difference.

From the lunar point of view, transcendence is just one part of the dialog; from the solar point of view, there is nothing but the solar. The two metaphysical dispositions create together seamlessly as they both suffer and harmonize with each other. The easiest example is the pattern of each day. We rise and focus on our work or sense of destiny, like the Sun, and in the evening we rest, play, participate, and share in a non-goal-oriented sphere. Some of us do this anyway!

None of this means that we don't live with a sense of self that sometimes forgets the interconnection we all share, that sometimes has to wake up to something transcendent, and none of this means that linear enlightenment-oriented evolution isn't an aspect of our spiritual reality. What it does mean is that we should try to imagine no source, no origin, no awakening, and no return, perhaps as often as we offer any spiritual answers based on solar thinking. If we don't do this, then I fear that the same solar religious impulse that has dominated mankind for thousands of years will similarly permeate New Age thinking and the subtle, unspeakable "yogic" potential of astrology will be compromised.

Five Ways to Spot the Infiltration of Extreme Solar Thinking

1. To imagine that the main project of human life is to awaken from separation consciousness (this is the same view as original sin). To talk about life as though it has a fundamental purpose toward which it is evolving or moving.

2. To imagine that the ego is an undesirable thing related to separation consciousness (let's not forget that the transcendent oneness drive or the awakening drive in us can be just as separate and deluded).

3. In astrology: to see the presence of this incarnation as a result of unresolved separation desires, to view incarnation as a result of desire, or to view the South Node of the Moon as a karmic past you are trying to evolve away from, as you move toward the North Node.

As the nodes of the Moon represent the intersection points between the Sun, Moon, and Earth (the points where eclipses are created), we can just as readily see the South Node and North Node as a balancing between the solar and lunar properties, like the breath in and the breath out. We don't need to see the Moon as the "separation jailed" ego and the Sun as the non-dual enlightened destiny, and we don't have to keep creating linear evolutionary stories about awakening to a higher self when we interpret the birth chart. We also don't need to imagine source and returning to source. Those concepts are sometimes unnecessary.

4. To talk about the battle for love and oneness or any kind of holy war we are waging toward a higher vibration. To stare down non-love with love.

5. To talk about having to work hard toward something on your spiritual path. To talk about the need to purge, clean, or continually heal yourself from negativities, astral attachments, lower or crossed energies, etc.

Five Pros and Cons of Solar Thinking

1. Awakening to larger, shared realities and essences is a wonderful part of life. Evolution and linear growth are also great parts of life, and it will be wonderful if we all grow and evolve toward something kinder and more peaceful, etc. On the other hand, sometimes awakening is nonsensical, ambitious, alienating, isolating, and delusional.

2. Thinking we are the center of the world is of course silly. Each of us has done this. But to make the struggle with the ego the center of the world is also silly.

3. To see real growth work in the birth chart is good, to see the awakening potentials in the birth chart is good—but it's not the only way to do astrology. We can also use the birth chart to describe the perfection of what's already

here. There is not always a need for evolutionary levels or hierarchical conceptions of how the soul evolves through the course of many lifetimes. The concept is void of meaning at least half of the time!

4. Sometimes spirituality is about psychic warfare and holy war, but just as often it's not.

5. Sometimes spirituality is hard work, and cleaning and purging from negativities is very real, and sometimes it's not at all.

In Conclusion—Toward a Solar/Lunar/Earth Balance

In my opinion (which, as I've said from the start, tends to change all the time), those of us who consider ourselves spiritual people are learning to carry the solar/lunar paradigms equally. We're all learning that reality is absolutely-relative. For the most part, we don't know quite how that paradox works, or why, or where it's heading, if anywhere at all. Suffice it to say, there have been just as many holy people saying there are no answers, there is no source, there is nothing to return to, as there have been spiritual masters who say we're all emanations of God, going out into the many, only to return to the one. The two ways of conceptualizing reality are dependent upon one another, it would seem, as dependent as two hearts—or like Steinhardt and Turoc's two membranes perhaps, beating together as one or colliding endlessly to create universes upon universes.

For the past few thousand years, we've been solarizing our consciousness. It's provided us with a great story of linear growth and evolution. We discovered that the Sun was the center, not the Earth, and we transcended. It was like a fresh breath in. Perhaps what's next is to surrender the conceptualizing of *centers* or *sources* in the first place. Like the breath out. Who knows what might happen when we surrender at least half of our solar source and singularity talk and come back down to Earth!

Endnotes

1. Joseph Campbell, *Acts of God*, Volume Three, *Occidental Mythology* (New York: Viking Penguin Inc., 1964), 26–27).
2. Ibid., 9.

15

Shamanic Astrology

Benjamin Bernstein

Overview

Shamanic astrology starts by acknowledging that each planet is an intelligent being. Not only do the planets have consciousness, they are also responsive to invocation. So the most distinctive feature of shamanic astrology is that it involves direct communication with a planetary consciousness. This is done in order to improve its functioning in the client's life. I know of several others who say that they practice "shamanic astrology," and each one does something quite different. So when I speak of shamanic astrology, I am referring only to the particular way that I practice it.

This chapter will open with a brief overview of shamanism, followed by an overview of the shamanic astrology process. I will then look at the origins and development of shamanic astrology and the process of planetary energy integration. Next I'll provide an example of a shamanic astrology consultation, followed by two shamanic astrology clients describing their sessions and their downstream effects. I finish with a 10-step summary, to give you an easy reference for doing your own shamanic astrology sessions.

Finally, a semantic note. I find it awkward to use phrases such as "he or she," "him or her" and "his or her" when referring to a person of unspecified gender. I have chosen to use gender-neutral plural pronouns such as "they" and "their" instead. While such usage may be grammatically incorrect, my hope is that it will give you a smoother reading experience.

Shamanism

Shamanism, which could be thought of as mankind's original global religion, is common to indigenous cultures worldwide. The word "shaman" commonly refers to any practitioner who moves into altered states of consciousness to interact with the spirit world.

A shaman embarks on these visionary journeys to heal individual or societal imbalances at the causative spiritual level. Once this is accomplished, health and harmony are re-established physically, emotionally and mentally. Because shamanism accesses the unlimited power of the divine realms, it can often accomplish cures and healings that modern Western medicine would consider impossible.

Shamanism holds an animistic worldview. From this perspective, everything is alive and conscious: not just humans, animals and plants, but rivers, mountains, trees and stones. Even the Earth herself has a vast global consciousness, which includes everything on the planet.

A shaman sees physical forms as the tip of the iceberg. In the non-physical dimensions, even tiny rocks and crystals can be perceived as huge beings who embody vast wisdom. These allies, as well as psychoactive master plants such as ayahuasca, San Pedro, and peyote, possess a power and intelligence unimaginably greater than our human brains' limited abilities. All of these allies can assist the shaman, who invokes them in his healing work.

Many humans have not yet awakened to the fact that we live in an ensouled, intelligent, and unconditionally loving universe. Fortunately, more and more of us are now experiencing this reality. I have had powerful experiences of this indescribable consciousness during shamanic ceremonies, and so speak from direct experience.

While I awakened to this broader reality with the help of ayahuasca and San Pedro, many people routinely experience these extraordinary states without the use of such entheogenic (God-revealing) plants. These other modalities include dancing, drumming, dream work, vision quests, fasting, meditation and more.

The Essential Role of Western Astrology

Although direct connection with a planetary consciousness is at the heart of shamanic astrology, conventional Western astrological analysis is still an indispensable component. When I do in-depth shamanic astrology with a client, most of the session still looks like a standard astrological consultation.

We examine the core meaning of a planet, as well as how it relates to the chart. This can include the planet's sign, house, aspects and house rulership(s).

As we do so, I dialogue with the client. I describe low and high-side manifestations that they are likely to have experienced, based on how that planet integrates into their chart.

For optimum results, it is important that the client openly shares details about how this planet has been operating in their life. Most critically, they must specify how the planet is currently challenging them, and describe the high-side behavior they would prefer it to manifest instead. This provides the information needed to construct an invocation, which will help harmonize the planet's behavior.

Origin and Development of Shamanic Astrology

I had to feel my way into practicing shamanic astrology, since I learned it on my own. This modality arose spontaneously as the shamanic plant spirit ceremonies I was attending opened my consciousness to other dimensions.

When I first started practicing shamanic astrology, each consultation could last two hours or more. We would invoke every planet in the chart, starting with the Sun and working our way out through Pluto. After invoking the energy of that many planets, both the client and I would end up in a profoundly altered state. If the client came in person, I had to make sure they were grounded enough to drive!

With experience, I discovered that it is not always necessary, or even desirable, to invoke every planet in the chart. For a competent astrologer, it is usually a straightforward process to translate a client's specific issues into their chart's archetypal forces. Then it is only necessary to invoke the relevant planets and/or points.

One thing I was pleasantly surprised to discover is that one can invoke virtual points as well as physical planets. These can include the Ascendant, IC, Descendant, Midheaven, and the Lunar Nodes. As with the planets, each of these points has a distinctive energetic feel that becomes familiar over time.

One change I incorporated as I developed shamanic astrology was how actively I involved the client in the invocations. Initially, I did them on my own, while the client simply listened and received the planetary energies. While this worked, I observed that invocations are even more effective when the client actively participates. So now I say a few words of the invocation at a time then have the client repeat them. An invocation can be very detailed, and can take several minutes to verbalize.

Planetary Energy Integration

In the final part of the invocation process, we invite the planet's energy to enter the client's body. My shamanic astrology clients have been able to sense the energy of each invoked planet merging with them. And each invoked planet feels distinctly different. (I empathically experience the planets' energy signatures along with my clients.)

The integration of the planetary energies into the body usually takes a few minutes. I can feel when the integration process is complete. Sometimes, if the process is far enough along, it can keep running in the background as the client and I turn our attention elsewhere.

The more passive the client remains as the planetary energy integrates, the better the process works. I instruct my clients to focus on the simple sensation of their inhalations and exhalations. I tell them to let their breath do whatever it wishes, and to simply be aware of it.

As the planetary energy integrates, there's no need for the client to think about what's happening. Any mental activity whatsoever—no matter how helpful it may seem—creates "static" that makes it more difficult for the planetary energy to enter.

I don't want to set up an impossible expectation. So I tell my clients that they will almost certainly become distracted away from their breath as the planet integrates. I instruct them not to fight against the distraction, or try to change it in any way. What you resist persists: any energy directed toward a distraction just makes it stronger. Instead, I suggest to my clients that once they're aware of a distraction, they should "turn their back on it" and gently refocus their attention on the breath.

Even when a client is successfully focusing on the breath, they're often peripherally aware of other phenomena including bodily sensations, emotions, colors, visions and inner voices. I suggest to my clients that they treat these phenomena as if they were being projected onto a movie screen. They can watch, but should not jump into the screen!

And no matter how alluring the phenomena, the client should keep most of their attention on their breath. Remaining keenly aware of their inhalations and exhalations is what keeps the process moving forward, much like pushing a car's gas pedal.

A Shamanic Astrology Consultation

Let's illustrate shamanic astrology in action with an example. Rather than transcribe an actual session, with its inevitable digressions and tangents, what follows is a fictional transcript which concisely and accurately demonstrates the process. The client's chart (February 14, 1960, 5:15 pm, Norman, Oklahoma) is one I know well.

Since shamanic astrology is based on standard Western astrology, much of the session sounds just like a standard astrology consultation. I have included this material to give you a feeling for a typical shamanic astrology session. Specifically, I wanted to show the dynamic interchange that is so important in laying the groundwork for an optimal planetary invocation.

Astrologer: Let's figure out what planet in your natal chart is the most ripe for invocation. What's the most pressing issue in your life right now?

Client: Relationships. I just had another one fall apart, and I'm 50 years old. I'm wondering if I should even bother trying anymore.

A: Your chart certainly has a lot of relationship energy. Do you prefer men or women?

C: Women.

A: Have you been married?

C: Married and divorced four times.

230

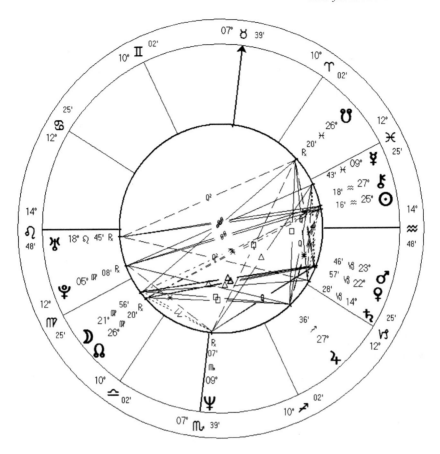

Figure 1 - Client

A: I understand. So we need to see what planets are energetically connected to your seventh house, which relates to important relationships. Your seventh house has Aquarius on the cusp. So we'll have a look at Aquarius' ruling planets, Saturn and Uranus. Venus, everyone's natural relationship ruler, is also a prime suspect. And your Sun can also represent relationships, since it's in your seventh house.

C: Okay.

A: All of the planets I've mentioned carry relationship energy. But I'd like to start with your seventh house Sun, which has the most aspects. The very presence of the Sun in the seventh house creates dynamic tension. The Sun can

231

represent the core of your ego—and, ultimately, your awakening beyond ego into divine consciousness—while the seventh house represents others. So there can be a part of you that doesn't feel legitimized until someone else gives you their stamp of approval. This can create a desire to always be in relationship so you can receive ongoing validation.

C: I can see how I've done that.

A: Your seventh house Sun is in Aquarius, the sign of awakening and paradigm shift; you most likely to put energy into a relationship if it helps accelerate your personal growth. If things start getting stagnant, you'll either try to stir things up or move on to another relationship. Is that correct?

C: That impulse is certainly there, but I don't jump ship that easily. In fact, my pattern has been to stay in relationships well past the point when I probably should have bailed.

A: I understand, but that impulse to stay the course has more to do with Saturn, Venus and Mars, your sixth house planets in Capricorn. I don't want to get sidetracked on them. But in a nutshell, they represent a lot of energy in your psyche saying that you should stand your ground and ride out the storm.

C: Sounds about right.

A: So let me guess: you stay loyal as long as you can, then end the relationship abruptly when you just can't stand it anymore?

C: Not something I'm proud to admit, but that sounds about right, too.

A: So let's look deeper. Your seventh house Sun's two most important aspects are its conjunction to Chiron and its opposition to Uranus. We'll take these one at a time. The Chiron conjunction is tight, and Chiron is also an Aquarian planet in the seventh house. The way I would expect the planet of the wounded healer to manifest in the early part of your life would be through wounding. This can be physical, but emotional and psychological wounds are more typical. Did you get your emotional needs met as a child?

C: Well, I knew my mom loved me, but I never really felt much love from my father. And that was the love that really mattered to me, because he was my big role model. He usually didn't want to be disturbed, even when he was home.

A: Physically present but emotionally absent?

C: There were emotions, but they usually weren't pleasant. I can't remember Mom and Dad ever expressing any genuine affection for each other. Instead, there were lots of arguments and hostility.

A: I understand. How about his emotions toward you?

C: He was basically impossible to please. No matter how well I did, in school or anything else, he just kept raising the bar.

A: So you were trained to please your father. Have you carried this pattern over into your romantic relationships?

C: In my marriages, I've always tried to keep my wives happy the best I could. But after a while I would start feeling frustrated, because I wasn't making enough time for the things that were important to me.

A: Okay, I'm getting a sense of how Chiron's wounds manifested for you. When someone has Chiron this strong in their chart, they often have mentoring and healing gifts. Is this true for you?

C: Well, I'm a counselor, and I also do some energy healing. And people do ask me for advice a lot.

A: Classic upside Chiron. Would you say that your development as a counselor unfolded as a result of the healing you had to do around your childhood wounds?

C: I'd say so, yes.

A: Beautiful. Let's move on to the next strongest aspect, the Sun's opposition to Uranus. As I mentioned earlier, Uranus is the modern ruler of Aquarius, and both the planet and the sign embody the same archetypal meaning. I've already mentioned the Aquarian/Uranian attributes of awakening and paradigm shift. But when things aren't unfolding as your higher self wishes, Uranus can throw a whole kitchen sink full of chaos, shock and crazy at you. And it can strike like a lightning bolt.

C: I've had that kind of experience a time or two.

A: But Uranus will only bring this kind of challenge when necessary. First, it will try to give you a heads-up about the change that's needed with an intuitive flash. You can think of this as a text message from God. Uranus also represents becoming an authentic expression of the personality you incarnated to be. And here it is, opposing your most powerful seventh house planet.

C: Sounds like trouble!

A: Potentially, but not necessarily. The word "opposition" sounds adversarial, but it can just as easily be harmonious. It's just the 180° aspect of relationship. So this setup in your chart—Uranus opposing your seventh house Sun—introduces another element of dynamic tension. Uranus says, "I want to do my own thing." The seventh house Sun says, "I need to devote myself to my partner." This theme is reinforced by their house placements. Uranus is in the 1st House of "me, myself and I," while the Sun is the seventh house of others. Any questions about this?

C: No.

A: I know we've done a lot of talking about how the Sun is set up in your chart. But all this probing and analysis is necessary if we want to get the maximum benefit out of your Sun invocation. I've been taking notes as we've gone along, but I never write out planetary invocations word for word. That's because part of my job is to be intuitively guided as the wording of the invocation comes together. So I can't give you an exact preview of what the wording is going to be.

C: I can live with that.

A: The invocation will have maximum power if you speak the words yourself. So this is going to proceed like a wedding vow: I say a few words, you repeat them, I say a few more, you repeat those, and so on. Is that okay with you?

C: Sure.

A: Since I'm not previewing the invocation language with you, it's possible that I may say something that you *don't* wish to invoke. This rarely happens, but if it does, interrupt me immediately. We can then have a brief discussion about what language is acceptable to you, and continue the invocation from there. The Sun won't mind, and the power of the invocation won't be compromised. Okay?

C: Okay.

A: Our final step before invoking is to outline the main changes you're asking for in your relationships. For starters, you're looking for a relationship with staying power?

C: Yes.

A: And not just one you have to slog through, but one that positively and delightfully stimulates your personal and spiritual growth?

235

C: Right.

A: Are you dead set on "as long as we both shall live"? You've already been married four times, so that obviously hasn't been your reality so far. But frankly, it often isn't with a lot of Aquarian energy in the seventh house. One attitude is that a relationship is a failure if it doesn't last until one of you dies. Another is that a relationship is successful if it provides positive growth experiences, no matter how long it lasts. What are you shooting for?

C: I'm tired of playing relationship roulette. I really want a partner for life.

A: Your Saturn, Venus and Mars in Capricorn are speaking loud and clear. Do you want to get married again or just live together?

C: Get married.

A: Okay. By the way, all that Aquarian energy in your seventh house also describes the type of partner who's best for you. I take it you want to call for a partner who's wonderfully unique and unconventional?

C: Absolutely.

A: One who's constantly reinventing herself so that you can never outgrow her? And one who supports you in your own growth process?

C: That would be fantastic.

A: We talked about receiving self-validation through relationships. Do you want to invoke being complete unto yourself, rather than depending on your partner to complete you?

C: That would be wonderful.

A: And do you want the same to be true of her?

C: Yes.

A: Aquarius also represents equality. Do you want to call for an equal partnership, where you get as good as you give?

C: You bet.

A: With a Sun–Chiron conjunction in the seventh, getting triggered by those close to you is, frankly, something you "signed up" for. So to invoke that you attract a partner who doesn't act as a catalyst in this way isn't realistic. But you can call for a partner who never hurts you on purpose. And you can call for the quick and efficient release of the old wounds that get triggered. How does that sound?

C: Okay, if that's the best I can do.

A: Of course, that same Sun–Chiron conjunction describes a partner who can be a healer and mentor to you. Sound good?

C: Sure!

A: The Sun–Uranus opposition really just repeats the Aquarian seventh house themes, which we've already covered. That's everything I can think of to include in the invocation. Anything else you'd like to add?

C: No, I'd say you've covered all the bases.

A: Great. Are you ready to do the actual invocation?

C: Let's do it!

A: All right. Get comfortable and close your eyes. Take a moment to feel your body. Note your current feeling state. We'll check it again after the invocation to see if you feel any different. Have you noted how you feel right now?

C: Yes.

A: Good. Now, get ready to repeat what I say. Here we go: "I hereby invoke my natal Sun."

C: I hereby invoke my natal Sun.

[Client repeats each of the following phrases.]

A: "Sun, I hereby call upon you...to transform your functioning in my life...in the following ways...to the greatest extent...that serves the highest good.... Sun...you're in Aquarius...and in my seventh house.... I hereby call for a unique and unconventional romantic partner...ideally suited to me...who will stay happily married to me...until death do us part.... This woman...constantly paradigm shifts and reinvents herself.... She powerfully and positively supports...my personal and spiritual growth.... Please help me to become...whole and complete unto myself...just as she is whole and complete unto herself.... We support and enrich each other's lives...by being together.... We enjoy a partnership of true equality... where each of us gets as good as we give.... I follow the guidance of my intuitive flashes...in my relationship...and in all things." Everything okay so far?

C: Yes.

A: Good, then we'll continue. "Sun...you're conjunct Chiron in the seventh house.... My beloved...acts as a mentor and healer to me...and empowers my own abilities...as a mentor and healer.... When she unintentionally triggers me...it does me the favor...of reactivating old wounds...that are ready for release.... I release these old wounds...quickly and efficiently." Anything you want to add or change before we actually call in the Sun?

C: No, that sounds great.

A: All right, here we go. "Sun...I hereby invoke you...to make these shifts...in my being...to the greatest extent...that serves the highest good...starting now.... Thank you."

At this point, I guide the client in how to most easily receive the planetary energy, as described in the "Planetary Energy Integration" section above. At the conclusion of the integration process, I have them compare their feeling states before and after, and invite them to describe their experience of the planetary integration. I've empathically felt plenty of extraordinary shifts and heard lots of amazing stories!

Client Experiences

Here are experiences that two actual clients shared with me after I led them in shamanic astrology sessions. These are condensed from the original emails. I did both these sessions on the phone, showing that the astrologer and client need not be in the same place for the work to be effective.

> The first planet we invoked was my natal Sun in Scorpio. Benjamin put together a very powerful and detailed invocation for my Sun to come in to serve me in my pursuit of my higher purpose and accelerated velocity along my life path. During his invocation, I actually began to feel the heat of the Sun coming into me and bathing me with celestial radiance. It took me a few breaths afterward to be able to tell Benjamin that I was ready to go on.
>
> Halfway through the session, **I was "higher" and more "expanded" than any drug or meditation has ever taken me,** and the experience I had with each planet was unique and profound. Each time I could feel the forces coming into me and, in a very real way, assembling themselves and combining with my DNA to become a physical part of my structure. The experience left me feeling extremely full, and I had to take a nap afterward to just let things begin to integrate!
>
> **Since the Shamanic Astrology Consultation, I have felt much more steady, strong, and at peace in myself and just**

more "me." I've been better able to hold my own personal ground and centeredness, while still being the loving and caring person that I am.

The dreams I've had since the session have been off the charts. So much that was hidden or not clear for me has begun to reveal itself in ways I can work with and transform into practical magic and manifestation for myself.

It hasn't just been on the emotional/spiritual level either. After our session, I had a dream in which Benjamin was telling me that I deserved to be financially successful and abundant. Since that dream, **my business and referrals from past clientele have taken a steep upward climb, and my financial situation has improved quite measurably. In less than a week, the money I invested in Benjamin's Shamanic Astrology Consultation has been returned several times over on the material side of things, and immeasurably on the emotional/spiritual side.**

– Hal Bahr, Phoenix, Oregon

Since doing our Shamanic Astrology Consultation two days ago, **I've felt energized, more joyful, peaceful and focused, and less attached to my persona.**

Each planet that we invoked had a different feel to it. Invoking the Sun made me feel that I was actually feeling the Sun on my skin. Neptune felt like waves, and Venus made my heart chakra spin! And **listening to each planetary invocation on the consultation recording brings it all back.**

The entire experience was a big wow, and unlike anything else I've ever done! It was energizing, comforting and soothing all at the same time. **It was an amazing paradigm shift to *feel* the planets and not just think about them rationally.**

Your shamanic astrology work really has been **life-changing** for me. It changed me at a very subtle but important level, as if my neural brain connections have been altered somehow.

240

There were some immediate changes, including some positive dietary shifts that surprised me. I had been drinking one or two Diet Cokes a week, but now I find it disgusting. I had been slowly getting meat out of my diet, and it's now completely unpalatable to me.

One of the most important things that's happened has been a detachment from myself. I'm no longer so caught up in my persona, and in defining myself by what I do or think. **I have a greater feeling of oneness, and a more spiritual perspective. Plus, I've had a tremendous amount of joy,** and have been grinning a lot.

Three months later, this client followed up:

During our session you invoked my Mars, specifying the most important qualities of my ideal male partner and calling him in for me. Two days later, I got a call from a very special man who embodies those qualities. That was fast!!! Things immediately began to heat up between us, and are still going great three months later!"

- Trish V., Lauderdale-by-the-Sea, Florida

Summary: Shamanic Astrology, Step by Step

So, in summary, here's how to do a shamanic astrology session:

1. Using your astrological knowledge, identify which planet(s) and/or point(s) in the client's chart are creating the greatest challenges. (To keep things simple, we'll assume here that we're talking about a natal planet.)
2. Interpret the planet's stand-alone meaning, sign, house and rulership(s) as deeply as time allows. Dialogue with the client to uncover the specific challenges they're experiencing, as well as the positive changes they desire. Take keyword notes as you go.
3. After your interpretation of the planet is complete, get the client's agreement on the changes they want the invocation to initiate. Make

sure you're clear what planetary shifts you'll be requesting before you begin.

4. Tell the client that they will be repeating the invocation out loud as you lead them through it a few words at a time. Instruct them to interrupt you immediately if they have a problem with any of your phrasing.

5. Tell your client to get comfortable, close their eyes, and note their current feeling state. The client can be sitting up or lying down.

6. Lead the client through the invocation. Invoke from your keyword notes, not a written-out script. Stay open to intuitive inspiration as you go. Don't talk about the challenges the planet has brought; only invoke the planet's new high-side functioning. Clarify any phrasing issues that may arise during the invocation, then continue with the invocation from that point.

7. After completing the invocation, tell the client to remain as passive as possible. Tell them to focus on the sensation of the breath entering and leaving their body on its own. Tell them to deal with any distractions by simply refocusing on their breath.

8. As the planet integrates, the client may experience unusual bodily sensations, emotions, colors, visions and/or inner voices. Tell them to treat these phenomena as if they were being projected onto a movie screen. They can watch but not interact.

9. If you're empathic, monitor the integration's progress based on what you're feeling. If you're not empathic, have the client inform you when they feel that the integration has finished.

10. After the integration is complete, ask the client to share what they experienced (if they weren't narrating as it happened). Have them check their feeling state and verbalize any differences. Dialogue as necessary to help them integrate the experience, and let them know that the changes they requested may unfold gradually over time.

Conclusion

I've been dealing exclusively with the natal chart so far, but planetary invocation doesn't stop there! You can just as easily invoke planets that are moving by transit, secondary progression, solar arc, or any other movement system.

Using the information given in this chapter, you can begin using shamanic planetary invocation whenever you're ready. Start by invoking the most important planets and/or points in your own chart. Once you've experienced these energies for yourself, begin practicing with others. In time, you may find, as I have, that planetary invocation can add a powerful healing component to your astrological work.

16

Astrology: The Noetic Science

Rafael Nasser

"The five universal forces include the gravitational force, the weak force, the electromagnetic force, the strong force, and consciousness."

– Quote attributable to any science textbook published in a hundred years

The Noetic Enlightenment

As I begin to contemplate this piece, I close my eyes. Ideas swirl, and without warning, I am swept away by a wild imaginary undertow and carried to another place and another time. As this inner world comes into sharper view, I gain my bearings and realize that I have been carried five centuries into the future. Large incandescent letters hang high overhead in a darkening sky. They read: Welcome to the annual conference of the Historical Society of Modernity. And below them the date, April 21, 2501 AD. I recognize the place. I am at the Garden of the Gods, a nature reserve in Colorado Springs that consists of a gallery of colossal ruddy sandstone formations formed eons ago by the massive uplift of a rising mountain and sculpted by the timeless winds. It's 7:45 PM, and as the last lingering traces of daylight vanish under the advance of night, the towering outlines take on the appearance of a coterie of primordial deities.

I'm lofted skyward by an invisible force and drift towards the suspended letters. I come to rest hundreds feet above the earthen gods, my body comfortably propped up by an invisible field that molds around the contours of my body like an ergonomic theater seat. Other people are streaming upwards and filling up the vacant spaces around me. Rows form and before long an amphitheater is hovering above the gods of rock and under the watchful eye of those other gods, the ones made of light—the planets.

Please join me. I reserved a space for you. It's perfectly safe up here. Nano-gusts of warm air will shelter the audience from the brisk Colorado night. I'm glad you agreed to attend this event. Any minute now, Professor Magnus Opum, a frizzy, white-haired octogenarian regarded as the leading expert on the history of the Modern Age, is going to make the keynote presentation. Opum is an eccentric genius who makes his presentations dressed up as notable characters that helped shape the Modern Age. On one occasion he wore a shoulder-length cloak, breeches, knee-high boots and a wide plumed hat that covered a wig of long dark hair, and a dark mustache. Of course, he was impersonating René Descartes (1596–1650), the amiable philosopher who fathered modernity.

Descartes lived at a time when tensions between religion and science were brewing. Being both religious and scientifically minded, he attempted to ease that tension by dividing reality into two independent realms: the intentional–mental realm that he assigned to theologians, and the extensional–material realm that came under the jurisdiction of a new breed of learned individuals, the natural philosophers who studied the laws of nature and the body.

Descartes believed that this ontological fence would make good neighbors out of religion and science, but his philosophical stratagem backfired. Descartes' fundamental split between God–mind and nature–body, though well intentioned, resulted in a dualistic universe that brought about a monumental philosophical problem. If mind and matter represent separate realities, then how do they interact? Through what mechanism does God manipulate the material world? Through what mechanism does the mind control the body? The emergence of the mind–body (and God–nature) split signaled the birth of the Modern Age.

Professor Opum, in the guise of Descartes, explained that the Modern Age underwent three basic stages of development, and that at each stage, an attempt was made to resolve the mind–body problem using a different strategy. The philosophers of early modernity tried to mend the dualistic rift in the fabric of reality in a variety of ways, all of them unconvincing, and ultimately, intellectually unsatisfying. Nicholas Malbranche (1638–1715), for example, argued that God micromanages the cosmos and synchronizes the workings of the mind with the events in nature. If your mind decided to move your little finger, and your little finger moved, according to Malbranche, it was because God made it happen. As modern philosophy matured, philosophers rejected Descartes' dualism, arguing that reality was fundamentally whole and that only one of the two realms could exist. A philosophical contest began between those who championed the mental realm, such as Bishop Georges Berkeley (1685–1753) who proposed a theory of "immaterialism"; and those who championed the material realm, such as Jean Meslier (1664–1729), a Catholic priest whose posthumously published book revealed him to be a staunch atheist and materialist.

The middle phase of modernity gained momentum as the materialists won the battle, largely due to a series of scientific discoveries that shook the foundation of the their religiously minded counterparts. The cosmological paradigm embraced by the all three monotheistic faiths envisioned Creation as a geocentric, spherical, and finite structure with the Earth situated at the center of the world and God abiding at the topmost level of the cosmos. But the findings of Copernicus, Galileo, and Kepler suggested that the solar system was heliocentric, irregular, and infinite. The cosmological model that emerged during middle modernity chipped away the religious cosmological model. The coup de grace was the publication of Isaac Newton's (1642–1727) Philosophiæ Naturalis Principia Mathematica, which proved that the same universal laws could be used to describe celestial and terrestrial phenomena. God was deemed either unable or unwilling to change the laws discovered by science, and therefore irrelevant with respect to the way nature behaved.

One time, Professor Opum made a presentation wearing a top hat, a dark double-breasted tailcoat, and long white pantaloons neatly strapped around black leather shoes. He was impersonating Pierre-Simon Laplace (1749–1827), a French mathematician who embodied the materialistic worldview that dominated the peak of the Modern Age. The story told is that Laplace presented a copy of his book on the system of the universe to Napoleon Bonaparte. Reputedly, Napoleon remarked that the work lacked any mention of God, to which Laplace replied, "Sir, I had no need for that hypothesis."

By the start of the 20th century, materialism reigned supreme in the industrialized world. But that reign was short-lived. Albert Einstein's (1879–1955) theory of relativity equated matter and energy and suggested that time

246

was a relative phenomenon. Einstein's vision of the cosmos transformed Newton's solid and dependable universe into rubbery space that behaved differently according to one's perspective. Consequently, the clockwork universe of materialism morphed into a surreal space reminiscent of Salvador Dali's molten timepieces.

Einstein's vision blunted the materialist worldview, but it was quantum mechanics that undermined that perspective. Professor Opum once did a presentation titled The Beginning of the End of Modernity wearing a gray two-piece suit, a starchy white shirt, and a dark pinstriped tie. He was impersonating Werner Heisenberg, the pioneering theoretical physicist whose uncertainty principle is legend in the lore of quantum physics. Heisenberg championed the radical notion that the observer changed the observed merely through the act of observing. The idea was viewed as preposterous by mainstream science, but irksome scientific experiments validated the uncertainty principle. Materialists grumbled. Professor Opum capped his presentation by quoting Heisenberg in a practiced 20th century German accent: "Zee first gulp from the glass of natural sciences will turn you into an atheist, but at zee bottom of zee glass, God is waiting for you."

Quantum mechanics set the stage for the demise of materialism. That perspective had inspired the compulsive drive that propelled the Modern Age into dizzying heights of scientific and technological achievement, but at a dear price. Interior experience was marginalized, spirituality was infantilized, astrology was disparaged, and in the extreme, consciousness was reduced to an epiphenomenon—the curious side effect of chemical reactions occurring inside the brain. Quantum mechanics brought a modicum of dignity back to human consciousness, at least with respect to the subatomic realm where human consciousness appeared to have an impact on reality.

Oh, look, the lights are flashing. I'd better stop lecturing. Professor Opum's keynote is about to begin. A drumroll and the clash of nano-cymbals quiver the air. The audience quiets and focuses on the figure of Magnus Opum rising through the air. Tonight he is wearing in a brown cardigan, a tan shirt buttoned up to the neckline, and dark slacks. He is sporting a neatly trimmed white beard and holding a blue book. A rousing round of applause accompanies his ascent. After reaching his destination on the invisible magnetic stage, Opum rests the

247

blue book down on a translucent lectern, waves appreciatively, and addresses the audience.

"Thank you, fellow modernologists, and welcome to tonight's presentation, The Noetic Enlightenment. This evening I stand before you dressed in the manner of a scientist that lived during Late Modernity, and whose pioneering work helped to usher the historical period we know as the Noetic Enlightenment. I am referring to William Tiller, Professor Emeritus, Chair of Material Sciences and Engineering at Stanford University—an institution that continues to shine half a millennium later.

"To appreciate the pivotal role Professor Tiller played in the scheme of human emergence, we must first come to understand the view of reality entrenched in the popular culture during Late Modernity. It is nearly impossible for humans living in the 26th century to fully appreciate the tight weave of materialism during the 20th and early 21st centuries, before the Noetic Enlightenment shifted the paradigm.

"The values of modernity centered on a worldview that privileged the primacy of matter and material goods above all else. As we know, quantum mechanics began to undermine materialism in some scientific circles, but the theory was abstract and too far removed from the common shores of human experience to carry much weight in popular culture. It wasn't until the pioneering research of William Tiller reached the mainstream that the Noetic Enlightenment began in earnest.

"The word 'noetic' would have meant little to the average person living in the Modern Age. That word, as any 26th century third grader knows, derives from the ancient Greek word for mind, nous, and in our broader contemporary usage includes all facets of mental and emotional activity such as our thoughts and feelings, those imagined and enacted, consciously and unconsciously.

"Shocking as it may sound, most Late Moderns were convinced that thoughts and feelings had no influence on the environment. Consequently, the average Joe and the plain Jane of the Modern Age lived out their lives believing that their psychological processes had no bearing whatsoever on the world around them.

"But William Tiller was an exception. Allow me to quote from the preface to his book Conscious Acts of Creation, published in 2001, precisely five hundred years ago.

248

'This book marks a sharp dividing line between old ways of scientific thought and old experimental protocols, wherein, human qualities of consciousness, intention, emotion, mind, and spirit cannot significantly affect physical reality, and a new paradigm wherein they can robustly do so!'"

Professor Opum closed the book and cleared his throat before continuing. "Conscious Acts of Creation is a fascinating compendium of experiments that Tiller conducted. The results he documented indicated that focused human consciousness impacted material reality, significantly. In one classic experiment, Tiller and three other participants sat around a table and focused a specific intention on a specially designed electrical device created for the purpose of this study. They called this device an intention imprinted electrical device or IIED for short. The specific intention they focused on the device was to raise the pH of a water solution by a unit of one, a significant change by any standard. Each person spoke their intention and the group focused meditatively on the IIED for 15 minutes. Then a second intention was spoken out loud to seal the first intention into the IIED. Then they placed the IIED in a room beside the water solution and tracked the pH over time.

"The results were astounding. The pH of the water gradually increased by a unit of one, just as the meditators had intended. They repeated the same experiment, only this time they set the opposite intention: To lower the pH of the water solution by a unit of one. They were equally successful in that endeavor. In both experiments, they also placed a control solution at another location far away from the IIED and tracked it. In both instances, the control did not change pH.

As impressive as these results were, the best was yet to come. Tiller repeated the experiment in the same room that had contained the IIED long after the device had been removed from the premises and, incredibly, he recorded the same results. Additional experiments showed that the intention had spread and was transforming the pH of water solutions 150 feet away. Tiller concluded that the fabric of space is malleable to intention and that space remembers.

Professor Opum closed Tiller's book. "Historians of modernity often argue about the defining moment when the Noetic Enlightenment began in earnest.

Tonight I would like to present my definitive position. The Noetic Enlightenment began on the day that a distinguished professor of applied material sciences living in the Late Modern Age proclaimed that the mind matters."

Mind Matters

Our evening with Professor Opum will resume a little later. But right now, return to the present moment and consider that notion that our culture stands on the cusp of a paradigm shift relating to the nature of consciousness. Most of us are aware of this emergent shift to some degree, at least intellectually. But a paradigm shift truly occurs only when the whole body is swept away by a novel realization and not just the intellect. A few years ago, I was shown a Qigong exercise by Master Robert Peng that resulted in my personal noetic "enlightenment," and I'd like to share this exercise with you in the hope that it inspires your own noetic satori. This exercise resembles William Tiller's experiment but the results take place in a matter of minutes and you can vouch for them yourself without the need of any fancy monitoring equipment. Reading about Tiller's work impressed me intellectually, but Robert's exercise shook me to the core. After this experience, my view of consciousness was radically altered, as was my understanding of astrology. The exercise is called A Game of Qi Power and it involves using your intention to transform the taste of brandy (if you are a teetotaler or underage you may substitute fresh-squeezed lemon juice for the brandy). The instructions are listed below and I recommend that you check the endnotes for a link to a follow-along video.[1]

1. Pour a few ounces of brandy into two glasses and place one of the glasses off to the side. Place the other glass directly in front of you.
2. Rub your hands together vigorously for twenty seconds, then hold them about a foot apart on either side of the glass in front of you as you create a field of Qi energy between your palms. Feel your energy penetrate the liquid inside the glass.

1.   2.

3. Pick up the glass. Visualize a brilliant light beaming down from your hand into the liquid and beyond it. Feel your energy inside the liquid. Purify the brandy by draining away the dark, and heavy quality of the alcohol. Visualize the alcohol becoming brighter and lighter. Continue doing this for at least thirty seconds.

4. Next, imagine beams of golden Qi shooting from your fingertips and stir the brandy energetically to refine it. Visualize the brandy becoming smoother and smoother. Smile as you continue doing this, steady and relaxed, for at least thirty seconds. Finish by imagining a Yin Yang symbol projecting from your palm right into the glass to seal your work.

3   4

5. Finally, sip the brandy from the glass that you just worked on. And then taste the brandy from the other glass.

5.

Did you notice a difference? Many people gag after sipping the brandy from the second glass due to its harsh taste. If you don't believe what your own taste buds are telling you, let another person sip both glasses. Robert Peng explains that the more powerful the intention, the more dramatic the effect. He claims that some Qigong Masters are powerful enough to project their intention across the room, across town, or even across the planet.

Let's consider the implications of this experiment. If your conscious intention can transform the taste of brandy in about a minute, then consider how the thoughts and feelings that you recycle continuously throughout the day transform your immediate environment. If focalized consciousness influences the quality of matter, then your clothes, accessories, and even your bed sheets are saturated with the impressions of your mind. And based on the results of Tiller's experiment, we can presume that these noetic imprints are going to spread beyond the confines of your personal space. If you live in an apartment building, your noetic impressions are going to extend into your neighbors' space, and their noetic impressions are going to radiate into your apartment. Additionally, the noetic footprints of previous tenants will interpenetrate these fields as well.

Take this idea one step further. If an individual's consciousness is powerful enough to "charge" an object noetically, what do you suppose happens when a group of people focus their intention at the same time? In his remarkable book,

The Conscious Universe, parapsychologist Dean Radin describes a series of experiments designed to measure the effect of focalized group consciousness on random number generators. The results are astounding. During large-scale events such as the opening ceremony of the Olympics or the Academy Awards, the random number generators produced ordered number sequences to a statistically significant degree. Radin writes:

> The results of these experiments also bear some resemblance to Jung's concept of "synchronicity," or meaningful coincidences in time. As with synchronicity, we seem to be witnessing meaningful relationships between mind and matter at certain times. But synchronicity, according to Jung, involves acausal relationships, and here we are able to predict synchronistic-like events. Jung believed that people could experience but not understand in causal terms how synchronicities occurred... We are more confident than Jung about what may be possible because it appears that with clever experimental designs, some aspects of Jung's unus mundus (one world) are in fact responsive to experimental probes, and some forms of synchronistic events can be—paradoxically—planned.[2]

Fascinating, all of it. But, you may be wondering, what does all of this information have to do with astrology? Everything, dear friend. Astrologers, like everyone else, are inadvertently subject to the biases of the materialistic paradigm that shapes the conventional view of reality. To break free of the juggernaut of culture requires radical insight and new language, and hopefully, Professor Opum's presentation, Peng's exercise, and the Tiller and Radin experimental results have expanded your view of consciousness. Perhaps you now realize more completely that your thoughts and feeling influence the world in a subtle but real way. With this understanding, we can begin to build a radical new understanding of astrology, for if projected consciousness imprints itself on the world, then we are going to have to account for the continual stream of prayers, supplications, and myths directed at the planets by billions of people over thousands of years, especially during intense moments of religious fervor

253

and duress. Indeed, after your noetic enlightenment, scrutinize at the sky anew and you'll soon realize that the planets are staring back at you through the eyes of the past.

The Noetic Planets

The year is 17,624 BCE, sometime around the peak of the last ice age, somewhere in Southern France, and although it is the height of summer, the temperature barely tips fifty degrees Fahrenheit. Life in the Paleolithic Age is harsh and unforgiving. The winter is bitterly cold and food is scarce. Predators abound. The extended families living in this habitat are subject to a perpetual sense of vulnerability, and consequently, their core value is safety. But amidst the chaotic and unpredictable life conditions, a profound discovery has been made: The menstrual cycle and the lunation cycle share the same periodicity. The synchrony between human and cosmos inspires the religious impulse of the age.

It is nighttime. A dozen menstruating women clad in furs stand in a circle around a central fire under the full Moon. They direct their attention at the corpulent sphere of light in the sky. She is Big Mother, the goddess who watches over the tribe, ensures the continuity of life, and brings comfort and security. Tonight they consecrate the blood they shed to renew their heavenly bond. Holding hands, they implore,

> Big Mother, protect us from the beasts
> Big Mother, shelter us from winter
> Big Mother, fill our bellies with warm food
> Big Mother, embrace us, your bleeding daughters, in your arms
> of light

Now, visualize this heartfelt supplication as a noetic laser beam energizing the Moon with their conscious intention just as you energized the glass of brandy with your conscious intention. But here, the energy directed at Big Mother is qualified by the fundamental values that defined Paleolithic culture—shelter, family, food, and safety.

Much about prehistoric culture remains unknown, but archeological evidence suggests that a Paleolithic religion that stretching from Western Europe all the way to China existed and worshipped a goddess figure believed to be associated with the Moon. Without written records we can only speculate about prehistoric culture, but with reasonable confidence, we can imagine countless souls directing the dominant needs, concerns, and desires of Paleolithic culture at the Moon repeatedly over thousands of years. Through this process, the Moon would have become imbued with the collective consciousness of the age, and since noetic fields perpetuate over time, we may also surmise that the noetic Moon continues radiate this field and generate order in the form of "lunar" synchronicities.

An anthropologist surveying the astrological meaning the planets would readily recognize the similarities between the core values of the Paleolithic and the themes associated with the astrological Moon: Mother, home, shelter, food, family or tribe, vulnerability and safety. The elements that defined Paleolithic culture are clearly reflected by the qualities associated with the astrological Moon. And while we may no longer be living in an ice age, we continually run across situations that cast us back into the same mood of deep vulnerability that colored the Paleolithic soul. The structure of consciousness forged during that epoch remains deeply nestled within our psyche, and when the noetic Moon triggers us, those primal energies surge and we seek safety through various coping strategies.

Paleolithic consciousness represents only one stage of human emergence. Dr. Don Beck, co-developer of a developmental model known as *Spiral Dynamics*[4], has elegantly mapped out the trajectory of sociocultural development, describing the life conditions and values that defined consecutive stages. While researching his conceptual framework, it became increasingly apparent that the stages of human emergence described by Dr. Beck bear an uncanny resemblance to the meanings of the planets that constitute the astrological pantheon. These planets also reflect a developmental arc. The Moon was worshipped as the primary deity during the Paleolithic, and later, as temperatures warmed and life conditions improved, the Neolithic emerged. The Sun became the primary deity during this age of heroes and kings. In antiquity, logic and order were instituted as the highest values. During this period the five points of light known as the conventional planets (Mercury,

Venus, Mars, Jupiter, and Saturn) came into vogue and reason, justice, warfare, religion, and rulership underwent a profound developmental shift. It was during this stage that the Zodiacal mandala—a novel structure that reflected cosmic order—was popularized. Under the progressive drive for knowledge of modernity, Uranus was discovered and during the nebulous and artistic post-modern period it was Neptune. More recently, a new stage of human emergence has been identified that some call post-postmodernity or the Integral Age that stresses the need for radical transformation as a way of life. Pluto was discovered within the first few decades of this stage.

Researching human emergence after my "noetic enlightenment," I discerned a causal link between the core values of each stage of human emergence and the core meaning of the astrological planets. That link being the unique form of consciousness that was directed by the collective at the planets during each discrete period. What follows is a brief overview of human emergence and the emergence of the noetic planets. We begin with the dawn of our species and continue right up to the present day.[3] Then, in the next section, we explore the emergence of the noetic Zodiac.

I.   Archaic humans (200,000–50,000 years ago): Our species appears in the fossil record about 200,000 years ago. For the first 150,000 years, our ancestors exhibited behavioral patterns and utilized the same kinds of tools used by earlier humans dating back a million years. These pre-cultural humans lived like sophisticated animals, relying on instinct and reflexes to adapt to the immediate environment. They banded in clans and, although they did not exhibit signs of culture, religion, music or art, they understood the relationship between the four elements and mastered fire.

II.   The Paleolithic Age, Safety, and the Moon (50,000–12,000 years ago): During the last ice age life conditions worsened. A group of humans developed symbolic thinking and language as a means to cope with the existential challenge. Geneticists claim that every human alive today descends from this ancestral group. Symbolic language enabled humans to create imaginary realms vested with meaning. Myths, religion, art, and culture emerged from this imaginal wellspring, and human consciousness projected symbolic meaning on to the

256

environment. As part of this process, humans discovered the link between the lunar and the menstrual cycles and projected their safety needs at the Moon. The spirit of the Paleolithic Age is embodied by the noetic Moon.

III.   The Neolithic Age, Power, and the Sun (12,000–2,500 years ago): This epoch coincides with the Neolithic Age and the Bronze Age. About 12,000 years ago, the last ice age ended and life conditions improved. The Sun came into prominence and food became vastly more abundant. Settlements formed, and to sustain the growing populations horticulture was invented. Settlements grew and when resources became scarce again metallurgy was invented and agriculture developed. Cities developed and eventually the great river valley civilizations emerged. Granaries were built to store surplus goods, and metal was forged into weapons to protect walled cities and food supplies.

The transformation of consciousness that accompanied these developments was the emergence of the ego. An attitude of power, confidence, and strength displaced the sense of vulnerability that had dominated human consciousness during the Paleolithic. Power subverted safety as the dominant value, and the Sun, the embodiment of power itself, became the dominant deity. Kingship—institutionalized egoism—emerged during this stage of human development. These qualities were projected at the Sun during this stage of human emergence, and consequently, the noetic Sun embodies the qualities of power, confidence, domination, majesty, glory, heroism, kingship, and the ego. The spirit of this age is embodied by the noetic Sun.

IV.   The Classical Age, Antiquity, and the Middle Ages; Reason; and the five points of light and the Zodiac (2,500–400 years ago): Around 2,500 years ago, Thales of Miletus, the father of philosophy, predicted a solar eclipse. The freewheeling gods in the sky, it turned out, were regulated by a higher power whose rational will could be discerned through the application of logic and reason. This supreme organizing principle came to be known as God or the Logos, and humans now sought to understand divine will through the workings of the intellect.

During this epoch, the familiar twelve-sign Zodiac was invented in the Near East and spread east and west to Europe and India. The Zodiac represented the divine logos and as the planets moved around this celestial mandala they reflected God's will which manifested on Earth. While the position of the Sun and the Moon could be easily predicted, the retrograde motion of the five other heavenly wanderers—Mercury, Venus, Mars, Jupiter, and Saturn—made determining their positions more complicated. If only their positions could be known in advance, the future could be foretold. The quest for foreknowledge of the divine plan brought these five planets into prominence during this age.

The reason used to determine the position of the planets, was also projected into their meaning. These planets came to be seen as the purveyors of divine order in our lives. The noetic qualities assigned to these conventional planets derived from their distinguishing characteristics. Mercury, the fastest of the bunch, was associated with communication, merchants, and fast-talkers. Venus, appearing in the sky like a pearly jewel at dawn or dusk, became associated with beauty, pleasure, and love. Ruddy Mars became associated with blood, war, and conflict. Bright Jupiter became the king of the gods and associated with providence and good fortune. The movement of these four planets was regulated by Saturn, the slowest planet. Envisioned as the elder, Saturn was also associated with time, structure, order, authority, seniority, convention, responsibility and hardship in general. During this stage of human emergence, as order displaced power as the highest good, astrology was elevated to the status of a divine science since it was viewed as the mechanism through which God's will was instituted on Earth. As rationality and order infused into astrology, the spirit of this age was noetically transferred to the conventional planets and the noetic Zodiac.

V. The Modern Age, Innovation, and Uranus (starting 400 years ago): René Descartes' philosophy, in conjunction with the astronomical discoveries that emerged over the course of the early Modern Age, served to deconstruct the pre-modern worldview. Many of the absolute truths dictated by pre-modern reason were disproved by modern empiricism. As new facts trumped the old logic, the presumptive authority of the past became increasingly delegitimized. The Modern Age was forward-looking, stressed scientific advancement, and convinced that humanity could innovate its way to a better future. The philosophical salons of 19th century Paris, the Industrial Revolution in Great Britain, and the American and French Revolutions reflected the optimism, spirit of innovation, and the quest for freedom that characterize modernity.

At the peak of modernity, the planet Uranus was discovered and astrologers living through this stage of human emergence attributed the spirit of the age to the planet. The qualities of progress, freedom, innovation, technology, liberalism, and revolution were projected onto Uranus and the spirit of the age was noetically transferred to the planet. This process continues to unfold.

VI. The Postmodern Age, Inner Awareness, and Neptune (starting 200 years ago): At the turn of the 19th century, life conditions in the industrialized world became intolerable. Urban centers swelled with unsightly factories that soiled the skies with smoke and streets with soot. Many felt betrayed by modernity and its promise of a better life.

Romanticism emerged as an early countermovement to modernity. Romantics envisioned utopian realities grounded in ideals that transcended the industrial world and privileged the inner life and the imagination over empiricism and technological progress. They idealized art, and over the course of the 19th century, artistic expression veered away from realism. The novel emerged as a new art form that highlighted the inner life of the individual. One of the first novels, *Frankenstein*, by Mary Shelley, was intended as a social critique of science and warned of the dangers inherent in modern values.

The focus of postmodernity shifted to the inner dimension, and the modern ideal of progress was internalized by various spiritual movements that emerged during this stage. Some individuals shunned external success and sought instead spiritual growth and spiritual wealth through the exploration of the inner worlds. Spiritualism, Theosophy, and then later the New Age movement lauded the virtue of spiritual knowledge and the ideal of spiritual purity and perfection.

259

Socialism sought to redress the inequities created by modernity that favored the few at the expense of the many. Socialists sought to allocate the wealth and resources compiled by modernity more equitably. Over time, various technologies emerged that facilitated the communication of interiority, including photography, film, and television—and more recently blogs and social media—which created a space where individuals could express their innermost self to the rest of the planet. As humans encountered each other's inner lives and stories, they became increasingly sensitive and less tolerant of personal suffering and inequity. Values such as egalitarianism and humanitarianism emerged as popular ideals that fueled movements that sought to redress social injustice and alleviate suffering such as civil rights, woman's rights, gay rights, animal rights. The values of this stage also gave rise to political correctness.

Postmodernism is a loose term that bundles together various perspectives that recognize that to a large extent, human reality is defined subjectivity, interiority, and the stories that constitute our worldview. Postmodernism redirected attention to the symbolic dimension of culture and language and embraced the relativism that separated different points of view. Within the purview of postmodernism it became possible to identify with others that were significantly different than ourselves. This perspective enabled the capacity for universal inclusion to emerge as a core value. This sentiment expressed itself socially as multiculturalism.

The memes and movements that emerged during the postmodern age include romanticism, art, spirituality, inner worlds, purity, mysticism, spirituality, socialism, relativity, novels, stories, photography, movies, egalitarianism, humanitarianism, sensitivity, inclusion, symbolism, the inner self, inner knowledge, purity, and social justice. These are also keywords associated with Neptune, which was discovered in 1846. The spirit of this relatively recent age was noetically transferred to the planet and this process continues to unfold.

VII.   The Integral Age, Transformation, and Pluto (starting 100 years ago): The discovery of the subconscious mind—the invisible repository of repressed and suppressed psychic material that controls the conscious

260

mind—struck a devastating blow at the modernist and postmodernist worldviews which prided themselves on rationality and human dignity. The power of the irrational underbelly of consciousness was highlighted by World War I, a brutal war driven by an emotional agenda that resulted in the deaths of millions at the hands of lethal modern technologies such as the machine gun and poison gas. After the pointless decimation, few could deny that pathology existed at the level of collective consciousness. Within a few years Nazism emerged as a national movement and by the end of World War II it became clear to all that even the most rational, cultured and sophisticated groups were capable of absurd destructive behavior of the highest order.

The usage of nuclear weapons at the end World War II and their subsequent proliferation during the Cold War forced humanity to confront mortality at a species-wide level. Weapons of mass destruction inspired both awesome power and a crushing sense of powerlessness. The trauma of the two World Wars and the prospect of nuclear annihilation spawned various ideologies. For the nihilists, life became inherently meaningless and hopelessness. For the existentialists, meaning in life became self-created and various schools of psychology developed practical methods to pacify the subconscious and integrate it with awareness in order to actualize mental health. Therapy became a way of life for millions.

Shortly after World War I, astronomer Edwin Hubble collected evidence that substantiated the theory of the Big Bang. The universe appeared to have a center from which it originated and therefore a beginning and an evolutionary history. The laws of science were eventually traced back to that origin, but scientists soon realized that nothing could be known about the nature of reality before the Big Bang occurred. It turned out that consciousness and the cosmos sprung out of unknowable mysteries. Quantum mechanics deepened those mysteries by describing an acausal connection between mind and matter.

For some, this connection inspired a new way of thinking. The exploration of consciousness and the actualization of its evolutionary potential became a prime directive. Evolutionary minded individuals investigated the span of consciousness that ranged from lower to higher levels of complexity along various lines of development. Progress could be made along this continuum through various kinds of transformative practices and the goal of these evolutionary minded individuals became the self-initiated transformation of human consciousness at the individual and collective levels. The healthy transformation of consciousness came to be seen as the highest good and an inseparable aspect of cosmic evolution.

The memes and movements that emerged during the Integral Age include psychology, the subconscious, irrationality, power and powerlessness, pathology, shadow work, therapy, nuclear weapons, death, mass destruction, nihilism, existentialism, quantum mechanics, the evolution of consciousness, transformative practices, and transformation as a core value. All of these keywords are terms associated with Pluto. The spirit of the burgeoning Integral Age have been noetically directed at the planet for the better part of the last century, and that process continues today.

In the ancient world, hand-carved idols were painted, dressed, and adorned meticulously. But they only became viable objects of worship after specially trained priests "opened" their eyes and ears by reciting magical incantations and enacting special rituals. This empowerment transformed the inanimate figures into powerful gods. From the perspective of noetic astrology, the inanimate balls of rock and the spheres of gas orbiting the Earth were empowered through a similar process. We dressed the planets in archetypal garb, adorned them in colorful myths, and empowered them by directing prayer and myth at them repeatedly over the course of human emergence. The noetic planets circling the Earth were created by our species. The qualities they reflect our journey and embody our values. As our adventure continues, new chapters will be written. Novel worldviews will arise. New gods will emerge from the imaginal womb of collective consciousness and join the other wanderers in the never-ending procession around the velvety vault of night.[5]

The Noetic Zodiac

A noetic astrologer would dismiss the notion that the Zodiac was created by a super-human force like God or infra-human forces like rays originating from the subatomic world. Both of these perspectives admit to a Zodiac that is "pre-given" and predates human emergence. A noetic astrologer would make a distinction between the ecliptic that certainly precedes the birth of our species and the Zodiac that does not. From the noetic perspective, the Zodiac is a noetic structure that was appended to the ecliptic by collective consciousness. The process that led to the creation of the noetic planets is simple to understand since the planets are tangible objects that are visible to the naked eye or telescope. The Zodiac, on the other hand, is an abstract structure and this raises a question: How did collective consciousness create the noetic Zodiac and why? The next step on our exploration of noetic astrology is to consider the historical dynamics that gave rise to this band of symbols that circles the sky and crosses our lives.

To track the mechanism that generated the noetic Zodiac, start by recalling Tiller's experiment. To refresh your memory, Tiller and his team focused their intention on an Intention Imprinted Electrical Device (IIED) to raise the pH of a water solution, and the solution changed its pH over time. And recall that even after the IIED was removed, the room continued to change the pH of other water solutions placed there and that this effect spread up to 150 feet from the location where the original experiment was conducted. Tiller concluded that space is malleable to intention and possesses memory.

Now, let's transpose the rubric of this experiment into our understanding of history and astronomy. While all ancient societies depended on knowledge of the seasonal cycle for their survival, agricultural societies were especially dependent on an intimate relationship to the cycles of nature. Mistiming planting season or a harvest would result in disastrous consequences for the entire population. Consequently, agricultural societies developed an elaborate seasonal calendar and religious festivals to inaugurate the major phases of the seasonal cycle.

With this background in mind, consider the noetic dynamics of agricultural society. As the Sun moved around the ecliptic, human consciousness moved along with it. Unwittingly, the Sun became a celestial IIED that conditioned space with the qualities that the yearly cycle inspired in the minds and hearts of millions. During springtime, wild excitement was projected skyward as the days grew longer and warmer and nature animated with the promise of new possibilities. In summer, it was radiant joy that was directed skyward as fruit ripened and nature became lush. In autumn, it was restraint and moderation as nights grew longer and the ground hardened. And in winter, it was hope and fear, as the ground lay desolate and bare. We divide the year into four seasons but agriculturalists attuned to the seasonal cycle subdivided the year into twelve basic units, each one presaging unique seasonal and cultural changes.

Consider Aries, the astrological sign that symbolizes the archetype of the warrior. Aries coincided with the time of the year when agricultural societies embarked on military campaigns. Virgo, the maiden of the wheat field, coincided with the time of the harvest. Libra, the sign of beauty coincided with the most beautiful time of the year. And Scorpio, the sign of death, coincided with the time of the year when nature starts to whither and die. Most astrologers tend to feel comfortable with this notion that the qualities of the signs correspond to the qualities of the year, and yet, the correlation between the signs and the seasons also poses a troubling theoretical problem.

Astrologers are fond of quoting Hermes Trismegistus' aphorism: as above, so below. But actually, if you think about it, while there is only one "above," but there are two "belows." We live on a sphere and the seasonal phases in each hemisphere are in perpetual opposition. Summer in New York; winter in Australia. Autumn in Paris; spring in Rio De Janeiro. Logically, there should be two Zodiacs, a northern Zodiac that reflects the seasonal phases manifesting in the Northern Hemisphere, and a southern Zodiac that reflects the seasonal phases manifesting in the Southern Hemisphere. But there is only one Zodiac and it blatantly privileges the Northern Hemispheric point of view.

The twelve astrological signs clearly reflect the cycles of nature north of the equator. Consider Leo, the sign associated by rulership to the Sun. Leo coincides with the hottest time of the year, in the Northern Hemisphere. The correspondence between Leo, the Sun, and summer is congruent above the equator. In the Southern Hemisphere, the Sun rules the coldest month of the year, July. Or consider the Sun's exaltation in Aries, the sign that corresponds to the start of spring in the Northern Hemisphere. Aries symbolizes the irrepressible excitement that accompanies new beginnings and resonates with the qualities evoked by springtime. The meaning of Aries remains the same in the Southern Hemisphere even though the Sun passes through Aries in the autumn as the Sun's power is rapidly waning. Or consider Capricorn, the sign of adversity and difficulty. In the Northern Hemisphere Capricorn coincides with winter, the harshest time of the year. The meaning of Capricorn harmonizes with the mood of the season. But in the Southern Hemisphere, Capricorn coincides with summer. As you scrutinize the meaning of the signs, it becomes increasingly apparent that their qualities are congruent with the seasonal phases of the Northern Hemisphere and incongruent with the seasonal phases of the Southern Hemisphere.

The Zodiac is biased. It privileges the Northern Hemisphere. (This inclination transcends astrology. Have you ever seen a map or image of the planet with South America above and North America below? The way we frame our relationship to the cosmos in general favors a northern hemispheric perspective.) And yet, this perspectival idiosyncrasy makes perfect sense in the context of noetic astrology given the historical fact that the Zodiac was developed in Mesopotamia by the culture that invented agriculture, and Mesopotamia happens to lie in the Northern Hemisphere. From there, the Zodiac spread along an east–west axis that extended to Greece and India. The system found appeal exclusively in agricultural societies situated above the equator that had developed the skill to chart the movement of the planets. Significantly, the twelve-fold Zodiac did not spread below the equator. And while indigenous forms of astrology developed in the Southern Hemisphere, none of them included a Zodiac that reflected the seasonal phases of the Northern Hemisphere.

What would have happened if Mesopotamia been located below the equator? I suspect that the meanings of the signs would be reversed to reflect the seasonal cycle experienced in the Southern Hemisphere. And had Mesopotamia straddled the equator, extending prominently into the northern and southern latitudes, instead of one Zodiac, today we might have two. One for each hemisphere.

Another theoretical problem faced by modern astrologers face is the troubling fact that the Zodiac is unabashedly geocentric despite the fact that we live in a Sun-centered neighborhood. The geocentric orientation of the Zodiac is a popular argument used by detractors of astrology who deride the Earth-centered perspective of astrology as an anachronism. But that objection falls away in the context of the noetic astrological paradigm. While it is true that objectively the Earth orbits the Sun, it is equally true that subjectively, the Sun orbits the Earth. Neurologically and psychologically we are hardwired to perceive the Sun going around the Earth and not the other way around. Therefore, we would expect the noetic Zodiac to reflect a geocentric perspective, and it does. The deeper we delve into the intricacies of noetic astrology, the more sense astrology begins to makes both rationally and intuitively. As I tune into this perspective, I sense the redemption of astrology nearing and deepen my intimate connection to the cosmos.

Venture outdoors after dusk on a clear night and witness the noetic sky. Behold the Moon, goddess of the Paleolithic who embodies the need for safety, the core value of the epoch. She is coursing along the ecliptic and passing through the sign Capricorn, the sign of winter that inspired trepidation in the hearts of farmers whose subsistence depended on warmth and sunlight. As these two noetic fields interpenetrate, a mood arises. Enter this place in consciousness and experience the melding together of Paleolithic consciousness and winter consciousness in the form of the desire for safety in the face of sobering hardship. Behold the Sun, god of the Neolithic who embodies power, the core value of the epoch. He is passing through Leo, the sign of summer. A different mood arises now. In this place in consciousness, we find the radiant joy of the season melding with heroic confidence that beckons bold and dramatic action.

As the solar system spirals through space, the noetic planets pass through the noetic signs, and at any given moment, this whirling mass defines a unique array of noetic fields. You incarnated into this swirling vortex, and at the instant of your first breath, you internalized an impression of that archetypal array just like a clay jar baked in an oven internalizes an impression of the Earth's magnetic field the moment it hardens. You personify a psychedelic blend of the variegated colors of consciousness symbolized by the glyphs scattered across your birth chart, the stamp of collective consciousness on your soul. Over time, as the noetic sky comes into harmonic resonance with the seeds of consciousness that you harbor, meaningful moments arise and life-shaping paths are revealed. Dare to follow those synchronistic trails. Your days will overflow with meaning and purpose. Dare to express your creative genius into the world. Feed the sky your consciousness and imprint yourself into the heart of future souls. The future embodies the past and both are rooted in the present. So the next time you open an ephemeris to check on the position of the planets, realize that they are located in your consciousness. Understand that as the sky revolves, humankind evolves, and that as humankind evolves, so does the cosmos.

Placing the Crown Back on the Head of Astrology

If you observed the shadow of a modern astrologer on a sunny afternoon, you would also notice the shadow of a large elephant trailing closely behind. The mammoth problem that plagues astrologers living in the modern age is the jarring fact that astrology can't be reconciled with the dominant materialistic worldview, and a certain degree of shame arises from this dissonance. The lack of scientific legitimacy causes astrologers distress. But in the light of the emergent noetic paradigm that validates consciousness as a force able to influence material reality, astrologers can relax into an attitude of confidence sustained by the realization that far from being the relic of a bygone age, astrology represents the future of a new kind of science. Indeed, Professor Magnus Opum is about to highlight this very point in his closing remarks. And here we are again, suspended atop the Garden of the Gods in the 26th century. Professor Magnus is recounting his distant past, our immediate future.

"During the Noetic Enlightenment humanity finally realized that consciousness is a fundamental force, and within the first few decades of the 21st century, everything changed. Noetic science shook the ground of knowledge. Noetic scientists investigated every field of inquiry. They mapped the properties of consciousness across every discipline. This scientific revolution led to the emergence of new fields such as bionoetics, physionoetics, and genonoetics among many others.

"But perhaps the greatest leap for humanity occurred when noetic cosmologists realized that the most potent and robust noetic fields ever created exist in the sky in the form of the noetic planets and the noetic Zodiac. And we all know what transpired next—the Astrological Revolution of the 21st century. After six long centuries, we placed the crown back on the head of astrology.

267

Tonight, let us acknowledge the contributions of the pioneers that ushered the Noetic Enlightenment, those intrepid souls that enabled us to admire the glorious heavens and proclaim, behold the children of humanity, behold the gods!"

The presentation ends with Professor Magnus Opum raising his head, followed by rows of mimicking craniums craning skyward, collective consciousness touching the cosmos and placing another fingerprint on the body of night.

Endnotes

1. https://www.youtube.com/watch?v=gdIrz-kaH94.

2. Dean Radin, *The Conscious Universe* (San Francisco: Harper Edge, 1997), p.173.

3. A more detailed account of human emergence can be found at the following link:

4. http://www.archive-ilr.com/archives-2007/2007-01/2007-01-nasser.php.

5. Don Beck and Christopher Cowen, *Spiral Dynamics* (Oxford: Blackwell,1996)

6. I consider the Asteroids, Chiron, and other recently formed noetic planetary fields adjuncts to existing structures of consciousness as opposed to symbols that embody a radical new worldview. For this reason, I did not include them in this brief overview of noetic astrology.

17

Postscript

The chapters in this book are not the first writings about transpersonal astrology, and they will certainly not be the final word on the topic. Outcroppings have presented themselves over the centuries, and although they have met with some approval, they have rarely seeded much in the way of a change in business as usual. Why? It has to do with the consciousness of the astrologer, as the practice of astrology is defined by its practitioners. For many reasons, astrologers have largely operated within the prevailing cultural attitudes and expectations. As a result, astrology has been slow to fully embrace the transpersonal. Given the essentially transpersonal nature underpinning not only what we do as astrologers but also the theoretical framework that we operate within, there is some irony to this situation.

To many people, it is apparent that we are living through a spiritual renaissance. There is an explosion of interest in contemplative pursuits and spiritual paradigms and an increase in literature concerning transcendent experiences. This book is a reflection of a collective reach beyond the status quo that tends to marginalize our spiritual roots. Mirroring this shift in focus in the broader populace, increasing numbers of those drawn to astrology are experiencing some degree of awakening beyond separation consciousness. Thus, many astrologers cannot help but scratch the itch which asks, "What are we *really* doing with our astrology?"

It is our responsibility to question, to venture, and to wonder. Historically, astrologers have been concerned with the application of theory for clients and students who demand precision and results, leaving the consideration of the sacred to those within the religious ranks. Today, more people are looking beyond organized religion and finding greater meaning in the direct experience of Spirit. Consistent with this is an increasing demand for a transpersonal astrology. After all, the field of astrology is a reflection of our collective consciousness. The shift to incorporating the transpersonal becomes cemented when astrology truly supports people who struggle with the broader existential questions that underpin their very legitimate everyday concerns.

Transpersonal astrology doesn't lose sight of the everyday but uses a broader perspective to understand it. As we are within the vehicles of separate selves, each of us does have a unique perspective. And we can extend this to other points of reference. The inclusion of the transpersonal informs us that the universe looks different from Neptune than it does from Pluto. Transpersonal explorers and theorists have tended to chide astrology for its determination to come up with a single right answer, to reduce the multifaceted world of meaning to simple formulas. This is what we might call Saturnian astrology, and the authors in this book have attempted to pass beyond that boundary. Yet there is also awareness of the opposite tendency, to slip into solipsism (roughly, "It's true if you believe it"). An authentic transpersonal approach avoids ungrounded arbitrariness and grasps the necessary limitations of mundane reality.

Ultimately, Saturn serves as a gateway to what's beyond, not a wall. Once we head through this passage, life potentially becomes exponentially more expanded, nuanced, multi-dimensional, and perhaps somewhat dreamlike. Once the doors are opened to the transpersonal, we do let in *some degree* of chaos (Uranus) to the established order—perhaps the price for incorporating more of the mystery. Over time, what is initially disruptive becomes commonplace. We are continually integrating what is beyond (Uranus) into what is manifest (Saturn)—an ongoing process of evolution without a foreseeable end. Who can claim that we have exhausted all possibilities when we're discovering new planetoids, moons, or other interesting objects regularly?

If we really are spiritual beings having human experiences, then the transpersonal becomes primary, and the everyday (relative) world is understood as the movement of pieces in a far larger theater. From this view, we reframe our familiar astrological interpretations. The implication is an entire new wave of astrological study and practice, created by those who set out on the journey.

If we are willing to explore, astrology has the potential to make staggering connections: increased utilization of consciousness studies, spiritually focused technologies, guidance for contemplative pursuits, and bridges across other disciplinary fields that address the transpersonal. Astrology as spiritual tool would flourish—a true roadmap for exploring both the inner and outer cosmos, which turn out to be the same thing.

We are stepping into increasingly less familiar territory for astrology. Others have come here before and have established camps (if not permanent dwellings), and we are entering an epic of acceleration in this endeavor.

Our thanks to the authors in this volume for taking up the challenge...and to the reader for joining us on this exploration.

Contributors

Eric Meyers holds an M.A. in Transpersonal Counseling Psychology from Naropa University. He has written 5 astrology books: *The Astrology of Awakening: Eclipse of the Ego*, *Elements & Evolution: The Spiritual Landscape of Astrology*, *Uranus: The Constant of Change*, *Between Past & Presence: A Spiritual View of the Moon & Sun*, and *The Arrow's Ascent*. His chapter, *The Planets & Awakening* was included in the *Astrology: The New Generation* compilation in 2012. He is a graduate of the Steven Forrest Apprenticeship Program; an evolutionary astrologer with an emphasis on spiritual awakening. Eric's main emphasis is on clarifying a spiritual paradigm for astrology, one that literally orbits around spiritual realization instead of ego. He has been published in *The Mountain Astrologer* and has lectured at several conferences.

He can be contacted directly via email at eric@soulvisionconsulting.com or on the web at www.SoulVisionConsulting.com

Jessica Murray has been writing cultural commentary and practicing astrology for thirty-five years. After graduating from Brown University in psychology, fine arts and linguistics, Jessica toured with a political theatre troupe before moving to San Francisco in 1975, where a study of Jung led her to astrology. Jessica's website, MotherSky.com, offers topical blogs, a monthly Skywatch and a lecture series that addresses the astrology of today. Her latest book, *At the Crossroads: An Astrologer's Look at Turbulent Times*, is about the world-altering transits of our era. She is also a contributor to Reality Sandwich, DaykeeperJournal.com and *the Mountain Astrologer Magazine*.

Jessica can be contacted at jessica@mothersky.com or through her website www.mothersky.com.

Armand Diaz, Ph.D., is a professional astrologer whose work emphasizes the development of consciousness in its interaction with astrology. He is the author of *Integral Astrology: Understanding the Ancient Discipline in the Contemporary World* as well as articles in publications including *The Mountain Astrologer*, *The Journal of the Astrological Association of Great Britain*, and *ReVision*. In addition to consulting and writing, Armand devotes time to teaching astrology and leading workshops and talks. His dissertation, in the field of transformative studies,

272

was on the lives and worldviews of psychic-mediums, and his subsequent research efforts have expanded this theme to astrologers. He can be reached through his website, www.IntegralAstrology.net

Bill Streett holds degrees from the University of Vermont (B.A., Psychology), the California Institute of Integral Studies (M.A., Philosophy and Religion) and John F. Kennedy University (M.A., Counseling Psychology). While attending the California Institute of Integral Studies, Bill developed an avid interest in the astrological perspective. Over the past several years, he has written several articles for astrological websites, focusing primarily upon the astrology of current events. He has also written for *The Mountain Astrologer* and was the co-editor of collection of essays uniting astrology and the movies, *The Astrology of Film*. Currently, Bill serves as Assistant Editor for *Archai: The Journal of Archeytpal Cosmology*.

Dena DeCastro, M.A., has been a professional astrologer since 1998. She attended Steven Forrest's Apprenticeship Program from 2002-2004, and bases her approach upon the principles of Evolutionary Astrology. She holds two Master's degrees: one in English from California State University Sacramento, and one in Interdisciplinary Studies from Marylhurst University. Dena is also a former college writing instructor, and she worked for three years as an Associate Editor for *The Mountain Astrologer*. In 2007, she started one of the earliest astrology podcasts, now titled "Sirius Astrology Podcast." Over the years, the show has featured interviews with fellow astrologers, as well as her own exploration of various topics of astrology and divination. She lives in Portland, Oregon, and provides readings both in person and long distance via phone or Skype.

Mark Jones is an Evolutionary Astrologer, Psychosynthesis Therapist and Hypnotherapist working in private practice in Bristol, England. Mark is the main teacher of Evolutionary Astrology in the U.K. and is a regular speaker and workshop leader. Mark's first book, *Healing the Soul: Pluto, Uranus and the Lunar Nodes*, explains his method and his second book, *Therapeutic Astrology* expands on that method within the counseling dynamic of a reading. Mark also has chapters in *Astrology: the New Generation* and *Insights into Evolutionary Astrology*.

Mark is available for readings, Astrology tuition and Astrological Counseling and has many resources for students on his website: www.plutoschool.com. His email address is markjones@plutoschool.com

Faye Cossar has been an astrologer for personal and business clients for over 25 years. She runs the Amsterdam School of Astrology (www.asastrology.nl), lectures worldwide, and holds an MA in Cultural Astronomy and Astrology from Bath Spa University (UK). Her interest in looking at the transpersonal started when she was researching one of her academic papers on the history of Uranus. Faye is also at home in the world of psychology and is in private practice as a therapist. She wrote a chapter for the book *From Here to There: An Astrologer's Guide to Astro-Mapping*, edited by Martin Davis, where she looked at using Astro*carto*graphy in business. In 2012 she published *Using Astrology to Create a Vocational Profile: Finding the Right Career Direction* and she offers an online apprenticeship using this book as a basis, leading students through a process of working with their own clients in the vocational profiling process.

Faye can be contacted at faye@asastrology.nl for more information. Visit her website at http://www.fayecossar.com, or her consultancy site for business at www.juxtaposition.nl where she has links to her blog and offers a free E-zine, *The Monthly Planet*.

Maurice Fernandez is a leading evolutionary astrologer and author of the books *Neptune, the 12th House, and Pisces* and *Astrology and the Evolution of Consciousness—Volume One*. Maurice teaches astrology in a holistic way that addresses mind, body, heart and spirit to generate a more comprehensive learning experience. He directs a correspondence and on-location professional certification program and organizes spiritual retreats in sacred places around the world, combining astrology, Kundalini yoga, health consciousness, ceremony and animal communication. He is also the organizer of The River of Stars astrology conference, the first astrology conference to incorporate the principles described above. Currently based in Hawaii, he has forged over the years a worldwide reputation of depth and excellence as a counselor, teacher and organizer.

Visit the free learning forum on his website: www.mauricefernandez.com

Maurice is on Facebook at: www.facebook.com/Maurice.Fernandez.Cosmic

Andrew Smith discovered astrology in 1993 whilst in his final year reading Geography through Natural Sciences in Trinity College, Dublin. He is a full time professional astrologer since 1995, running a very busy international private practice from South Dublin, Ireland. He writes prolifically for his clients and various magazines and online websites. He is formally both a director of the Dublin Astrological Centre and editor of the Dublin Astrologer journal, which he left in 1998 to focus on his client practice. Along with his astrologer wife, Karen Morgan, he runs weekly classes and monthly workshops, designed in a way that balances the rigor of the intellect and the soul of the imagination.

Since Andrew's practice has emerged solely through referrals he has no website, but can be contacted via email on dastroc@gmail.com. He also has a web presence on www.facebook.com/andrewdhsmith and on LinkedIn.

Julene Packer-Louis is a full time professional astrologer for the past eleven years, living in Avon Lake, Ohio with her husband, two teenage children, and two dogs. She holds a diploma from the International Academy of Astrology and certifications from the National Counsel for Geocosmic Research and a CAP from the International Society for Astrological Research. She has been a serious student of both Astrology & Yoga since 1998. She has been teaching at the International Academy of Astrology since 2000, serving on the school's Board of Directors since 2002.

Her website for more details: www.yogicastrology.com or contact her via email at julene.packer@gmail.com

Adam Gainsburg is an author, teacher and consulting astrologer. He founded Soulsign Astrology to illuminate the sentient interface of astrology and astronomy through his private practice and astrological training programs. His books include *The Soul's Desire for Wholeness, Pluto & the Lunar Nodes* and the popular *Chiron: The Wisdom of a Deeply Open Heart*. His most recent book, *The Light of Venus*, delivers a complete system for delineating the 13 Venus Phases. Adam is a regular guest on astrology and consciousness-related radio, and offers advanced classes on many topics. He has presented his original research

275

at conferences and chapters around the US and has contributed astrology articles for many websites and newsletters. Adam is also the creator of the Sky Engine software, the world's first program for instantly finding heliacal and synodic phases.

Adam can be found on the web at the following websites - www.SoulsignAstrology.com and www.SkyEngine.us, or email him at mail@soulsignastrology.com

Margaret Gray has an MSW in Clinical Social Work, a B.A in Sociology from Trinity College, Dublin and a Diploma in Psychological Astrology from the CPA London, where she studied with Liz Greene and Melanie Reinhart. Margaret works full time as a professional astrologer offering consultations, courses, workshops and mentoring to astrologers and therapists in Hawaii, Ireland, and the US mainland, as well as teaching online for IAA.

Margaret has published astrology articles in the AA and NCGR journals, the Irish psychotherapy publication '*Inside Out Ireland*', as well as writing a regular astrology article for the general public in *Positive Life Ireland* and currently in *Network Ireland Magazine*. She is a member of the ISAR board as well as the book reviewer for the ISAR journal and has been a speaker at several astrology conferences including NORWAC, ISAR and the UK AA conference

Her website for more details: www.astrologypsychological.com

Sherene Schostak, M.A. is a Jungian therapist and astrologer who specializes in helping creative artists transform their addictions and blocks. She has been in private practice in New York City for the past sixteen years consulting, writing and teaching and is now based in San Francisco. She is the creator and editor of the online astrology magazine, Constellation Mag, and the Zodiac Dance DVD and the authentic movement workshops from which it was derived. She is the co-author of Surviving Saturn's Return: Overcoming the most tumultuous time of your life (McGraw Hill) as well as the *The Fate of Your Date* (Chronicle Books). She holds a Master's Degree from New York University in Clinical Psychology, and pursued advanced graduate work in the former psychoanalytic studies program at what was formerly known as The New School for Social Research. She is currently the resident astrologer at Elle

276

UK magazine and www.Elleuk.com; and formerly wrote the astrology column for Teen Vogue. Her work has been featured on writing credits/features include: The Benjamin Moore Aurascope Campaign; Pottery Barn astrology calendar; Bravotv.comLifescript, Astrology.com; "Star Signs" for NBC/iVillage; and reviews in The Mountain Astrologer. Sherene teaches classes and workshops internationally.

Sherene can be found on the web at www.shereneschostak.com and at www.jungianauthenticmovement.com/project40/

Adam Elenbaas is the critically acclaimed author of *Fishers of Men: The Gospel of an Ayahusaca Vision Quest,* and one of the founding writers at RealitySandwich.com. Elenbaas holds an MA and MFA in English and is the director and founder of the Nightlight Astrology School and Sky House Yoga Studio. Adam currently lives in Washington D.C. and is working on his new book, a psychedelic zodiac story called "Jungle. Star. Medicine."

He can be reached via email at nightlightastrology@gmail.com or via the web at www.nightlightastrology.com and www.facebook.com/adam.elenbaas.3.

Benjamin Bernstein, founder of AstroShaman.com in Asheville, North Carolina, is an experienced, professionally certified astrologer who has done about 5000 sessions with a global clientele. He hosts *This Week in Astrology*, iTunes' #1 astrology podcast, and has lectured at national astrology conferences. Benjamin is also a shaman who consistently facilitates powerful healings and expanded spiritual consciousness in his clients.

Benjamin can be reached at info@AstroShaman.com or (+1) 828-338-9852.

Rafael Nasser grew up in a multicultural home and globetrotted around the world during his formative years. Circumstances, in addition to an exceedingly mutable birth chart, resulted in the formation of a chameleon like identity that reflected his cultural milieu. Only after discovering astrology and meditation was he able to identify with an authentic self that transcended childhood conditioning and social programming. The interplay between astrology, Qi energy, and the evolution of consciousness became a source of fascination. After narrowly missing being a passenger on one of the fated flights of September 11th, 2001, his life took a sharp turn, and thereafter, he

277

devoted his energies to the exploration of consciousness. As part of that process, he authored *Under One Sky* (Seven Paws Press), and co-authored *The Master Key* (Sounds True, 2014). Rafael is currently enrolled in the massage program at Pacific College of Oriental Medicine. After graduating, he intends to develop a healing method that integrates Eastern and Western bodymind practices along with the deep wisdom of astrology.

He can be reached at rafinasser@gmail.com.

CPSIA information can be obtained at www.ICGtesting.com
Printed in the USA
BVOW01s0007221113

336882BV00007B/104/P